The C.I.A. and the U-2 Program

1954–1974

Volumes in the Top Secret series,
Published by New Century Books:

World War Two:
U.S. Military Files on the Invasion of Japan

The F.B.I. Files on Elvis Presley

The Vietnam War:
Confidential Files on the Siege and Loss of Khe Sanh

The F.B.I. Files on the Lindbergh Baby Kidnapping

The C.I.A. and the U-2 Program

1954–1974

Thomas Fensch, Editor

New Century Books

New Century Books
P.O. Box 7113
The Woodlands, Texas, 77387-7113

Library of Congress Number: 2001117311
ISBN: Hardcover 0-930751-09-4
Softcover 0-930751-10-8

Introduction

To paraphrase Franklin Delano Roosevelt, May 1, 1960 was "a day that will live in infamy." That was the day the American people felt betrayed by their own government; and even President Dwight Eisenhower had to lie to the American people and to the world for several days because he was not fully informed until after the fact that on May 1, 1960, a U-2 high altitude spy plane, from Peshawar Pakistan, overflying much of eastern Russia toward Bodo, Norway, was shot down over Sverdlovsk, Russia. Not even Eisenhower knew the U-2 was in the sky that day; he was preparing for a Summit meeting with Soviet premier Nikita Khrushschev scheduled for two weeks later. Eisenhower had known of the U-2 spy plane program and had approved previous flights. But he and his administration believed that, in the event a U-2 was lost, no pilot would survive. Francis Gary Powers, the pilot of the U-2 downed over Sverdlovsk did, in fact, survive to be placed on trial before the Military Division of the Soviet Supreme Court, in Moscow, August 17, 18 and 19, 1960.

The U-2 incident fractured U.S.-Soviet relations. It put the Eisenhower administration in the uncomfortable position of lying about the U-2 then backtracking and it gave Nikita Khrushchev the upper hand in accusing the U.S. of invading soviet airspace—and provably so—just before an all-important peace Summit. It gave the American people a little-known spy program to discuss and moralize about: the name U-2 and the pilot Francis Gary Powers.

And what of the aircraft known as the U-2?

An early book about the U-2 by Chris Pocock was titled *Dragonfly* and that name was extraordinarily apt. The U-2 was such a fragile aircraft that one U-2, buffeted by the turbulence of a U.S. escort jet, broke apart in flight and the pilot was killed.

The technology of designing an aircraft to fly hour after hour at 70,000 feet was daunting. In *May-Day: Eisenhower, Khrushchev and the U-2 Affair,* Michael Beschloss writes:

> In the thin air over seventy thousand feet, jet engines scarcely ran. Since the new plane could hardly touch down at Leningrad or Minsk for a friendly refueling, it had to be able to stay in the air for up to ten hours. The Catch-22 was that at such altitude and distance, the engine would probably burn so much fuel that no standard fuel tank would be large enough. Any tank large enough would weigh the plane down so badly that it could not stay so high in the air.
>
> They solved the puzzle with a design that was less a jet airplane than a glider with a Pratt & Whitney turbojet engine attached. To conserve fuel, the engine would turn on and off: the plane would alternately fly and glide through the stratosphere for almost eleven hours and 4,750 miles on little more than a thousand gallons of fuel. The men pared every conceivable ounce from their design and built a craft of spectacular grace, which they named the Angel.
>
> The Angel was made of titanium and other lightweight materials. Wingspan was roughly twice the length of the fuselage. The razorlike tail was joined to the rest of the plane by just three bolts. The aircraft was slung so low that on the runway, its nose was only the height of a man. It

was so light that later, at first glimpse, pilots wondered whether this was intended to be the world's first disposable plane, built for only one flight.

Other components were perfected. James Baker of Land's intelligence panel worked on a new telescopic lens. Eastman Kodak devised a new Mylar film thin enough to be carried aloft in large quantities. Under Land's oversight, Trevor Gardner's old firm Hycon built the massive cameras that swung from horizon to horizon, covering a swath of land literally 750 miles wide—about one tenth of this in three dimensions. With 12,000 feet of film, the cameras were considered able to photograph a path from Washington to Phoenix in one flight.

Some in the CIA and Air Force still doubted that "Dulles's Folly" or "Bissell's Bird" would ever fly, but in February 1955, eighty-eight days after the program's inception, Kelly Johnson called Bissell in Washington to say that the experimental model was ready. Final cost: $190 million.

The plane still needed a name. The Angel would not do (nor would Dulles's Folly, for that matter). Bissell and Johnson might have given the plane the prefix "X," which as used for other experimental aircraft like Chuck Yeager's fabled X-1, but that would draw too much attention: people might wonder just what barrier this plane was designed to smash, and why. Reconnaissance planes often had the prefix "R," but that would also give away the secret. So Johnson's plane was assigned to the catch-all category of "U —utility planes—and named the U-2.

This choice was not as clever as it may have seemed. The name U-2 had already been taken by the Soviets, who had used it on a single-engine biplane before the Second World War. (pp. 92–93).

Since the U-2 incident, there have been only a handful of books about the U-2 program: *The U-2 Affair* by David Wise and Thomas B. Ross; *May-Day* by Michael Beschloss, which is devoted to the relationship between the U.S. and the Soviet Union immediately following the U-2 incident; Francis Gary Powers' autobiography *Operation Overflight* and a couple of books about the technology of the U-2 aircraft.

But there has never been a complete public — declassified — accounting for the U-2 program from any government agency.

Until now.

The Central Intelligence Agency assigned two staff historians, Gregory W. Pedlow and Donald E. Welzenbach of the Center for the Study of Intelligence, to document the history of the U-2. Their manuscript, *The CIA and the U-2 Program, 1954–1974,* was declassified in 1998, but never made generally available.

This book is the declassified report.

Readers will observe that there are deletions through the book; legally they are *redactions*, material blacked out prior to publication. In a few cases, names can be determined from cross-checking with the previously-published books about the U-2 affair. In other cases, there is still no indication to what the redactions referred.

Did U-2 flights continue after May, 1960? Readers may be fascinated to know that they did. There were reconnaissance flights over Cuba, during the Cuban Missile Crisis, in Asia and during the Vietnam war years. There are many more redactions concerning the latter years of the U-2 programs than during the Gary Powers' years.

And, it may be suspected, there well could be substantially more material about the U-2 spy program which did not appear in this C.I.A.-authorized history.

Until such additional material is released, this may be the definitive government document about the aircraft and the 20 year history of the U-2 program.

Pedlow and Welzenbach wrote (prior to de-classification):

The CIA and the U-2 Program, 1954–1974

This volume presents to scholars and the public the CIA's newly declassified internal history of the U-2 program. The original study, written by Gregory W. Pedlow and Donald E. Welzenbach for the CIA History Staff in the 1980s, was published in 1992 under the title *The Central Intelligence Agency and Overhead Reconnaissance: The U-2 and OXCART Programs, 1954–1974*. Sections of that study on the U-2 program have been included here to mark the occasion of the September 1998 conference "The U-2: A Revolution in Intelligence." The entire study is being reviewed under the provisions of the Freedom of Information Act.

The product of a remarkable collaboration between the Central Intelligence Agency, the United States Air Force, Lockheed Corporation, and other suppliers, the U-2 collected intelligence that revolutionized American intelligence analysis of the Soviet threat. Although the U-2 has been one of America's best known intelligence achievements, significant aspects of the U-2's story have remained unknown outside the US Government. This volume tells much of that story in a clear and engaging manner, providing a fuller context for understanding some of the most dangerous

> moments of the Cold War. The U-2 stand as a monument to the many ways in which intelligence has upheld the security of the United States and furthered the possibilities for peace around the world.

Nothing has been changed in this volume, except the Annotated Bibliography, which has been added.

And what did Francis Gary Powers think of the flight over the Soviet Union? Michael Beschloss quotes him:

> I knew that flying over the Soviet Union without permission was spying. I *knew* that it was. But I really didn't think that in the true sense of the word spy I ever considered myself a spy. I was a pilot flying an airplane and it just so happened that *where* I was flying made what I was doing spying. (pp. 17)

—*Thomas Fensch*

The C.I.A. and the U-2 Program

1954–1974

Contents

* Project Oxcart was the development of the SR-71 Blackbird, which was eventually capable of flying at Mach 3. Flight records of the Blackbird: New York to London in one hour and 59 minutes; London to Los Angeles in three hours and 47 minutes; Los Angeles to Washington, D.C., in 64 minutes. The Blackbird was 40 percent faster than the Concorde, which flew seven years later. The Blackbird was designed and built by the Skunk Works, at Lockheed. See Rich and Janos, *Skunk Works*, pp. 201–261. — TF.

TOP SECRET

Foreword

This History Staff Monograph offers a comprehensive and authoritative history of the CIA's manned overhead reconnaissance program, which from 1954 to 1974 developed and operated two extraordinary aircraft, the U-2 and the A-12 OXCART. It describes not only the program's technological and bureaucratic aspects, but also its political and international context. The manned reconnaissance program, along with other overhead systems that emerged from it, changed the CIA's work and structure in ways that were both revolutionary and permanent. The formation of the Directorate of Science and Technology in the 1960s, principally to develop and direct reconnaissance programs, is the most obvious legacy of the events recounted in this study.

The authors tell an engrossing story. The struggle between the CIA and the US Air Force to control the U-2 and A-12 OXCART projects reveals how the manned reconnaissance program confronted problems that still beset successor programs today. The U-2 was an enormous technological success: its first flight over the USSR in July 1956 made it immediately the most important source of intelligence on the Soviet Union Using it against the Soviet target it was designed for nevertheless produced a persistent tension between its program managers and the President. The program managers, eager for coverage, repeatedly urged the President to authorize frequent missions over the Soviet Union President. Eisenhower, from the outset doubtful of the prudence and propriety of invading Soviet airspace, only reluctantly allowed any overflights at all. After the Soviets shot down Francis Gary Powers' U-2 on 1 May 1960, President Eisenhower forbade any further U-2 flights over the USSR. Since the Agency must always assess a covert operation's potential payoff against the diplomatic or military cost if it fails, this account of the U-2's employment over the Soviet Union offers insights that go beyond overhead reconnaissance programs

Indeed, this study should be useful for a variety of purposes. It is the only history of this program based upon both full access to CIA records and extensive classified interviews of its participants. The authors have found records that were nearly irretrievably lost and have interviewed participants whose personal recollections gave information available nowhere else. Although the story of the manned reconnaissance program offers no tidy model for imitation, it does reveal how resourceful managers coped with unprecedented technological challenges and their implications for intelligence and national policy. For this reason, the program's history provides profitable reading for intelligence professionals and policymakers today.

Many people made important contributions to the production of this volume. In the History Staff's preparation of the manuscript, Gerald Haines did the final revision, (name deleted) again demonstrated her high talent as a copy editor, and (name deleted) provided staunch secretarial support throughout. As usual, we are indebted to more members than we can name from the Publications, Design, and Cartography Centers in the Office of Current Production and Analytic Support, whose lively interest in the publication went far beyond the call of duty. Their exceptional professional skill and the masterly work of the Printing and Photography Group combined to create this handsome volume.

Donald E. Welzenbach, who began this study, and Gregory W. Pedlow, who completed it, brought complementary strengths to this work. A veteran of CIA service since 1960, Mr. Welzenbach began research on this study in 1983, when he joined the DCI History Staff on a rotational assignment from the Directorate of Science and Technology. After tireless documentary research and extensive interviewing, he finished a draft manuscript of the history before returning to his directorate. In early 1986, Gregory W. Pedlow, a new member of the DCI History Staff, was assigned to complete the study. A Johns Hopkins University Ph.D. who has served as an Army intelligence officer and University of Nebraska professor of history, Dr. Pedlow undertook important research in several new areas, and reorganized, edited, and revised the entire manuscript before leaving CIA to become NATO Historian in late 1989. The final work, which has greatly benefited from both authors' contributors, is the CIA's own history of the world's first great overhead reconnaissance program.

J. Kenneth McDonald
Chief, CIA History Staff

April 1992

Preface

When the Central Intelligence Agency came into existence in 1947, no one foresaw that, in less than a decade, it would undertake a major program of overhead reconnaissance, whose principal purpose would be to fly over the Soviet Union. Traditionally, the military services had been responsible for overhead reconnaissance, and flights deep into unfriendly territory only took place during wartime. By the early 1950s, however, the United States had an urgent and growing need for strategic intelligence on the Soviet Union and its satellite states. At great risk, US Air Force and Navy aircraft had been conducting peripheral reconnaissance and shallow-penetration overflights, but these missions were paying a high price in lives lost and increased international tension. Furthermore, many important areas of the Soviet Union lay beyond the range of existing reconnaissance aircraft. The Air Force had therefore begun to develop a high-altitude reconnaissance aircraft that would be able to conduct deep-penetration reconnaissance missions over the Soviet Union. President Dwight D. Eisenhower and his civilian scientific advisers feared that the loss of such an aircraft deep in Soviet territory could lead to war and therefore authorized the development of new nonmilitary aircraft, first the U-2 and later the A-12 OXCART, to be manned by civilians and operated only under cover and in the greatest secrecy. Primary responsibility for this new reconnaissance program was assigned to the Central Intelligence Agency, but the Air Force provided vital support.

The Agency's manned overhead reconnaissance

program lasted 20 years. It began with President Eisenhower's authorization of the U-2 project in late 1954 and ended with the transfer of the remaining Agency U-2s to the Air Force in 1974. During this period the CIA developed a successor to the U-2, the A-12 OXCART, but this advanced aircraft saw little operational use and the program was canceled in 1968 after the Air Force deployed a fleet of similar aircraft, a military variant of the A-12 called the SR-71.

Neither of these aircraft remains secret today. A great deal of information about the U-2 and its overflight program became known to the public after 1 May 1960, when the Soviet Union shot down a CIA U-2 and publicly tried its pilot, Francis Gary Powers. Four years later, at press conferences in February and July 1964, President Lyndon B. Johnson revealed the existence of the OXCART-type of aircraft, although only in its military YF-12A (interceptor) and SR-71 (strategic reconnaissance) versions.

The two CIA reconnaissance aircraft have also been the subject of a number of books, beginning with David Wise's and Thomas B. Ross's *The U-2 Affair* in 1962 and then Francis Gary Powers' memoirs, *Operation Overflight*, in 1970. Two recent books give many more details about the U-2 and OXCART aircraft: Michael Beschloss's *Mayday Eisenhower, Khrushchev* and the U-2 Affair (1986) and William Burrows's *Deep Black Space Espionage and National Security* (1987). Although well written and generally accurate, these books suffer from their authors' lack of access to classified official documentation. By drawing upon the considerable amount of formerly classified data on the U-2 now available to the public, Beschloss has provided an accurate and insightful depiction of the U-2 program in the context of the

Eisenhower administration's overall foreign policy, but his book does contain errors and omissions on some aspects of the U-2 program. Burrows's broader work suffers more from the lack of classified documentation, particularly in the OXCART/SR-71 section, which concentrates on the Air Force aircraft because little information about the Agency's aircraft has been officially declassified and released.

After the present study of the Agency's overhead reconnaissance projects was completed, a new book on the U-2 was published in the United Kingdom Chris Pocock's *Dragon Lady. The History of the U-2 Spyplane* [deleted] unclassified account of the U2 program. Pocock has been able to compensate for his lack of access to classified documents by interviewing many former participants in the program, especially former pilots. Pocock is also quite familiar with aircraft itself, for he had worked with Jay Miller on the latter's excellent technical study of the U-2 *Lockheed U-2* (1983).

There has also been a classified official study of the U-2 and OXCART programs. In 1969 the Directorate of Science and Technology published a *History of the Office of Special Activities* by [deleted]. This 16-volume Top Secret Codeword study of the Agency's reconnaissance aircraft provides a wealth of technical and operational information on the two projects but does not attempt to place them in their historical context. Without examining the international situation and bureaucratic pressures affecting the president and other key policymakers, however, it is impossible to understand the decisions that began, carried out, and ended the CIA's reconnaissance aircraft projects.

In preparing this study of CIA's overhead reconnaissance program, the authors drew on published sources, classified government documents, and interviews with key participants from the CIA, Air Force, contractors, scientific advisory committees, and the Eisenhower administration. The interviews were particularly important for piecing together the story of how the CIA became involved in overhead reconnaissance in the first place because Agency documentation on the prehistory of the U-2 project is very sketchy and there are no accurate published accounts. Research on the period of actual reconnaissance operations included the records of the Director of Central Intelligence, the Office of Special Activities in the Directorate of Science and Technology, and the Intelligence Community Staff, along with documents from the Eisenhower Presidential Library in Abilene, Kansas, and additional interviews.

Both authors are grateful for the assistance they have received from many individuals who played important roles in the events they recount. Without their help a good deal of this story could never have become known. The assistance of Agency records management officers in the search for documents on the overhead reconnaissance program is also greatly appreciated.

To ensure that this study of the Agency's involvement in overhead reconnaissance reaches the widest possible audience, the authors have kept it at the Secret classification level. As a result, some aspects of the overhead reconnaissance program, particularly those involving satellites and related interagency agreements, have had to be described in very general terms. The omission of such information is not significant for this book, which focuses on the Agency's reconnaissance aircraft.

1

Searching for a System

THE NEED FOR HIGH-ALTITUDE RECONNAISSANCE

For centuries, soldiers in wartime have sought the highest ground or structure in order to get a better view of the enemy. At first it was tall trees, then church steeples and bell towers. By the time of the American Civil War and the Franco-Prussian War of 1870–71, observers were using hot-air balloons to get up in the sky for a better view of the "other side of the hill". With the advent of dry film, it became possible to carry cameras into the sky to record the disposition of enemy troops and emplacements. Indeed, photoreconnaissance proved so valuable during World War I that in 1938 Gen. Werner von Fritsch, Commander in Chief of the German Army, predicted, "The nation with the best aerial reconnaissance facilities will win the next war."[1]

By World War II, lenses, films, and cameras had undergone many improvements, as had the airplane, which could fly higher and faster than the primitive craft of World War I. Now it was possible to use photoreconnaissance to obtain information about potential targets before a bombing raid and to assess the effectiveness of the bombing afterward.

Peacetime applications of high-altitude photography at first included only photomapping and surveying for transcontinental highways and mineral and oil exploration. There was little thought given to using photography for peacetime espionage until after World War II, when the Iron Curtain rang down and cut off most forms of communication between the Soviet Bloc of nations and the rest of the world.

By 1949 the Soviet Union and the states of Eastern Europe had been effectively curtained off from the outside world, and the Soviet military carried out its planning, production, and deployment activities with the utmost secrecy. All Soviet strategic capabilities — bomber forces, ballistic missiles, submarine forces, and nuclear weapons plants — were concealed from outside observation. The Soviet air defense system, a prime consideration in determining US retaliatory policies, was also largely an unknown factor.

Tight security along the Soviet Bloc borders severely curtailed the movement of human intelligence sources. In addition, the Soviet Union made its conventional means of communication — telephone, telegraph, and radio-telephone — more secure, thereby greatly reducing the intelligence available from these sources. The stringent security measures imposed by the Communist Bloc nations effectively blunted traditional methods for gathering intelligence secret agents using covert means to communicate intelligence, travelers to and from target areas who could be asked to keep their eyes open and report their observations later, wiretaps and other eavesdropping methods, and postal intercepts. Indeed, the entire panoply of intelligence tradecraft seemed ineffective against the Soviet Bloc, and no other methods were available.

Early Postwar Aerial Reconnaissance

Although at the end of World War II the United States had captured large quantities of German photos and documents on the Soviet Union, this material was rapidly becoming outdated. The main source of current intelligence on the Soviet Union's military installations was interrogation of prisoners of war returning from Soviet captivity. To obtain information about Soviet scientific progress, the intelligence community established several programs to debrief German scientists who had been taken to the Soviet Union after the end of the war but were now being allowed to leave[2].

[approximately nine lines deleted]

Interrogation of returning Germans offered only fragmentary information, and this source could not be expected to last much longer. As a result, in the late 1940s, the US Air Force and Navy began trying to obtain aerial photography of the Soviet Union. The main Air Force effort involved Boeing RB-47 aircraft (the reconnaissance version of the B-47 jet-propelled medium bomber) equipped with cameras and electronic "ferret" equipment that enabled aircrews to detect tracking by Soviet radars. At that time the Soviet Union had not yet completely ringed its borders with radars, and much of the interior also lacked radar coverage. Thus, when the RB-47s found a gap in the air-warning network, they would dart inland to take photographs of any accessible targets. These "penetration photography" flights (called SENSINT — sensitive intelligence — missions) occurred along the northern and Pacific coasts of Russia. One RB-47 aircraft even managed to fly 450 miles inland and photograph the city of Igarka in Siberia. Such intrusions brought protests from Moscow but no Soviet military response[2].

In 1950 there was a major change in Soviet policy Air defense units became very aggressive in defending their airspace, attacking all aircraft that came near the borders of the Soviet Union. On 8 April 1950, Soviet fighters shot down a US Navy Privateer patrol aircraft over the Baltic Sea. Following the outbreak of the Korean war in June 1950, the Soviet Union extended its "severe air defense policy" to the Far East. In the autumn of 1951, Soviet aircraft downed a twin-engine US Navy Neptune bomber near Vladivostok. An RB-29 lost in the Sea of Japan on 13 June 1952 was probably also a victim of Soviet fighters. The United States was not the only country affected by the new aggressive Soviet air defense policy, Britain and Turkey also reported attacks on their planes[4].

The Soviet Union's air defense policy became even more aggressive in August 1952, when its reconnaissance aircraft began violating Japanese airspace over Hokkaido, the northernmost Japanese home island. Two months later, on 7 October 1952, Soviet fighter aircraft stalked and shot down a US RB-29 flying over Hokkaido Aerial reconnaissance of the Soviet Union and surrounding areas had become a very dangerous business.

Despite the growing risks associated with aerial reconnaissance of the Soviet Bloc, senior US officials strongly believed that such missions were necessary. The lack of information about the Soviet Union, coupled with the perception that it was an aggressive nation determined to expand its borders — a perception that had been greatly strengthened by the Soviet-backed North Korean invasion of South Korea in June 1950 — increased US determination to obtain information about Soviet intentions and capabilities and thus reduce the danger of being surprised by a Soviet attack.

New Approaches to Photoreconnaissance

While existing Navy and Air Force aircraft were flying their risky reconnaissance missions over the Soviet Union, the United States began planning for a more systematic and less dangerous approach using new technology. One of the leading advocates of the need for new, high-altitude reconnaissance aircraft was Richard S. Leghorn, a Massachusetts Institute of Technology graduate and employee of Eastman Kodak who had commanded the Army Air Forces' 67th Reconnaissance Group in Europe during World War II. After the war he returned to Kodak but maintained his interest in photoreconnaissance. Leghorn strongly believed in the need for what he called pre-D-day reconnaissance, that is, reconnaissance of a potential enemy before the outbreak of actual hostilities, in contrast to combat reconnaissance in wartime. In papers presented in 1946 and 1948, Leghorn argued that the United States needed to develop such a capability, which would require high-altitude aircraft and high-resolution cameras. The outbreak of the Korean war gave Leghorn an opportunity to put his ideas into effect. Recalled to active duty by the Air Force, Lieutenant Colonel Leghorn became the head of the Reconnaissance Systems Branch of the Wright Air Development Command at Dayton, Ohio, in April 1951[5].

In Leghorn's view, altitude was the key to success for overhead reconnaissance. Since the best Soviet interceptor at that time, the MIG-17, had to struggle to reach 45,000 feet,[6] Leghorn reasoned that an aircraft that could exceed 60,000 feet would be safe from Soviet fighters. Recognizing that the fastest way to produce a high-altitude reconnaissance aircraft was to modify an existing aircraft, he began looking for the highest flying aircraft available in the Free World. This search soon led him to a British twin-engine medium bomber — the Canberra — built by the English Electric Company. The Canberra had made its first flight in May 1949. Its speed of 469 knots (870 kilometers per hour) and its service ceiling of 48,000 feet made the Canberra a natural choice for high-altitude reconnaissance work. The Royal Air Force quickly developed a reconnaissance version of the Canberra, the PR3 (the PR stood for photoreconnaissance), which began flying in March 1950[7].

At Leghorn's insistence, the Wright Air Development Command invited English Electric representatives to Dayton in the summer of 1951 to help find ways to make the Canberra fly even higher. By this time the Air Force had already adopted the bomber version of the Canberra, which the Glenn L. Martin Aircraft Company was to produce under license as the B-57 medium bomber. Leghorn and his English Electric colleagues designed a new Canberra configuration with very long high-lift wings, new Rolls-Royce Avon-109 engines, a solitary pilot, and an airframe that was stressed to less than the standard military specifications. Leghorn calculated that a Canberra so equipped might reach 63,000 feet early in a long mission and as high as 67,000 feet as the declining fuel supply lightened the aircraft. He believed that such a modified Canberra could penetrate the Soviet Union and China for a radius of 800 miles from bases around their periphery and photograph up to 85 percent of the intelligence targets in those countries.

Leghorn persuaded his superiors to submit his suggestion to the Pentagon for funding. He had not, however, cleared his idea with the Air Research and Development Command, whose reconnaissance division in Baltimore, headed by Lt. Col. Joseph J. Pellegrini, had to approve all new reconnaissance aircraft designs. Pellegrini's unit reviewed Leghorn's design and ordered extensive modifications According to Leghorn, Pellegrini was not interested in a special-purpose aircraft that was only suitable for covert peacetime reconnaissance missions, for he believed that all Air Force reconnaissance aircraft should be capable of operating under wartime conditions. Pellegrini therefore insisted that Leghorn's design meet the specifications for combat aircraft, which required heavily stressed airframes, armor plate, and other apparatus that made an aircraft too heavy to reach the higher altitudes necessary for safe overflights of the Soviet Bloc. The final result of Leghorn's concept after its alteration by Pellegrini's staff was the RB-57D in 1955, whose maximum altitude was only 64,000 feet. Meanwhile Leghorn, frustrated by the rejection of his original concept, had transferred to the Pentagon in early 1952 to work for Col. Bernard A. Schriever, Assistant for Development Planning to the Air Force's Deputy Chief of Staff for Development[8].

In his new position Leghorn became responsible for planning the Air Force's reconnaissance needs for the next decade. He worked closely with Charles F. (Bud) Wienberg — a colleague who had followed him from Wright Field — and Eugene P. Kiefer, a Notre Dame-educated aeronautical engineer who had designed reconnaissance aircraft at the Wright Air Development Center during World War II. All three of these reconnaissance experts believed that the Air Force should emphasize high-altitude photoreconnaissance.

Underlying their advocacy of high-altitude photoreconnaissance was the belief that Soviet radars would not be able to track aircraft flying above 65,000 feet. This assumption was based on the fact that the Soviet Union used American-built radar sets that had been supplied under Lend-Lease during World War II. Although the SCR-584 (Signal Corps Radio) target-tracking radar could track targets up to 90,000 feet, its high power consumption burned out a key component quickly, so this radar was normally not turned on until an early warning radar had detected a target. The SCR-270 early warning radar could be left on for much longer periods and had a greater horizontal range (approximately 120 miles) but was limited by the curvature of the earth to a maximum altitude of 40,000 feet. As a result, Leghorn, Kiefer, and Wienberg believed that an aircraft that could ascend to 65,000 feet before entering an area being swept by the early warning radar would go undetected, because the target-tracking radars would not be activated[9].

The problem with this assumption was that the Soviet Union, unlike Britain and the United States, had continued to improve radar technology after the end of World War II. Even after evidence of improved Soviet radar capabilities became available, however, many advocates of high-altitude overflight continued to believe that aircraft flying above 65,000 feet were safe from detection by Soviet radars.

The Air Force Search for a New Reconnaissance Aircraft

With interest in high-altitude reconnaissance growing, several Air Force agencies began to develop an aircraft to conduct such missions. In September 1952, the Air Research and Development Command gave the Martin Aircraft Company a contract to examine the high-altitude potential of the B-57 by modifying a single aircraft to give it long, high-lift wings and the American version of the new Rolls-Royce Avon-109 engine. These were the modifications that Richard Leghorn had suggested during the previous year.[10]

At about the same time, another Air Force office, the Wright Air Development Command (WADC) in Dayton, Ohio, was also examining ways to achieve sustained flight at high altitudes. Working with two German aeronautical experts — Woldemar Voigt and Richard Vogt — who had come to the United States after World War II, Air Force Maj. John Seaberg advocated the development of a new aircraft that would combine the high-altitude performance of the latest turbo-jet engines with high-efficiency wings in order to reach ultrahigh altitudes. Seaberg, an aeronautical engineer for the Chance Vought Corporation until his recall to active duty during the Korean war, was serving as assistant chief of the New Developments Office of WADC's Bombardment Branch.

By March 1953, Seaberg had expanded his ideas for a high-altitude aircraft into a complete request for proposal for "an aircraft weapon system having an operational radius of 1,500 nm [nautical miles] and capable of conducting pre- and post-strike reconnaissance missions during daylight, good visibility conditions." The requirement stated that such an aircraft must have an optimum subsonic cruise speed at altitudes of 70,000 feet or higher over the target, carry a payload of 100 to 700 pounds of reconnaissance equipment, and have a crew of one.[11]

The Wright Air Development Command decided not

to seek proposals from major airframe manufacturers on the grounds that a smaller company would give the new project a higher priority and produce a better aircraft more quickly. In July 1953, the Bell Aircraft Corporation of Buffalo, New York, and the Fairchild Engine and Airplane Corporation of Hagerstown, Maryland, received study contracts to develop an entirely new high-altitude reconnaissance aircraft. In addition, the Glenn L Martin Company of Baltimore was asked to examine the possibility of improving the already exceptional high-altitude performance of the B-57 Canberra By January 1954 all three firms had submitted their proposals. Fairchild's entry was a single-engine plane known as M-195, which had a maximum altitude potential of 67,200 feet; Bell's was a twin-engine craft called the Model 67 (later the X-16), which had a maximum altitude of 69,500 feet, and Martin's design was a big-wing version of the B-57 called the Model 294, which was to cruise at 64,000 feet. In March 1954, Seaberg and other engineers at Wright Field, having evaluated the three contending designs, recommended the adoption of both the Martin and Bell proposals. They considered Martin's version of the B-57 an interim project that could be completed and deployed rapidly while the more advanced concept from Bell was still being developed.[12]

Air Force headquarters soon approved Martin's proposal to modify the B-57 and was very much interested in the Bell design. But word of the competition for a new reconnaissance airplane had reached another aircraft manufacturer, the Lockheed Aircraft Corporation, which submitted an unsolicited design.

Lockheed had first become aware of the reconnaissance aircraft competition in the fall of 1953. John H. (Jack) Carter, who had recently retired from the Air Force to become the assistant director of Lockheed's Advanced Development Program, was in the Pentagon on business and dropped in to see Eugene P. Kiefer, an old friend and colleague from the Air Force's Office of Development Planning (more commonly known as AFDAP from its Air Force office symbol) Kiefer told Carter about the competition for a high-flying aircraft and expressed the opinion that the Air Force was going about the search in the wrong way by requiring the new aircraft to be suitable for both strategic and tactical reconnaissance.

Immediately after returning to California, Carter proposed to Lockheed Vice President L. Eugene Root (previously the top civilian official in the Air Force's Office of Development Planning) that Lockheed also submit a design Carter noted that the proposed aircraft would have to reach altitudes of between 65,000 and 70,000 feet and correctly forecast, "If extreme altitude performance can be realized in a practical aircraft at speeds in the vicinity of Mach 0 8, it should be capable of avoiding virtually all Russian defenses until about 1960." Carter added, "To achieve these characteristics in an aircraft which will have a reasonably useful operational life during the period before 1960 will, of course, require very strenuous efforts and extraordinary procedures, as well as nonstandard design philosophy." Some of the "nonstandard" design characteristics suggested by Carter were the elimination of landing gear, the disregard of military specifications, and the use of very low load factors Carter's memorandum closed with a warning that time was of the essence. "In order that this special aircraft can have a reasonably long and useful life, it is obvious that its development must be greatly accelerated beyond that considered normal."[13]

Lockheed's senior officials approved Carter's proposal, and early in 1954 the corporation's best aircraft designer — Clarence L. (Kelly) Johnson — began working on the project, then known as the CL-282 but later to become famous under its Air Force designator — the U-2. Already one of the world's leading aeronautical engineers, Kelly Johnson had many successful military and civilian designs to his credit, including the P-38, P-80, F-104, and Constellation. Johnson quickly came up with a radical design based upon the fuselage of the F-104 jet fighter but incorporating a high-aspect-ratio sailplane wing. To save weight and thereby increase the aircraft's altitude, Johnson decided to stress the airframe to only 25 units of gravity (g's) instead of the military specification strength of 5.33 g's. For the power plant he selected the General Electric J73/GE-3 nonafterburning turbojet engine with 9,300 pounds of thrust (this was the same engine he had chosen for the F-104, which had been the basis for the U-2 design).[14] "Many of the CL-282's design features were adapted from gliders. Thus, the wings and tail were detachable. Instead of a conventional landing gear, Johnson proposed using two skis and a reinforced belly rib for landing — a common sailplane technique — and a jettisonable wheeled dolly for takeoff. Other features included an unpressurized cockpit and a 15-cubic-foot payload area that could accommodate 600 pounds of sensors. The CL-282's maximum altitude would be just over 70,000 feet with a 2,000-mile range. Essentially, Kelly Johnson had designed a jet-propelled glider.[15]

Early in March 1954, Kelly Johnson submitted the CL-282 design to Brig Gen. Bernard A. Schriever's Office of Development Planning. Eugene Kiefer and

Bud Wienberg studied the design and recommended it to General Schriever, who then asked Lockheed to submit a specific proposal. In early April, Kelly Johnson presented a full description of the CL-282 and a proposal for the construction and maintenance of 30 aircraft to a group of senior Pentagon officials that included Schriever's superior, Lt. Gen. Donald L. Putt, Deputy Chief of Staff for Development, and Trevor N. Gardner, Special Assistant for Research and Development to the Secretary of the Air Force. Afterward Kelly Johnson noted that the civilian officials were very much interested in his design but the generals were not.[16]

The CL-282 design was also presented to the commander of the Strategic Air Command (SAC), Gen. Curtis E. LeMay, in early April by Eugene Kiefer, Bud Wienberg, and Burton Klein from the Office of Development Planning. According to Wienberg, General LeMay stood up halfway through the briefing, took his cigar out of his mouth, and told the briefers that, if he wanted high-altitude photographs, he would put cameras in his B-36 bombers and added that he was not interested in a plane that had no wheels or guns. The general then left the room, remarking that the whole business was a waste of his time.[17]

Meanwhile, the CL-282 design proceeded through the Air Force development channels and reached Major Seaberg at the Wright Air Development Command in mid-May. Seaberg and his colleagues carefully evaluated the Lockheed submission and finally rejected it in early June. One of their main reasons for doing so was Kelly Johnson's choice of the unproven General Electic J73 engine. The engineers at Wright Field considered the Pratt and Whitney J57 to be the most powerful engine available, and the designs from Fairchild, Martin, and Bell all incorporated this engine. The absence of conventional landing gear was also a perceived shortcoming of the Lockheed design.[18]

Another factor in the rejection of Kelly Johnson's submission was the Air Force preference for multi-engine aircraft. Air Force reconnaissance experts had gained their practical experience during World War II in multiengine bombers. In addition, aerial photography experts in the late 1940s and early 1950s emphasized focal length as the primary factor in reconnaissance photography and, therefore, preferred large aircraft capable of accommodating long focal-length cameras. This preference reached an extreme in the early 1950s with the development of the cumbersome 240-inch Boston camera, a device so large that the YC-97 Boeing Stratocruiser that carried it had to be partially disassembled before the camera could be installed. Finally, there was the feeling shared by many Air Force officers that two engines are always better than one because, if one fails, there is a spare to get the aircraft back to base. In reality, however, aviation records show that single-engine aircraft have always been more reliable than multiengine planes. Furthermore, a high-altitude reconnaissance aircraft deep in enemy territory would have little chance of returning if one of the engines failed, forcing the aircraft to descend.[19]

In 7 June 1954, Kelly Johnson received a letter from the Air Force rejecting the CL-282 proposal because it had only one engine and was too unusual and because the Air Force was already committed to the modification of the Martin B-57.[20] By this time, the Air Force had also selected the Bell X-16; the formal contract calling for 28 aircraft was signed in

September. Despite the Air Force's selection of the X-16, Lockheed continued to work on the CL-282 and began seeking new sources of support for the aircraft.

Lockheed CL-282 Supporters and the CIA

Although the Air Force's uniformed hierarchy had decided in favor of the Bell and Martin aircraft, some high-level civilian officials continued to favor the Lockheed design. The most prominent proponent of the Lockheed proposal was Trevor Gardner, Special Assistant for Research and Development to Air Force Secretary Harold E. Talbott. Gardner had many contacts in west coast aeronautical circles because before coming to Washington he had headed the Hycon Manufacturing Company, which made aerial cameras in Pasadena, California. He had been present at Kelly Johnson's presentation on the CL-282 at the Pentagon in early April 1954 and believed that this design showed the most promise for reconnaissance of the Soviet Union. This belief was shared by Gardner's special assistant, Frederick Ayer, Jr, and Garrison Norton, an adviser to Secretary Talbott.[21]

According to Norton, Gardner tried to interest SAC commander LeMay in the Lockheed aircraft because Gardner envisioned it primarily as a collector of strategic, rather than tactical, intelligence. But General LeMay had already shown that he was not interested in an unarmed aircraft. Gardner, Ayer, and Norton then decided to seek CIA support for the high-flying aircraft. At that time the Agency's official involvement in overhead reconnaissance was limited to advising the Air Force on the problems of launching large camera-carrying balloons for reconnaissance flights over hostile territory (for the details of this program, see chapter 2). The Chief of the Operations

Staff in the Office of Scientific Intelligence, Philip G. Strong, however, served on several Air Force advisory boards and kept himself well informed on developments in reconnaissance aircraft.[22]

Gardner, Norton, and Ayer met with Strong in the Pentagon on 12 May 1954, six days before the Wright Air Development Command began to evaluate the Lockheed proposal. Gardner described Kelly Johnson's proposal and showed the drawings to Strong. After this meeting, Strong summarized his impressions of the Air Force's search for a high-altitude reconnaissance aircraft.

> *Proposals for special reconnaissance aircraft have been received in the Air Staff from Lockheed, Fairchild, and Bell.*
>
> *The Lockheed proposal is considered to be the best. It has been given the type designation of CL-282 and in many respects is a jet-powered glider based essentially on the Lockheed Day Fighter XF-104. It is primarily subsonic but can attain transonic speeds over the target with a consequent loss of range. With an altitude of 73,000 feet over the target it has a combat radius of 1,400 nautical miles. The CL-282 can be manufactured mainly with XF-104 jigs and designs. The prototype of this plane can be produced within a year from the date of order. Five planes could be delivered for operations within two years.*
>
> *The Bell proposal is a more conventional aircraft having normal landing gear. As a result, its maximum altitude over target is 69,500 feet and the speed and range are not as good as the Lockheed CL-282.*[23]

Gardner's enthusiasm for the CL-282 had given

Strong the false impression that most Air Force officials supported the Lockheed design. In reality, the Air Force's uniformed hierarchy was in the process of choosing the modified version of the Martin B-57 and the new Bell X-16 to meet future reconnaissance needs.

During their meeting with Strong, Trevor Gardner, Frederick Ayer, and Garrison Norton explained that they favored the CL-282 because it gave promise of flying higher than the other designs and because at maximum altitude its smaller radar cross section might make it invisible to existing Soviet radars. The three officials asked Strong if the CIA would be interested in such an aircraft. Strong promised to talk to the Director of Central Intelligence's newly hired Special Assistant for Planning and Coordination, Richard M. Bissell, Jr, about possible Agency interest in the CL-282.[24]

Richard Bissell had already had an active and varied career before he joined the CIA. A graduate of Groton and Yale, Bissell studied at the London School of Economics for a year and then completed a doctorate at Yale in 1939. He taught economics, first at Yale and then from 1942 at the Massachusetts Institute of Technology (MIT), where he became a full professor in 1948. During World War II, Bissell had managed American shipping as executive officer of the Combined Shipping Adjustment Board. After the war, he served as deputy director of the Marshall Plan from 1948 until the end of 1951, when he became a staff member of the Ford Foundation. His first association with the Agency came in late 1953, when he undertook a contract study of possible responses the United States might use against the Soviet Bloc in the event of another uprising such as the East Berlin riots of June 1953. Bissell quickly concluded that there was not much hope for clandestine operations against Bloc nations. As he remarked later "I know I emerged from that exercise feeling that very little could be done." This belief would later make Bissell a leading advocate of technical rather than human means of intelligence collection.[25]

Bissell joined the Agency in late January 1954 and soon became involved in coordination for the operation aimed at overthrowing Guatemalan President Jacobo Arbenz. He was, therefore very preoccupied when Philip Strong approached him in mid-May 1954 with the concept of the proposed spyplane from Lockheed. Bissell said that the idea had merit and told Strong to get some topflight scientists to advise on the matter. Afterward he returned to the final planning for the Guatemalan operation and promptly forgot about the CL-282.[26]

Meanwhile, Strong went about drumming up support for high-altitude overflight. In May 1954 he persuaded DCI Allen W. Dulles to ask the Air Force to take the initiative in gaining approval for an overflight of the Soviet guided-missile test range at Kapustin Yar. Dulles's memorandum did not mention the CL-282 or any of the other proposed high-altitude aircraft CIA and Air Force officials met on several occasions to explore the overflight proposal, which the Air Force finally turned down in October 1954.[27]

Although Allen Dulles was willing to support an Air Force overflight of the Soviet Union, he was not enthusiastic about the CIA undertaking such a project. Few details about Dulles's precise attitude toward the proposed Lockheed reconnaissance aircraft are available, but many who knew him believe that he did not want the CIA to become involved in projects that belonged to the military, and the Lockheed CL-282 had been designed for an Air Force requirement. Moreover, high-altitude reconnaissance of the Soviet Union did not fit well into Allen Dulles's perception of the proper role of an intelligence agency. He tended to favor the classical form of espionage, which relied on agents rather than technology.[28]

At this point, the summer of 1954, Lockheed's CL-282 proposal still lacked official support. Although the design had strong backers among some Air Force civilians and CIA officials, the key decisionmakers at both Air Force and CIA remained unconvinced. To make Kelly Johnson's revolutionary design a reality, one additional source of support was necessary prominent scientists serving on government advisory boards.

SCIENTISTS AND OVERHEAD RECONNAISSANCE

Scientists and engineers from universities and private industry had played a major role in advising the government on technical matters during World War 11. At the end of the war, most of the scientific advisory boards were disbanded, but within a few years the growing tensions of the Cold War again led government agencies to seek scientific advice and assistance. In 1947 the Air Force established a Scientific Advisory Board, which met periodically to discuss topics of current interest and advise the Air Force on the potential usefulness of new technologies. The following year the Office of Defense Mobilization established the Scientific Advisory Committee, but the Truman administration made little use of this new advisory body.[29]

The BEACON HILL Report

In 1951 the Air Force sought even more assistance from scientists because the Strategic Air Command's requests for information about targets behind the Iron Curtain could not be filled. To look for new ways of conducting reconnaissance against the Soviet Bloc, the Air Force's Deputy Chief of Staff for Development, Maj. Gen. Gordon P. Saville, added 15 reconnaissance experts to an existing project on air defense known as Project LINCOLN, then under way at the Massachusetts Institute of Technology. By the end of the year, these experts had assembled in Boston to begin their research. Their headquarters was located over a secretarial school on Beacon Hill, which soon became the codename for the reconnaissance project. The consultants were called the BEACON HILL Study Group.

The study group's chairman was Kodak physicist Carl F.P. Overhage, and its members included James G. Baker and Edward M. Purcell from Harvard; Saville Davis from the *Christian Science Monitor,* Allen F. Donovan from the Cornell Aeronautical Laboratory, Peter C. Goldmark from Columbia Broadcasting System Laboratories, Edwin H. Land, founder of the Polaroid Corporation, Stewart E. Miller of Bell Laboratories, Richard S. Perkin of the Perkin-Elmer Company, and Louis N. Ridenour of Ridenour Associates, Inc. The Wright Air Development Command sent Lt. Col Richard Leghorn to serve as its liaison officer[30].

During January and February 1952, the BEACON HILL Study Group traveled every weekend to various airbases, laboratories, and firms for briefings on the latest technology and projects. The panel members were particularly interested in new approaches to aerial reconnaissance, such as photography from high-flying aircraft and camera-carrying balloons. One of the more unusual (albeit unsuccessful) proposals examined by the panel was an "invisible" dirigible. This was to be a giant, almost flat-shaped airship with a blue-tinted, nonreflective coating; it would cruise at an altitude of 90,000 feet along the borders of the Soviet Union at very slow speeds while using a large lens to photograph targets of interest.[31]

After completing these briefings at the end of February 1952, the BEACON HILL Study Group returned to MIT, where the panel members spent the next three months writing a report detailing their recommendations for ways to improve the amount and quality of intelligence being gathered on the Soviet Bloc. Published as a classified document on 15 June 1952, the *BEACON HILL Report* advocated radical approaches to obtain the information needed for national intelligence estimates. Its 14 chapters covered radar, radio, and photographic surveillance, examined the use of passive infrared and microwave reconnaissance, and discussed the development of advanced reconnaissance vehicles. One of the report's key recommendations called for the development of high-altitude reconnaissance aircraft.

> *We have reached a period in history when our peacetime knowledge of the capabilities, activities and dispositions of a potentially hostile nation is such as to demand that we supplement it with the maximum amount of information obtainable through aerial reconnaissance. To avoid political involvements, such aerial reconnaissance must be conducted either from vehicles flying in friendly airspace, or — decision on this point permitting — from vehicles whose performance is such that they can operate in Soviet airspace with greatly reduced chances of detection or interception.*

Concern About the Danger of a Soviet Surprise Attack

The Air Force did not begin to implement the ideas of the *BEACON HILL Report* until the summer of 1953. By this time interest in reconnaissance had increased after Dwight D. Eisenhower became President in January 1953 and soon expressed his dissatisfaction with the quality of the intelligence estimates of Soviet strategic capabilities and the paucity of reconnaissance on the Soviet Bloc.[33]

To President Eisenhower and many other US political and military leaders, the Soviet Union was a dangerous opponent that appeared to be moving inexorably toward a position of military parity with the United States. Particularly alarming was Soviet progress in the area of nuclear weapons. In the late summer of 1949, the Soviet Union had detonated an atomic bomb nearly three years sooner than US experts had predicted. Then in August 1953 a scant nine months after the first US test of a hydrogen bomb — the Soviet Union detonated a hydrogen bomb manufactured from lithium deuteride, a technology more advanced than the heavy water method used by US scientists. Thus, new and extremely powerful weapons were coming into the hands of a government whose actions greatly disturbed the leaders of the West. Only two months before the successful hydrogen bomb test, Soviet troops had crushed an uprising in East Berlin. And, at the United Nations, the Soviet Bloc seemed bent on causing dissension between Western Europe and the United States and between the developed and undeveloped nations. This aggressive Soviet foreign policy, combined with advances in nuclear weapons, led officials such as Secretary of State John Foster Dulles to see the Soviet Union as a menace to peace and world order.

The Soviet Union's growing military strength soon became a threat not just to US forces overseas but to the continental United States itself. In the spring of 1953, a top secret RAND study pointed out the vulnerability of the SAC's US bases to a surprise attack by Soviet long-range bombers.[34]

Concern about the danger of a Soviet attack on the continental United States grew after an American military attache sighted a new Soviet intercontinental bomber at Ramenskoye airfield, south of Moscow, in 1953. The new bomber was the Myasishchev-4, later designated Bison by NATO. Powered by jet engines rather than the turboprops of Russia's other long-range bombers, the Bison appeared to be the Soviet equivalent of the US B-52, which was only then going into production. Pictures of the Bison taken at the Moscow May Day air show in 1954 had an enormous impact on the US intelligence community. Unlike several other Soviet postwar aircraft, the Bison was not a derivative of US or British designs but represented a native Soviet design capability that surprised US intelligence experts. This new long-range jet bomber, along with the Soviet Union's large numbers of older propeller and turboprop bombers, seemed to pose a significant threat to the United States, and, in the summer of 1954, newspapers and magazines began publishing articles highlighting the growing airpower of the Soviet Union. Pictures of the Bison bomber featured prominently in such stories.[35]

The Air Force Intelligence Systems Panel

Even before the publication of photographs of the Bison raised fears that the Soviet bomber force might eventually surpass that of the United States, the Air Force had already established a new advisory body to look for ways to implement the main recommendation of the BEACON HILL Report — the construction of high-flying aircraft and high-acuity cameras. Created in July 1953, the Intelligence Systems Panel (ISP) included several experts from the BEACON HILL Study Group Land, Overhage, Donovan, and Miller. At the request of the Air Force, the CIA also participated in the panel, represented by Edward L. Allen of the Office of Research and Reports (ORR) and Philip Strong of the Office of Scientific Intelligence (OSI)[36].

The chairman of the new panel was Dr. James G. Baker, a research associate at the Harvard College Observatory. Baker had been involved in aerial reconnaissance since 1940, when he first advised the Army Air Corps on ways to improve its lenses. He then established a full-scale optical laboratory at Harvard — the Harvard University Optical Research Laboratory — to produce high-quality lenses. Since the university did not wish to continue manufacturing cameras and lenses after the end of the war, the optical laboratory moved to Boston University, which agreed to sponsor the effort as long as the Air Force would fund it. Baker decided to remain at Harvard, so his assistant, Dr. Duncan E. Macdonald, became the new head of what was now called the Boston University Optical Research Laboratory (BUORL). Baker's association with the Air Force did not end with the transfer of the optical laboratory to Boston University, because he continued to design lenses to be used in photoreconnaissance.[37]

The ISP first met at Boston University on 3 August 1953. To provide background on the poor state of US knowledge of the Soviet Union, Philip Strong informed the other panel members that the best intelligence then available on the Soviet Union's interior was photography taken by the German Luftwaffe during World War II. Since the German photography covered only the Soviet Union west of the Urals, primarily west of the Volga River, many vital regions were not included. The ISP would, therefore, have to look for ways to provide up-to-date photography of all of the Soviet Union. Several Air Force agencies then briefed the panel members on the latest developments and proposed future projects in the area of aerial reconnaissance, including new cameras, reconnaissance balloons, and even satellites. Among the Air Force reconnaissance projects discussed were multiple sensors for use in existing aircraft such as the RB-47, RB-52, and RB-58; Project FICON — an acronym for "fighter conversion" — for adapting a giant, 10-engine B-36 bomber to enable it to launch and retrieve a Republic RF-84F. Thunderflash reconnaissance aircraft, reconnaissance versions of the Navejo and Snark missiles, the high-altitude balloon program, which would be ready to go into operation by the summer of 1955, and research for a new high-altitude reconnaissance aircraft[38].

The wide variety of programs discussed at the conference were all products of the Air Force's all-out effort to find a way to collect intelligence on the Communist Bloc. Some of the schemes went beyond the existing level of technology, others, like the camera-carrying balloons, were technically feasible but involved dangerous political consequences.

British Overflight of Kapustin Yar

The British were also working on high-altitude reconnaissance aircraft. In 1952 the Royal Air Force (RAP) began Project ROBIN, which was designed to modify the Canberra bomber for high-altitude reconnaissance. This project was probably inspired by

Richard Leghorn's collaboration with English Electric Company designers in 1951, when they calculated ways to increase the altitude of the Canberra. The RAF equipped the new Canberra PR7 with Rolls-Royce Avon-109 engines and gave it long, fuel-filled wings. The range of this variant of the Canberra was now 4,300 miles, and, on 29 August 1955, it achieved an altitude of 65,880 feet[39].

Sometime during the first half of 1953, the RAF employed a high-altitude Canberra on a daring overflight of the Soviet Union to photograph the missile test range at Kapustin Yar. Because of advanced warning from either radar or agents inside British intelligence, the overflight did not catch the Soviet Union by surprise. Soviet fighters damaged and nearly shot down the Canberra[40]. Rumors about this flight reached Washington during the summer of 1953, but official confirmation by the United Kingdom did not come until February 1954. While on a six-week tour of Europe to study aerial reconnaissance problems for the US Air Force's Scientific Advisory Board, James Baker was briefed by RAF intelligence officials on the Canberra overflight of the Soviet Union. On 22 and 23 March 1954, he reported on it to the full Scientific Advisory Board at Langley AFB, Virginia.

Baker also chaired the next meeting of the Air Force's Intelligence Systems Panel in late April 1954 but could not tell its members about the British overflight of Kapustin Yar because they were not cleared for this information. The panel did, however, discuss the modifications for high-altitude flight being made to the US Canberra, the B-57.[41]

The Intelligence Systems Panel and the CL-282

The next Intelligence Systems Panel meeting took place on 24 and 25 May at Boston University and the Polaroid Corporation Panel member Allen F. Donovan from the Cornell Aeronautical Laboratory evaluated the changes being made to the B-57 by the Martin Aircraft Company. Even without Martin's specifications or drawings, Donovan had been able to estimate what could be done to the B-57 by lengthening the wings and lightening the fuselage. He had determined that alterations to the B-57 airframe would not solve the reconnaissance needs expressed in the *BEACON HILL Report.* Theoretically, he explained to the panel, any multiengine aircraft built according to military specifications, including the B-57, would be too heavy to fly above 65,000 feet and hence would be vulnerable to Soviet interception. To be safe, Donovan explained, penetrating aircraft would need to fly above 70,000 feet for the entire rnission.[42]

Development of such an aircraft was already under way, Donovan continued, for Philip Strong of the CIA had told him that the Lockheed Aircraft Corporation had designed a lightweight, high-flying aircraft. ISP chairman Baker then urged Donovan to travel to southern California to evaluate the Lockheed design and gather ideas on high-altitude aircraft from other aircraft manufacturers.

When he was finally able to make this trip in late summer, Donovan found the plane that he and the other ISP members had been seeking. On the afternoon of 2 August 1954, Donovan met with L. Eugene Root, an old Air Force acquaintance who was now a Lockheed vice-president, and learned about the Air Force's competition for a high-altitude reconnaissance aircraft. Kelly Johnson then showed Donovan the plans for Lockheed's unsuccessful entry. A lifelong sailplane enthusiast, Donovan immediately recognized that the CL-282 design was essentially a jet-propelled glider capable of attaining the altitudes that he felt were necessary to carry out reconnaissance of the Soviet Union successfully.[43]

Upon his return east on 8 August, Donovan got in touch with James Baker and suggested an urgent meeting of the Intelligence Systems Panel. Because of other commitments by the members, however, the panel did not meet to hear Donovan's report until 24 September 1954 at the Cornell Aeronautical Laboratory. Several members, including Land and Strong, were absent. Those who did attend were upset to learn that the Air Force had funded a closed competition for a tactical reconnaissance plane without informing them. But once Donovan began describing Kelly Johnson's rejected design for a jet-powered glider, they quickly forgot their annoyance and listened intently.

Donovan began by stressing that high-altitude reconnaissance aircraft had to fly above 70,000 feet to be safe from interception. Next, he set out what he considered to be the three essential requirements for a high-altitude spyplane: a single engine, a sailplane wing, and low structural load factors. Donovan strongly favored single-engine aircraft because they are both lighter and more reliable than multiengine aircraft. Although a twin-engine aircraft could theoretically return to base on only one engine, Donovan explained, it could only do so at a much lower altitude, about 34,000 feet, where it was sure to be shot down.

The second of Donovan's essential factors, a sailplane wing (in technical terms a high-aspect-ratio, low-induced-drag wing), was needed to take maximum advantage of the reduced thrust of a jet engine operating in the rarefied atmosphere of extreme altitude. Because of the thinness of the atmosphere above 70,000 feet, engineers estimated that the power curve of a jet engine would fall off to about 6 percent of its sea-level thrust.

Finally, low structural load factors, like those used by transport aircraft, were necessary to reduce weight and thereby achieve maximum altitude. Donovan explained that strengthening wings and wingroot areas to withstand the high speeds and sharp turns mandated by the standard military airworthiness rules added too much weight to the airframe, thereby negating the efficiency of the sailplane wing.

In short, it was possible to achieve attitudes in excess of 70,000 feet, but only by making certain that all parts of the aeronautical equation were in balance: thrust, lift, and weight. The only plane meeting these requirements, Donovan insisted, was Kelly Johnson's CL-282 because it was essentially a sailplane. In Donovan's view, the CL-282 did not have to meet the specifications of a combat aircraft because it could fly safely above Soviet fighters.[44]

Donovan's arguments convinced the Intelligence Systems Panel of the merits of the CL-282 proposal, but this panel reported to the Air Force, which had already rejected the CL-282. Thus, even though the Lockheed CL-282 had several important sources of support by September 1954 — the members of the Intelligence Systems Panel and high-ranking Air Force civilians such as Trevor Gardner — these backers were all connected with the Air Force. They could not offer funds to Lockheed to pursue the CL-282 concept because the Air Force was already committed to the

Martin RB-57 and the Bell X-16. Additional support from outside the Air Force was needed to bring the CL-282 project to life, and this support would come from scientists serving on high-level advisory committees.

The Technological Capabilities Panel

The Eisenhower administration was growing increasingly concerned over the capability of the Soviet Union to launch a surprise attack on the United States. Early in 1954, Trevor Gardner had become alarmed by a RAND Corporation study warning that a Soviet surprise attack might destroy 85 percent of the SAC bomber force. Gardner then met with Dr. Lee DuBridge, President of the California Institute of Technology and Chairman of the Office of Defense Mobilization's Science Advisory Committee, and criticized the committee for not dealing with such essential problems as the possibility of a surprise attack. This criticism led DuBridge to invite Gardner to speak at the Science Advisory Committee's next meeting. After listening to Gardner, the committee members decided to approach President Eisenhower on the matter. On 27 March 1954, the President told them about the discovery of the Soviet Bison bombers and his concern that these new aircraft might be used in a surprise attack on the United States. Stressing the high priority he gave to reducing the risk of military surprise, the President asked the committee to advise him on this problem.[45]

The President's request led Chairman DuBridge to ask one of the most prominent members, MIT President James R. Killian, Jr, to meet with other Science Advisory Committee members in the Boston area to discuss the feasibility of a comprehensive scientific assessment of the nation's defenses. At their

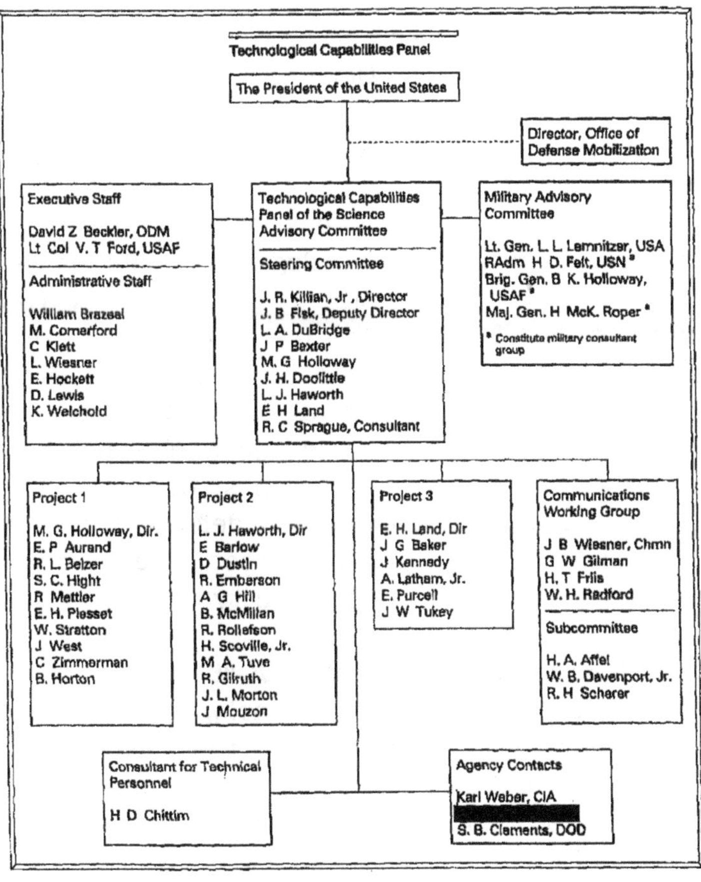
Technological Capabilities Panel
The President of the United States
Director, Office of Defense Mobilization
Executive Staff
David Z. Beckler, ODM
Lt Col V. T Ford, USAF
Administrative Staff
William Brazeal
M. Comerford
C Klett
L. Wiesner
E. Hockett
D. Lewis
K. Welchold
Technological Capabilities Panel of the Science Advisory Committee
Steering Committee
J. R. Killian, Jr, Director
J. B Fisk, Deputy Director
L. A. DuBridge
J P Baxter
M. G Holloway
J. H. Doolittle
L. J. Haworth
E H Land
R. C Sprague, Consultant
Military Advisory Committee
Lt. Gen. L. L. Lemnitzer, USA
RAdm H D. Felt, USN *
Brig. Gen. B K. Holloway, USAF *
Maj. Gen. H McK. Roper *
* Constitute military consultant group
Project 1
M. G. Holloway, Dir.
E. P Aurand
R. L. Belzer
S. C. Hight
R Mettler
E. H. Plesset
W. Stratton
J West
C Zimmerman
B. Horton
Project 2
L. J. Haworth, Dir
E Barlow
D Dustin
R. Emberson
A G Hill
B. McMillan
R. Rollefson
H. Scoville, Jr.
M A. Tuve
R. Gilruth
J. L. Morton
J Mouzon
Project 3
E. H. Land, Dir
J G Baker
J Kennedy
A. Latham, Jr.
E. Purcell
J W Tukey
Communications Working Group
J B Wiesner, Chmn
G W Gilman
H. T Friis
W. H. Radford
Subcommittee
H. A. Affel
W. B. Davenport, Jr.
R. H Scherer
Consultant for Technical Personnel
H D Chittim
Agency Contacts
Karl Weber, CIA
S. B. Clements, DOD

meeting at MIT on 15 April 1954, the group called for the recruitment of such a task force if the President endorsed the concept.

On 26 July 1954, President Eisenhower authorized Killian to recruit and lead a panel of experts to study "the country's technological capabilities to meet some of its current problems". Killian quickly set up shop in offices located in the Old Executive Office Building and organized 42 of the nation's leading scientists into three special project groups investigating US offensive, defensive, and intelligence capabilities, with an additional communications working group (see chart, next page). The Technological Capabilities Panel (TCP) groups began meeting on 13 September 1954. For the next 20 weeks, the members of the various panels met on 307 separate occasions for briefings, field trips, conferences, and meetings with every major unit of the US defense and intelligence establishments. After receiving the most up-to-date information available on the nation's defense and intelligence programs, the panel members began drafting their report to the National Security Council.[46]

Project Three Support for the Lockheed CL-282

Even before the final Technological Capabilities Panel report was ready, one of the three working groups took actions that would have a major impact on the US reconnaissance program. Project Three had the task of investigating the nation's intelligence capabilities. Its chairman was Edwin H. (Din) Land, the inventor of the polarizing filter and the instant camera. When James Killian asked Land to head Project Three, Land had to make a major decision about his career. At the time, the 45-year-old millionaire was on a leave of absence from Polaroid and was living in

Hollywood, advising Alfred Hitchcock on the technological aspects of making three-dimensional movies. Land decided to give up his interest in cinema's third dimension and return east to Polaroid and the panel appointment.[47]

Land's Project Three was the smallest of the three Technological Capabilities Panel projects, for he preferred what he called "taxicab committees" — committees small enough to fit into a single taxicab. The Project Three committee consisted of Land, James Baker and Edward Purcell of Harvard; chemist Joseph W. Kennedy of Washington University, St Louis, mathematician John W. Tukey of Princeton University and Bell Telephone Laboratories, and Allen Latham, Jr., of Arthur D. Little, Inc., an engineer and former treasurer of the Polaroid Corporation.[48]

In mid-August 1954, Land and Baker went to Washington to arrange for the various intelligence organizations to brief the Project Three study group. As the briefings progressed, the panel members became more and more distressed at the poor state of the nation's intelligence resources. Land later noted, "We would go in and interview generals and admirals in charge of intelligence and come away worried. Here we were, five or six young men, asking questions that these high-ranking officers couldn't answer." Land added that the Project Three members were also not overly impressed with the Central Intelligence Agency.[49]

Land learned the details of Lockheed's proposed CL-282 aircraft soon after he arrived in Washington. Philip Strong showed him Kelly Johnson's conceptual drawing of the plane and told him that the Air Force had rejected it. Although Land had heard Allen Donovan briefly mention a Lockheed design for a high-flying aircraft at the 24-25 May meeting of Baker's Intelligence Systems Panel, he did not realize that that plane and the one in Strong's drawing were the same. As soon as Land saw Strong's copy of the CL-282 drawing, however, he telephoned Baker to say, "Jim, I think I have the plane you are after."[50]

A few days later, when Land showed Kelly Johnson's conceptual drawing to Baker and the other Project Three members, they all became enthusiastic about the aircraft's possibilities. Although Baker had heard Allen Donovan's brief mention of the Lockheed design in May, he had not yet seen a drawing of the aircraft because Donovan did not report to the ISP on his early-August trip to Lockheed until 24 September. After seeing the CL-282 drawing, Baker began designing a camera and lens system that would fit in the Lockheed craft.[51]

At the end of August, Land discussed the CL-282 with Allen Dulles's Special Assistant for Planning and Coordination, Richard Bissell, who came away from the meeting without any definite ideas as to what Land wanted to do with the aircraft. Overhead reconnaissance was not uppermost in Bissell's mind at the time, and it was unclear to him why he had even been contacted.[52] Bissell's outstanding academic credentials, his acquaintanceship with James Killian through his previous teaching experience at MIT, and his direct access to DCI Dulles may have led the Technological Capabilities Panel members to consider him the best CIA point of contact.

Although surprised that he had become involved in the CL-282 project, Bissell's interest was piqued, and he set out to learn what he could about reconnaissance systems. In early September 1954, Bissell had [name deleted] a young Air Force officer on his staff, put together a general status report on air reconnaissance programs. Bissell forwarded the 16-page study to the Deputy Director of Central Intelligence (DDCI), Lt. Gen. Charles Pearre Cabell, USAF, on 24 September. In a covering memorandum, Bissell called Cabell's attention to a section of the report about a "stripped or specialized aircraft" called the Lockheed CL-282.[53]

By September 1954, Land's Project Three study group had become very much interested in the Lockheed C~282 design. Their interest grew even stronger when James Baker told them of Allen Donovan's strong case for the CL-282 at the 24-25 September meeting of the ISP. It is not possible to determine exactly when the Land committee decided to back the CL-282; in fact, there may never have been a formal decision as such. In view of Land's impulsive nature, he probably seized upon the CL-282 design as being a workable concept and immediately began developing it into a complete reconnaissance system.

During September and October the Project Three study group met frequently to discuss the Lockheed design and the reconnaissance equipment it would carry. Meetings were small, generally with fewer than 10 participants, Garrison Norton was often the only government official in attendance. At times outside experts joined in the proceedings. When the discussion turned to cameras and film, Land invited Dr. Henry Yutzy, Eastman Kodak's film expert, and Richard S. Perkin, President of the Perkin-Elmer Company, to participate. For discussions on the J57 engine, the panel members asked Perry W. Pratt, Pratt and Whitney's chief engineer, to attend. Kelly Johnson also met with the panel to review plans for the CL-282 system.[54]

By the end of October, the Project Three meetings had covered every aspect of the Lockheed design. The CL-282 was to be more than an airplane with a camera, it was to be an integrated intelligence-collection system that the Project Three members were confident could find and photograph the Soviet Union's Bison bomber fleet and, thus, resolve the growing "bomber gap" controversy. It was not just the Lockheed aircraft that had captured the Land group's fancy, the plane was seen as the platform for a whole new generation of aerial cameras that several committee members had been discussing since the BEACON HILL and Intelligence Systems Panel meetings James Baker was in the process of developing a revolutionary new camera with tremendously improved resolution and film capacity, and the Eastman Kodak company was working on new thin, lightweight film.[55]

By October 1954, the Project Three study group had drafted a complete program for an overhead reconnaissance effort based on the CL-282 aircraft .The one remaining question was who would conduct the overflights. The committee's members, particularly Land, were not in favor of the Air Force conducting such missions in peacetime. Firmly believing that military overflights in armed aircraft could provoke a war, they argued for civilian overflights in unarmed, unmarked aircraft. In their view, the organization most suited for this mission was the Central Intelligence Agency.[56]

In late October 1954, the Project Three panel discussed the CL-282 system concept with DCI Allen Dulles and the Secretary of the Air Force's Special Assistant for Research and Development, Trevor Gardner. Dulles was reluctant to have the CIA undertake the project. He did not like to involve the CIA with military projects, even ones that the military had rejected, like the CL-282. Furthermore, the DCI strongly believed that the Agency's mission lay in the use of human operatives and secret communications, the classic forms of intelligence gathering. Land came away from this meeting with the impression that Dulles somehow thought overflights were not fair play. Project Three committee members were nevertheless convinced that technology, particularly in the form of the CL-282 and the new camera designs, would solve the nation's intelligence problems.[57]

A Meeting With the President

Allen Dulles's reluctance to involve the C1A in the CL-282 project did not stop the Project Three committee from pursuing its aims because it was able to go over Dulles's head and appeal directly to the President. Having participated in the BEACON HILL Study and the Intelligence Systems Panel, several Project Three members had definite ideas on how to improve intelligence collection, ideas that they were determined to present to the highest levels of government They were able to do so because the Land committee was part of a panel commissioned by President Eisenhower to examine the nation's intelligence community and recommend changes. The committee thus had a direct line to the White House through James Killian's contacts there.

Early in November 1954, Land and Killian met with President Eisenhower to discuss high-altitude reconnaissance. Killian's memoirs contain an account of this crucial meeting.

Land described the [CL-282] system using an

> *unarmed plane and recommended that its developments be undertaken. After listening to our proposal and asking many hard questions, Eisenhower approved the development of the system, but he stipulated that it should be handled in an unconventional way so that it would not become entangled in the bureaucracy of the Defense Department or troubled by rivalries among the services.*[58]

The scientists from the advisory committees and the President were thus in agreement that the new reconnaissance program should be controlled by the CIA, not the military.

CIA and Air Force Agreement on the CL-282

Meanwhile Edwin Land and his Project Three colleagues were working to convince Allen Dulles that the CIA should run the proposed overflight program. On 5 November Land wrote to the DCI strongly urging that the CIA undertake the CL-282 project.

> *Here is the brief report from our panel telling why we think overflight is urgent and presently feasible. I [Land] am not sure that we have made it clear that we feel there are many reasons why this activity is appropriate for CIA, always with Air Force assistance. We told you that this seems to us the kind of action and technique that is right for the contemporary version of CIA a modern and scientific way for an Agency that is always supposed to be looking, to do its looking. Quite strongly, we feel that you must always assert your first right to pioneer in scientific techniques for collecting intelligence — and choosing such partners to assist you as may be needed. This present opportunity for aerial photogra-*

phy seems to us a fine place to start.[59]

The letter had two attachments: a two-page summary of a complete operational plan for organizing, building, and deploying the CL-282 within a period of 20 months at a cost of $22 million and a three-page memorandum, entitled "A Unique Opportunity for Comprehensive Intelligence."

Aware of Dulles's preference for classical intelligence work, the Project Three memorandum stressed the superiority of the CL-282 program over traditional espionage methods.

> *We believe that these planes can go where we need to have them go efficiently and safely, and that no amount of fragmentary and indirect intelligence can be pieced together to be equivalent to such positive information as can thus be provided.*[60]

The Land committee memorandum also stressed the need for the CIA to undertake such reconnaissance missions rather than the Air Force, noting that "For the present it seems rather dangerous for one of our military arms to engage directly in extensive overflight." The committee members also listed the advantages of using the CL-282 rather than an Air Force aircraft.

> *The Lockheed super glider will fly at 70,000 feet, well out of the reach of present Russian interceptors and high enough to have a good chance of avoiding detection. The plane itself is so light (15,000 pounds), so obviously unarmed and devoid of military usefulness, that it would minimize affront to the Russians even if through some remote mischance it were detected and identified.*[61]

One additional advantage of the Lockheed design over the Air Force's proposed high-altitude reconnaissance aircraft was a faster completion time. Kelly Johnson had promised the Land committee that his aircraft would be flying by August 1955, just eight months after he proposed to start construction. The Bell X-16 prototype was not scheduled for completion before the spring of 1956.

The strong advocacy of Killian and the other scientists on the various advisory committees concerned with overhead reconnaissance, combined with President Eisenhower's support, finally won over DCI Dulles, but a project of this magnitude also required the support of the Air Force Some Air Force officials, however, feared that a decision to build the CL-282 might jeopardize the Air Force's own RB-57 and X-16 projects. Just one month earlier, in October 1954, the Wright Air Development Command had appealed to the Air Force Deputy Chief of Staff for Development, Lt. Gen. Donald L. Putt, to oppose the adoption of the Lockheed design. The officials argued that the Bell X-16 was a better design because it was more airworthy than the CL-282 and could be used throughout the Air Force in different types of missions because it had two engines, wheels, and an armor-plated, pressurized pilot's compartment. If J57 engines were diverted to the CL-282, the appeal to General Putt warned, there would not be enough of these popular powerplants to meet the needs of the X-16 program.[62]

Having heard of the Wright Air Development Command attack on the CL-282, Allen Donovan of the Intelligence Systems Panel met with General Putt on 19 October to argue in favor of the Lockheed design. This discussion led General Putt to meet with 15 scientists from the Technological Capabilities Panel on 18

November 1954 to discuss the merits of the four proposed reconnaissance aircraft. Also present as a briefer was Maj. John Seaberg from the Wright Air Development Command, who later recalled

> *What I did was present the results of my comparative analysis of all four designs. I showed the relative high attitude performance capabilities of all four. I pointed out that aerodynamically the Bell, Fairchild, and Lockheed designs were close Martin's B-57, being a modification, was not quite as capable. I stated that, in my opinion, the J73 [General Electric engine] would not be good enough to do the job in Johnson's airplane. And further, I overlaid a curve showing that with the JS7 [Pratt & Whitney engine] installed, it would then be competitive with the Bell and Fairchild designs.*[63]

This meeting — along with the knowledge that President Eisenhower also supported the CL-282 — helped win over the Air Force. To be on the safe side, however, the Air Force did not abandon the X-16 program until the Lockheed aircraft had begun flying.

On 19 November, the day after Seaberg's briefing, the final decision on the CL-282 came at a luncheon hosted by Air Force Secretary Talbott. The participants — Dulles and Cabell from the CIA, Gardner, Ayer, and General Putt from the Air Force, Kelly Johnson, and Edwin Land — all agreed "that the special item of material described by Lockheed was practical and desirable and would be sought. It was agreed that the Project should be a joint Air Force-CIA one but that, regardless of the source of the funds, whether AF or CIA, [end of sentence deleted]

It is interesting to note that Lockheed, which had

originally developed the CL-282 on its own and had devoted considerable effort to promoting it, had to be persuaded to undertake the project in November 1954 because the company had become heavily committed to several other civilian and military projects. When Kelly Johnson received a call from Trevor Gardner on 17 November asking him to come to Washington for conversations on the project, his instructions from Lockheed's senior management were "to not commit to any program during the visit, but to get the information and return." When he returned to California, Johnson noted in his project log that "I was impressed with the secrecy aspect and was told by Gardner that I was essentially being drafted for the project. It seemed, in fact, that if I did not talk quietly, I might have to take a leave of absence from my job at Lockheed to do this special project."[65] Of course, Kelly Johnson did not need to be drafted or persuaded into undertaking such a bold step forward in aircraft design. He used Gardner's statement to convince Lockheed's senior management to approve the project, which they did after meeting with Johnson when he returned to California on the evening of 19 November.

Four days later, on 23 November, the Intelligence Advisory Committee (IAC) approved DCI Dulles's request to undertake the CL-282 project. The following day Dulles signed a three-page memorandum, drafted by DDCI Cabell, asking President Eisenhower to approve the overhead reconnaissance project. That same afternoon, at a meeting attended by the Secretaries of State and Defense and senior Air Force officials, Dulles and Cabell presented the document to the President and received verbal authorization to proceed. Eisenhower told Dulles that the project was to be managed by the Agency and that the Air Force was to provide any assistance needed to get it operational.[66]

Thus, it was that the CIA entered into the world of high technology primarily because of decisions and actions taken outside the Agency: the Air Force's refusal to build the CL-282 aircraft, President Eisenhower's desire to have a sensitive overflight project conducted by a civilian agency rather than the military, and, above all, the determination by a small group of prominent scientists that the Lockheed design represented the best possible overhead reconnaissance system.[67]

[1]Roy M. Stanley II, *World War II Photo Intelligence* (New York: Scribners, 1981), p. 16

[footnote deleted]

[3]A. L. George, *Case Studies of Actual Overflights*, 1930–1953, and Study RM-1349 (Santa Monica: Rand, 1955) (S) Arthur S Lundahl and Dino Brugioni, interview by Donald E. Welzenbach, tape recording, Washington, DC, 14 December 1983 (TS Codeword). Recordings, transcripts, and notes for the interviews conducted for this study are on file at the DCI History Staff.

[4]Jeffrey Richelson states on page 121 of *American Espionage and the soviet Target* (New York: Morrow, 1987) that "the first recorded attack by Soviet air defense forces, in this case fighters, occurred on October 22, 1949". In this incident, however, Soviet fighters did not attempt to hit the US aircraft; they merely fired warning shots. He real change in Soviet policy did not occur until the April 1950 downing of the US Navy Privateer George, *Case Studies*, pp. 1–2, 9–16, (S).

[4][footnote deleted]

[5]Richard S. Leghorn, interview by Donald E. Welzenbach, tape recording, Washington DC, 19 August 1985 (S).

[6]13,715 meters To avoid giving a false impression of extremely precise measurements, original English measuring system figures in round numbers have not been converted to the metric system. To convert feet to meters, multiply by 0 3048. To convert airspeeds in knots (nautical miles per hour) to kilometers per hour, multiply by 1 85.

[7]Dick van der Aart, *Aerial Espionage, Secret Intelligence Flights by East and West* (Shrewsbury, England: Airlife Publishing, 1985), p 18.

[8]Leghom interview (S)

[9]Ivan A Getting, interview by Donald E. Weizenbach, Los Angeles, 28 August 1988 (U)

[10]Philip G. Strong, Chief, Operations Staff, OSI, Memorandum for the Record, "Reconnaissance Capabilities," 21 August 1953 OSI records (S)

[11]Jay Miller, *Lockheed U-2,* Aerograph 3 (Austin, Texas: Aerofax, 1983), p. 10

[12]The request for proposal, known as "Design Study Requirements, Identification No 53WC-16507," has been reprinted in Miller, *Lockheed U-2,* pp. 10–11.

[13]Miller, *Lockheed* U-2, p. 12.

[14]Lockheed Corporation, "Strategic Reconnaissance and Intelligence," Development Planning Note #1, 30 November 1953 (U).

[15]Miller, *Lockheed U-2*, p. 12. For more details on Kelly Johnson's original proposal, see "Profile of CL-282 High Altitude Aircraft prepared by Lockheed Aircraft corporation, 5 March 1954" in [deleted] *History of the Office of Special Activities.* DS&T, Directorate of Science and Technology Historical series OSA-1, 16 vols (CIA: DS&T, 1969), chap 1, annex 2 (TS Codeword). The 16 volumes of this history contain 20 chapters, each paginated separately. Future references will be shortened to *OSA History*, followed by the relevant chapter and page numbers.

[16]Kelly Johnson Papers, "Log for Project X," April 1954, Lockheed Corporation. Advanced Development Projects Division, Burbank, California.

[17]C. F. Wienberg, telephone conversation with Donald E. Welzenbach, 23 July 1988 (U).

[18]Miller, *Lockheed U-2*, p. 12.

[19]Allen F. Donovan, interview by Donald E. Weizenbach, Corona del Mar, California, 20 May 1985 (S).

[20]Johnson, "Log for Project X," 7 June 1954.

[21]Garrison Norton, interview by Donald E. Welzenbach, tape recording, Washington, DC, 23 May 1983 (S); Michael R. Beschloss *Mayday Eisenhower, Khrushchev and the U-2 Affair* (New York Harper & Row, 1986), p. 79.

[22]Strong was a colonel in the Marine Corps Reserve and often used that title even though he was not on active duty. He later advanced to the rank of brigadier general in the reserve. For Strong's contacts with senior Air Force officials concerning the CL-282, see the Norton interview (S).

[23]Philip G. Strong, Memorandum for the Record, "Special Aircraft for Penetration Photo Reconnaissance," 12 May 1954, OSI records (now in OSR), [deleted] (S).

[24]Karl H. Weber, *The Office of Scientific Intelligence, 1949–68*, Directorate of science and Technology Historical Series OSI-I (CIA: DS&T, 1972), vol 1, tab A, pp. 16–17 (TS Codeword).

[25]Thomas Powers, *The Man Who Kept the Secrets: Richard Helms and the CIA* (New York: Alfred A. Knopf, 1979), p. 79. Beschloss, *Mayday*, pp. 86–89.

[26]Memorandum for H. Marshall Chadwell, Assistant Director/Scientific Intelligence, from Chief, Support Staff, OSI, "Review of OSA Activities Concerned with Scientific and Technical Collection Techniques," 13 May 1955, p. 6, OSI (OSWR) records, [deleted] (S); Richard M. Bissell, Jr., interview by Donald E. Welzenbach, tape recording, Farmington,

Connecticut, 8 November 1984 (S).

[27]Memorandum for Richard M. Bissell, Special Assistant to the Director for Planning and Coordination, from Philip G. Strong, Chief, Operations Staff, OSI, "Overflight of Kapustin Yar," 15 October 1954, OSI (OSWR) records, [deleted] TS, downgraded to S).

[28]Powers, *Man Who Kept the Secrets,* pp. 103–104; Edwin H. Land, interview by Donald E. Welzenbach, tape recording, Cambridge, Massachusetts, 17 and 20 September 1984 (TS Codeword); Robert Amory, Jr., interview by Donald E. Welzenbach and Gregory W. Pedlow, Washington, DC, 22 April 1987 (S).

[29]For more information on the Air Force's use of scientists see Thomas A. Sturm, *The USAF Scientific Advisory Board. Its First Twenty Years, 1944 1964* (Washington, DC: USAF Historical Office, 1967) (U)

[30]USAF, Project LINCOLN, *BEACON HILL Report: Problems of Air Force Intelligence and Reconnaissance,* Massachusetts Institute of Technology, 15 June 1952, pp. V, xi; app. A (S, downgraded to C).

[31]Allen F. Donovan, telephone conversation with Donald E. Welzenbach, 21 June 1985 (U); James G. Baker, interview by Donald E. Welzenbach, tape recording Washington, DC, 24 April 1985 (S).

[32]BEAC*ON HILL Report,* pp. 164, 167–168 (C). This section of the report was written by Allen Donovan and Louis Ridenour.

[33]Ludahl and Brugioni interview (TS Codeword).

[34]RAND Corporation, Plans Analysis Section, *"Vulnerability of US Strategic Power to a Surprise Attack in 1956."*RAND Special Memorandum No. 15, Santa Monica, California: the RAND Corporation, April 15, 1953 (TS, declassified May 1967).

[35]"AF Cities Red Bomber Progress," *Aviation Week,* May 24, 1954, p. 14; "Is Russia Winning the Arms Race?," *US News and World Report,* June 18, 1954, pp. 28–29; "Russia Parades Airpower as *'Big Stick',"* *Aviation Week,* June 28, 1954, p. 15; "Red Air Force: The World's Biggest," *Newsweek*, August 23, 1954, pp. 28–33.

[36]Memorandum for Robert Armory, Jr, Deputy Director, Intelligence from Edward L. Allen, Chief, Economic Research, ORR and Philip G. Strong, Chief, Operations Staff, OSI, "Meeting of the Intelligence Systems Panel of the Scientific Advisory Board, USAF," 26 August 1953, OSI (OSWR) records, [deleted] (S).

[37]Baker interview (S) In 1957 after the Air Force decided to cut back its funding of BUORL, Duncan Macdonald and Richard Leghorn (by then retired from the Air Force) formed their own corporation — Itek — and purchased the laboratory from Boston University (Leghorn interview [S().

[38]Memorandum for Robert Armory, Jr., Deputy Director, Intelligence, from Edward L. Allen, Chief, Economic Research, ORR, and Philip G. Strong, Chief, Operations Staff, OSI, "Meeting of the Intelligence Systems Panel of the Scientific Advisory Board, USAF," 26 August 1953; Memorandum for H Marshall Chadwell, Assistant Director/Scientific Intelligence, from Chief, Support Staff, OSI,"Review of OSA Activities Concerned with Scientific and Technical Collection Techniques," 13 May 1955, p. 6, OSI (OSWR) records, [deleted] (S);

Donovan interview, 22 May 1985 (S).

[39]Van der Aart, *Aerial Espionage*, p. 18; Philip G. Strong, Chief, Operations Staff, OSI, Memorandum for the Record, "Meeting of Air Force Scientific Advisory Board, 18–21 October 1953," 26 October 1953, OSI (OSWR) records, [deleted] TS, downgraded to S)

[40]Stewart Alsop, *The Center*, (New York Popular Library, 1968), p. 194; Beschloss, *Mayday*, pp. 78–79. Both of these books state that the project included the CIA, but there is no evidence to support this assertion.

[41]Baker interview (S).

[42]Donovan interview (S), Baker interview (S).

[43]Donovan interview (S).

[44]Donovan interview (S); Baker interview (S).

[45]Beschloss, *Mayday*, pp. 73–74; Technological Capabilities Panel of the Science Advisory Committee, *Meeting the Threat of surprise Attack,* 14 February 1955, p. 185 (hereafter cited as *TCP Report*) (TS/Restricted Data, downgraded to S)

[46]James R. Killian, Jr., *Sputnik, Scientists, and Eisenhower A Memoir of the First Special Assistant to the President for Science and Technology* (Cambridge: MIT Press, 1977), p. 68; Beschloss, *Mayday*, p. 74; *TCP Report*, pp. 185–186 (S).

[47]James R. Killian, Jr., interviewed by Donald E. Welzenbach, tape recording, Cambridge, Massachusetts, 2 November 1984 (S); Land interview (TS Codeword).

[48]*TCP Report,* p. 188 (S).

[49]Land interview (TS Codeword).

[50]Baker interview (S).

[51]Ibid.

[52]Bissell interview (S).

[53]Memorandum for DDCI Charles Pearre Cabell from R. M. Bissell, Special Assistant to the Director for Planning and Coordination, "Aerial Reconnaissance," 24 September 1954, DCI Records, [deleted] TS, downgraded to S).

[54]Killian, *Sputnik, Scientists, and Eisenhower,* p. 82.

[55]Land interview (TS Codeword).

[56]Land interview (TS Codeword); Baker interview (S).

[57]Lane interview (TS Codeword).

[58]Killian, *Sputnik, Scientists, and Eisenhower,* p. 82. The exact date of the meeting cannot be determined, but it occurred during the first half of November 1954.

[59]Letter, Project Three Panel to DCI Allen F. Dulles, 5 November 1954, in *OSA History*, chap 1, annex 1 (TS Codeword).

[60]Memorandum for DCI Allen F. Dulles from Project Three Panel, "A Unique Opportunity for Comprehensive Intelligence," 5 November 1954, p 3 (TS, downgraded to S) in *OSA History*, chap 1, annex 1 (TS Codeword).

[61]Ibid.

[62]Donovan interview (S).

[63]Quoted in Miller, *Lockheed U-2,* p. 13.

[64]Charles Pearre Cabell, Memorandum for the Record, "Luncheon

Meeting with the Secretary of the Air Force," 19 November 1954, in *OSA History,* chap. 2, annex 4 (TS Codeword)
[65]Johnson, "Log for Project X," 17 and 19 November 1954.
[66]Charles Pearre Cabell, Memorandum for the Record, "Meeting at the White House," 24 November 1954, in *OSA History*, chap. 2, annex 8 (TS Codeword); Beschloss, *Mayday*, pp. 82–83; Andrew J. Goodpaster, Memorandum of Conference with the President, 24 November 1954," White House Office of the Staff Secretary, Alpha Series, Dwight D. Eisenhower Library (hereafter cited as WHOSS, Alpha, DDEL) (TS, declassified).
[67]Scientists remained active in advising the government on overhead reconnaissance. In February 1955 the Technological Capabilities Panel issued its final report, which strongly urged the use of technology to gather intelligence. President Eisenhower strongly backed the panel's findings and directed government agencies to respond to the recommendations by June. The CIA's most important reaction to the technological Capabilities Panel report was to create its own Scientific Advisory Board composed of the members of the Project Three Study Group with the addition of James Killian and Jerome B. Wiesner, professor of electrical engineering at MIT. Edwin Land served as chairman of the CIA Scientific Advisory Board for the next 10 years, and it soon became known unofficially as the Land Panel. This panel provided important advice to the Agency, particularly in the field of overhead reconnaissance.

President Eisenhower also acted to increase the amount and quality of scientific advice he was receiving. In January 1956 he established the President's Board of Consultants on Foreign Intelligence Activities (renamed the President's Foreign Intelligence Advisory Board in 1961) to oversee the intelligence community and advise him on intelligence matters. The board's first chairman was James Killian. In 1957 the President reorganized and upgraded the Office of Defense Mobilization's Science Advisory Committee, which became the President's Science Advisory Committee. He also named James Killian to be the first Special Assistant to the President for Science and Technology. In this new position Killian served as the President's scientific advisor and the chairman of the President's Scientific Advisory Committee (Killian stepped down as chairman of the President's Board of Consultants on Foreign Intelligence Activities but remained a member). These actions by the President brought scientists into the White House and gave them considerable influence.

2

Developing the U-2

THE ESTABLISHMENT OF THE U-2 PROJECT

On 26 November 1954, the day after Thanksgiving, Allen Dulles called his special assistant, Richard Bissell, into his office to tell him that President Eisenhower had just approved a very secret program and that Dulles wanted Bissell to take charge of it. Saying it was too secret for him to explain, Dulles gave Bissell a packet of documents and told him he could keep it for several days to acquaint himself with the project. Bissell had long known of the proposal to build a high-altitude reconnaissance aircraft, but only in the most general terms. Now he learned in detail about the project that proposed sending aircraft over the Soviet Union.

Late on the morning of 2 December 1954, Dulles told Bissell to go to the Pentagon on the Following day to represent the Agency at an organizational meeting for the U-2[1] project. Before leaving, Bissell asked Dulles which agency was to run the project. The DCI replied that nothing had been clearly decided. Bissell then asked who was going to pay for the project. Dulles answered: "That wasn't even mentioned. You'll have to work that out."[2]

Bissell was accompanied by Herbert I. Miller, chief of the Office of Scientific Intelligence's Nuclear Energy Division, who soon became the executive officer of the overflight project. When Bissell and Miller arrived at the Pentagon on the afternoon of 3 December, they sat down with a group of key Air Force officials that included Trevor Gardner and Lt. Gen. Donald L. Putt. The participants spent very little time delineating Air Force and Agency responsibilities in the project, taking for granted that the CIA would handle the security matters. Much of the discussion centered on methods for diverting Air Force materiel to the program, particularly the Pratt & Whitney J57 engines, because a separate contract for the engines might jeopardize the project's security. The Air Force promised to turn over a number of J57 engines, which were then being produced for B-52s, KC-135s, E7-100s, and RB-57.s Eventually Bissell asked who was going to pay for the airframes to be built by Lockheed. His query was greeted with silence. Everyone present had their eyes on him because they all expected the Agency to come up with the funds. Bissell rose from his chair, said he would see what he could do, and the meeting adjourned.[3]

After the meeting, Bissell told Dulles that the CIA would have to use money from the Contingency Reserve Fund to get the project going. The DCI used this fund to pay for covert activities, following approval by the President and the Director of the Budget Dulles told Bissell to draft a memorandum for the President on funding the overflight program and to start putting together a staff for Project AQUATONE, the project's new codename.

At first the new "Project Staff" (renamed the Development Projects Staff in April 1958) consisted of

Bissell, Miller, and the small existing staff in Bissell's Office of the Special Assistant to the DCI. During the months that followed the establishment of the project, its administrative workload increased rapidly, and in May 1955 the project staff added an administrative officer, James A. Cunningham, Jr., a former Marine Corps pilot then working in the Directorate of Support. Cunningham stayed with the U-2 project for the next 10 years. Two other key project officials who began their duties early in 1955 were [name deleted] the finance officer, and [name deleted] the contracting officer.

[one-half page deleted — may have been a photograph)

During the first half of 1955, the project staff grew slowly; many of the individuals working on overhead reconnaissance remained on the rolls of other Agency components. To achieve maximum security, Bissell made the project staff self-sufficient Project. AQUATONE had its own contract management, administrative, financial, logistic, communications, and security personnel, and, thus, did not need to turn to the Agency directorates for assistance. Funding for Project AQUATONE was also kept separate from other Agency components, its personnel and operating costs were not paid out of regular Agency accounts. As approving officer for the project, Richard Bissell could obligate funds in amounts up to [number deleted] larger sums required the DCI's approval.[5]

At the end of April 1955, Bissell's staff developed, and the Deputy Director for Support approved, the first table of organization for Project AQUATONE. Once operational, the project would have a total [number deleted] personnel divided among project headquarters, a US testing facility, and [deletions] The Air Force personnel commitment was larger, [deletions] on the 1955 table of organization (this total does not include many other Air Force personnel, such as SAC meteorologists, who supported the U-2 project in addition to their other duties). The largest Project AQUATONE category was contract employees, [number deleted] positions in 1955. This category included maintenance and support personnel from Lockheed (five per aircraft), the pilots, and support personnel from other contractors for items such as photographic equipment.[6]

The first project headquarters was in CIA's Administration (East) Building at 2430 E Street, NW. Continued growth caused the AQUATONE staff to move several times during its first two years On 1 May 1955, the project staff moved to the third floor of a small red brick building (the Briggs School) at 2210 E Street, NW. Then on 3 October, the staff moved to Wings A and C of Quarters Eye, a World War II "temporary" building on Ohio Drive, NW, in the West Potomac Park area of Washington. On 25 February 1956, the project staff moved again, this time to the fifth floor of the Matomic Building at 1717 H Street, NW. Here the staff remained for the next six years until it moved into the new CIA Headquarters building at Langley in March 1962. The final move came in January 1968, when the project staff (by that time known as the Office of Special Activities) moved to [deleted].

Bissell reported directly to the DCI, although in reality the DDCI, Gen. Charles Pearre Cabell, was much more closely involved in the day-to-day affairs of the overhead reconnaissance project. Cabell's extensive background in Air Force intelligence, particularly in overhead reconnaissance, made him ideally qualified to oversee the U-2 project. Cabell frequently attended White House meetings on the U-2 for the DCI.

FUNDING ARRANGEMENTS FOR PROJECT AQUATONE

Although Allen Dulles had approved the [deleted] for the reconnaissance project, many financial details remained to be settled, including the contract with Lockheed. Nevertheless, work on the U-2 began as soon as the project was authorized. Between 29 November and 3 December 1954, Kelly Johnson pulled together a team [deleted] engineers, which was not easy because he had to take them off other Lockheed projects without being able to explain why to their former supervisors. The engineers immediately began to work 45 hours a week on the project. The project staff gradually expanded to a total [deleted] personnel, and the workweek soon increased to 65 hours.[8]

Kelly Johnson's willingness to begin work on the aircraft without a contract illustrates one of the most important aspects of this program: [end of one paragraph and the beginning of the next paragraph deleted]

use Public Law 110,approved by the 81st Congress on 20 June 1949, designates the Director of Central Intelligence as the only government employee who can obligate Federal money without the use of vouchers [about 12 lines deleted; probably financial costs of the programs or secret financing]

In mid-December 1954, President Eisenhower authorized DCI Dulles to use [deleted] from the Agency's Contingency Reserve Fund to finance the U-2 project. Then on 22 December 1954, the Agency signed a letter contract with Lockheed, using the codename Project OARFISH. The Agency had proposed to give Lockheed "performance specifications" rather than the standard Air Force "technical specifications," which were more rigid and demanding, and Kelly Johnson agreed that such a move would save a lot of money. Lockheed's original proposal to the Air Force in May 1954 had been [deleted] for 20 U-2s equipped with GE J73 engines. During negotiations with CIA General Counsel Lawrence R. Houston, Lockheed changed its proposal to [deleted] for 20 airframes plus a two-seat trainer model and spares; the Air Force was to furnish the engines. Houston insisted that the Agency could only budget [costs deleted] for the airframes because it needed the balance of the available [deleted] for cameras and life-support gear. The two sides finally agreed on a fixed-price contract with a provision for a review three-fourths of the way through to determine if the costs were going to exceed the [deleted] figure. The formal contract, No SP-1913, was signed on 2 March 1955 and called for the delivery of the first U-2 in July 1955 and the last in November 1956. Meanwhile, to keep work moving at Lockheed, Richard Bissell wrote a check [deleted] and mailed it to Kelly Johnson's home on 21 February 1955.[9]

As it turned out, no review of the contract was necessary at the three-fourths point. Lockheed delivered the aircraft not only on time but under budget. [approximately 10-12 lines deleted]

MAJOR DESIGN FEATURES OF THE U-2

Aware of the great need for secrecy in the new project, Kelly Johnson placed it in Lockheed's Advanced Development facility at Burbank, California, known as the Skunk Works.[10] Lockheed had established this highly secure area in 1945 to develop the nation's first jet aircraft, the P-80 Shooting Star. The small Skunk Works staff began making the detailed drawings for the U-2, which was nicknamed the "Angel" because it was to fly so high.

Kelly Johnson's approach to prototype development was to have his engineers and draftsmen located not more than 50 feet from the aircraft assembly line. Difficulties in construction were immediately brought to the attention of the engineers, who gathered the mechanics around the drafting tables to discuss ways to overcome the difficulties. As a result, engineers were generally able to fix problems in the design in a matter of hours, not days or weeks. There was no emphasis placed on producing neatly typed memorandums, engineers simply made pencil notations on the engineering drawings in order to keep the project moving quickly.[11]

A little more than a week after he had been authorized to begin the project, Kelly Johnson wrote a 23-page report detailing his most recent ideas on the U-2 proposal. The aircraft, he explained, would be designed to meet load factors of only 2 5 g's, which was the limit for transport aircraft rather than combat planes. The U-2 would have a speed of Mach 0 8 or 460 knots at altitude. Its initial maximum altitude would be 70,600 feet and the ultimate maximum altitude would be 73,100 feet. According to these early December 1954 specifications, the new plane would take off at 90 knots, land at 76 knots, and be able to glide 244 nautical miles from an altitude of 70,000 feet. After discussing the reconnaissance bay with James Baker, Johnson had worked out various equipment combinations that would not exceed the weight limit of 450 pounds. Johnson ended his report by promising the first test by 2 August 1955 and the completion of four aircraft by 1 December 1955.[12]

In designing the U-2 aircraft, Kelly Johnson was

confronted with two major problems — fuel capacity and weight. To achieve intercontinental range, the aircraft had to carry a large supply of fuel, yet, it also had to be light enough to attain the ultrahigh altitudes needed to be safe from interception. Although the final product resembled a typical jet aircraft, its construction was unlike any other US military aircraft. One unusual design feature was the tail assembly, which — to save weight — was attached to the main body with just three tension bolts. This feature had been adapted from sailplane designs.

The wings were also unique. Unlike conventional aircraft, whose main wing spar passes through the fuselage to give the wings continuity and strength, the U-2 had two separate wing panels, which were attached to the fuselage sides with tension bolts (again, just as in sailplanes). Because the wing spar did not pass through the fuselage, Johnson was able to locate the camera behind the pilot and ahead of the engine, thereby improving the aircraft's center of gravity and reducing its weight.

The wings were the most challenging design feature of the entire airplane. Their combination of high-aspect ratio and low-drag ratio (in other words, the wings were long, narrow, and thin) made them unique in jet aircraft design. The wings were actually integral fuel tanks that carried almost all of the U-2's fuel supply.

The fragility of the wings and tail section, which were only bolted to the fuselage, forced Kelly Johnson to look for a way to protect the aircraft from gusts of wind at altitudes below 35,000 feet, which otherwise might cause the aircraft to disintegrate. Johnson again borrowed from sailplane designs to devise a "gust control" mechanism that set the ailerons and horizontal stabilizers into a position that kept the aircraft in a slightly nose-up attitude, thereby avoiding sudden stresses caused by wind gusts. Nevertheless, the U-2 remained a very fragile aircraft that required great skill and concentration from its pilots.

The final major design feature was the lightweight, bicycle-type landing gear. The entire structure — a single oleostrut with two lightweight wheels toward the front of the aircraft and two small, solid-mount wheels under the tail — weighed only 208 pounds yet could withstand the force of touchdown for this 7-ton aircraft. Because both sets of wheels were located underneath the fuselage, the U-2 was also equipped with detachable pogos (long, curved sticks with two small wheels on them) on each wing to keep the wings level during takeoff. The pilot would drop the pogos immediately after takeoff so that they could be recovered and reused. The aircraft landed on its front and back landing gear and then gradually tilted over onto one of the wingtips, which were equipped with landing skids.[13]

THE DEVELOPMENT OF THE CAMERA SYSTEM

By December 1954, Kelly Johnson was at work on drawings for the U-2's airframe and Pratt & Whitney was already building the J57 jet-engine, but no firm plans existed for the all-important cameras. Existing cameras were too bulky and lacked sufficient resolution to be used in high-altitude reconnaissance.

The workhorses of World War II aerial photography had been the Fairchild K-19 and K-21 framing cameras with lenses of varying focal lengths from 24 to 40 inches. Late in the war, the trimetrogon K-17 mapping-camera system came into use. This system consisted of three separate cameras which made three photographs simultaneously: a vertical, an oblique to the left, and an oblique to the right. The major shortcomings of the trimetrogon system were the large amount of film required and the system's lack of sharp definition on the obliques.

The standard aerial cameras available in the early 1950s could achieve resolutions of about 20 to 25 feet (7 to 8 meters) on a side when used at an altitude of 33,000 feet (10,000 meters), or about 25 lines per millimeter in current terms of reference. Such resolution was considered adequate because aerial photography was then used primarily to choose targets for strategic bombing, to assess bomb damage after air raids, and to make maps and charts. Unfortunately, a camera with a resolution of only 20 to 25 feet at a height of 33,000 feet was too crude to be used at twice that altitude. Indeed, for intelligence purposes a resolution of less than 10 feet was necessary to discern smaller targets in greater detail. This meant that any camera carried to altitudes above 68,000 feet had to be almost four times as good as existing aerial cameras in order to achieve a resolution of less than 10 feet. As a result, some scientists doubted that useful photography could be obtained from altitudes higher than 40~000 feet.[14]

The first success in designing very-high-acuity lenses came in the mid-1940s, when James G. Baker of Harvard and Richard S. Perkin of the Perkin-Elmer (P-E) Company of Norwalk, Connecticut, collaborated on a design for an experimental camera for the Army Air Force. They developed a 48-inch focal-length scanning camera that was mounted in a modified B-36 bomber. When tested over Fort Worth, Texas, at 34,000 feet, the new camera produced photographs in which two golf balls on a putting green could be distinguished (in reality, however, the "golf balls" were 3 inches in diameter). These photographs demonstrated the high acuity of Baker's lens, but the camera weighed more than a ton and was much too large to be carried aloft in an aircraft as small as the U-2.

Realizing that size and weight were the major restraining factors in developing a camera for the U-2, James Baker began working on a radically new system in October 1954, even before the CIA adopted the Lockheed proposal Baker quickly recognized, however, that he would need almost a year to produce a working model of such a complex camera. Since Kelly Johnson had promised to have a U-2 in the air within eight months, Baker needed to find an existing camera that could be used until the new camera was ready. After consulting with his friend and colleague Richard Perkin, Baker decided to adapt for the U-2 an Air Force camera known as the K-38, a 24-inch aerial framing camera built by the Hycon Manufacturing Company of Pasadena, California.

Perkin suggested modifying several standard K-38 cameras in order to reduce their weight to the U-2's 450-pound payload limit. At the same time, Baker would make critical adjustments to existing K-38 lenses to improve their acuity. Baker was able to do this in a few weeks, so several modified K-38s, now known as A-1 cameras, were ready when the first "Angel" aircraft took to the air in mid-1955.[15]

CIA awarded Hycon a contract for the modified K-38 cameras, and Hycon, in turn, subcontracted to Perkin-Blmer to provide new lenses and to make other modifications to the cameras in order to make them less bulky. In its turn, Perkin-Elmer subcontracted to Baker to rework the existing K-38 lenses and later design an improved lens system. To keep his lens-designing efforts separate from his research associate duties at Harvard and his service on government advisory bodies, Baker established a small firm known as Spica, Incorporated, on 31 January 1955.

The A-1 camera system consisted of two 24-inch K-38 framing cameras. One was mounted vertically and photographed a 17 2° swath beneath the aircraft onto a roll of 9 5-inch film. The second K-38 was placed in a rocking mount so that it alternately photographed the left oblique and right oblique out to 36 5° onto separate rolls of 9 5-inch film. The film supplies unwound in opposite directions in order to minimize their effect on the balance of the aircraft. Both cameras used standard Air Force 24-inch focal-length lenses adjusted for maximum acuity by Baker. The development of the special rocking mount by Perkin-Elmer's Dr. Roderic M. Scott was a major factor in reducing the size and weight of the A-1 system, because the mount provided broad transverse coverage with a single lens, ending the need for two separate cameras.[16]

U-2s equipped with the A-1 camera system also carried a Perkin-Elmer tracking camera using 2 7S-inch film and a 3-inch lens. This device made continuous horizon-to-horizon photographs of the terrain passing beneath the aircraft. Because the A-1 system was new, it also included a backup camera system, a K-17 6-inch three-camera trimetrogon unit using 9-inch film.

While the A-1 system was still being developed, James Biker was already working on the next generation of lenses for high-altitude reconnaissance. Baker was a pioneer in using computers to synthesize optical systems. His software algorithms made it possible to model lens designs and determine in advance the effects that variations in lens curvatures, glass compounds, and lens spacings would have on rays of light passing through a lens. These "ray-tracing" programs required extensive computations, and, for this he turned to the most modem computer available, an IBM CPC (card-programmed calculator) installation at nearby Boston University.[17]

Baker's new lenses were used in a camera system known as the A-2, which returned to a trimetrogon arrangement because of problems with the A-1 system's rocking mount. The A-2 consisted of three separate K-38 framing cameras and 9 5-inch film magazines. One K-38 filmed the right oblique, another the vertical, and a third the left oblique. The A-2 system also included a 3-inch tracking camera. All A-2 cameras were equipped with the new 24-inch f/8.0 Baker-designed lenses. These were the first relatively large photographic objective lenses to employ several aspheric surfaces. James Baker personally ground these surfaces and made the final bench tests on each lens before releasing it to the Agency. These lenses were able to resolve 60 lines per millimeter, a 240-percent improvement over existing lenses.[18]

Once Baker and Scott had redesigned the 24-inch lens for the K-38 devices, they turned their attention to Baker's new camera design, known as the B model It was a totally new concept, a high-resolution panoramic-type framing camera with a much longer 36-inch f/10 0 aspheric lens. The B camera was a very complex device that used a single lens to obtain photography from one horizon to the other, thereby reducing weight by having two fewer lenses and shutter assemblies than the standard trimetrogon configuration. Because its lens was longer than those used in the A cameras, the B camera achieved even higher resolution — 100 lines per millimeter.

The B camera used an 18- by 18-inch format, which was achieved by focusing the image onto two counter-rotating but overlapping 9 5-inch wide strips of film. Baker designed this camera so that one film supply was located forward, the other aft. Thus, as the film supplies unwound, they counterbalanced each other and did not disturb the aircraft's center of gravity.

The B camera had two modes of operation. In mode I, the camera used a single lens to make seven unique exposures from 73 5° on the far right and far left obliques to vertical photos beneath the aircraft, effectively covering from horizon to horizon. Mode II narrowed the lateral coverage to 215° on either side of vertical. This increased the available number of exposures and almost doubled the camera's operating time. Three of the seven B-camera frames provided stereo coverage. The complex B cameras were engineered by Hycon's chief designer, William McFadden.[19]

James Baker's idea for the ultimate high-altitude camera was the C model that would have a 240-inch focal length. In December 1954, he made preliminary designs for folding the optical path using three mirrors, a prism, and an f/20 0 lens system. Before working out the details of this design, however, Baker flew to California in early January 1955 to consult with Kelly Johnson about the weight and space limitations of the U-2's payload compartment. Despite every effort to reduce the physical dimensions of the C camera, Baker needed an additional six inches of payload space to accommodate the bigger lens. When he broached this subject to Johnson, the latter replied, "Six more inches? I'd sell my grandmother for six more inches!"[20]

Realizing that the 240-inch lens was both too large and too heavy for the camera bay, Baker scaled the lens down to a 200-inch f/16 0 system. This was still too big. Further reductions followed, resulting by July 1955 in a 120-inch f/10 9 lens that met both the weight and space limitations. Later in the year, Baker decided to make the mirrors for the system out of a new, lightweight foamed silica material developed by Pittsburgh-Corning Glass Company. This reduced the weight significantly, and he was able to scale up the lens to a 180-inch f/13 85 reflective system for a 13- by 13-inch format. In the past, the calculations for such a complex camera lens would have taken years to complete, but thanks to Baker's ray-tracing computer program, he was able to accomplish the task in just 16 days.

When a C camera built by Hycon was flight-tested on 31 January 1957, project engineers discovered that its 180-inch focal length, which was five times longer than that of the B camera, made the camera very sensitive to aircraft vibration and led to great difficulty in aiming the C camera from altitudes above 68,000 feet. The engineers, therefore, decided to shelve the camera. More than five years later, a redesigned C camera was employed during the Cuban Missile Crisis in October 1962, but the results were not very satisfactory.

The failure of the C camera design was not a serious setback to the high-altitude reconnaissance program, because the B camera proved highly successful. Once initial difficulties with the film-transport system were overcome, the B camera became the workhorse of high-altitude photography. An improved version known as the B-2 is still in use. Both of the earlier A-model cameras were phased out after September 1958.

During the period when he was designing lenses for the CIA's overhead reconnaissance program, James Baker was also working on classified lens designs for the Air Force and unclassified designs for the Smithsonian Institution. To protect the security of Baker's work for the Agency, Herbert Miller of the Development Projects Staff told Baker to work on lenses for the U-2 in the open and not make any effort to classify the documents connected with the project. Miller believed that by not calling attention to the effort through the use of special security measures, the project could be completed faster and still not be compromised. This "hiding in the open" strategy proved very successful.[21]

In addition to the camera systems, the U-2 carried one other important item of optical equipment, a periscope. Designed by James Baker and built by Walter Baird of Baird Associates, the optical periscope helped pilots recognize targets beneath the aircraft and also proved to be a valuable navigational aid.[22]

PREPARATIONS FOR TESTING THE U-2

As work progressed in California on the airframe, in Connecticut on the engines, and in Boston on the camera system, the top officials of the Development Projects Staff flew to [The deletions on this page seem to refer to the testing ground for the U-2, which was Groom Lake, Nevada, 100 miles northwest of Las Vegas. See Beschloss, pp. 93.] search for a site where the aircraft could be tested sagely and secretly. On 12 April 1955 Richard Bissell and Col. Osmund Ritland (the senior Air Force officer on the project staff) flew [deleted] with Kelly Johnson in a small Beechcraft plane piloted by Lockheed's chief test pilot, Tony LeVier. They spotted what appeared to be an airstrip [deleted] After debating about landing on the old airstrip, LeVier set the plane down [deleted] From the air the strip appeared to be paved, but on closer inspection it turned out to have originally been fashioned from compacted earth that had turned into ankle-deep dust after more than a decade of disuse. If LeVier had attempted to land on the airstrip, the plane would probably have nosed over when the wheels sank into the loose soil, killing or injuring all of the key figures in the U-2 project.[23]

Bissell and his colleagues all agreed that [deleted] would make an ideal site for testing the U-2 and training its pilots. Upon returning to Washington, Bissell discovered that [approximately 6-8 lines deleted]

Although [deletions also apparently refer to room Lake] could have served as a landing strip, project managers decided that a paved runway was needed so that testing could also take place during the times when rainwater runoff from nearby mountains [deleted] and Agency, Air Force, and Lockheed personnel began moving in.

SECURITY FOR THE U-2 PROJECT

On 29 April 1955, Richard Bissell signed an agreement with the Air Force and the Navy (which at that time was also interested in the U-2) in which the services agreed that the CIA "assumed primary responsibility for all security" for the overhead reconnaissance project (AQUATONE). From this time on, the CIA has been responsible for the security of overhead programs. This responsibility has placed a heavy burden on the Office of Security for establishing procedures to keep large numbers of contracts untraceable to the Central Intelligence Agency. The Office of Security has also had to determine which contractor employees require security clearances and has had to devise physical security measures for the various manufacturing facilities. Keeping the U-2 and subsequent overhead systems secret has been a time-consuming and costly undertaking.[25]

The most important aspect of the security program for the U-2 project was the creation of an entire new compartmented system for the product of U-2 missions. Access to the photographs taken by the U-2 would be strictly controlled, which often limited the ability of CIA analysts to use the products of U-2 missions.

[about one third page deleted]

Even the aircraft's onboard equipment required the involvement of CIA security planners. Thus, when Kelly Johnson ordered altimeters from the Kollman Instrument Company, he specified that the devices had to be calibrated to 80,000 feet. This immediately raised eyebrows at Kollman because its instruments only went to 45,000 feet. Agency security personnel quickly briefed several Kollman officials and produced a cover story that the altimeters were to be used on experimental rocket planes.[27]

THE CIA-AIR FORCE PARTNERSHIP

At the initial interagency meetings to establish the U-2 program in December 1954, the participants did not work out a clear delineation of responsibilities between the CIA and the Air Force. They agreed only that the Air Force would supply the engines and the Agency would pay for the airframes and cameras. With a myriad of details still unsettled, CIA and Air Force representatives began to work on an interagency agreement that would assign specific responsibilities for the program. These negotiations proved difficult. Discussions on this subject between DCI Allen Dulles and Air Force Chief of Staff Nathan Twining began in March 1955. Twining wanted SAC, headed by Gen. Curtis E. LeMay, to run the project once the planes and pilots were ready to fly, but Dulles opposed such an arrangement. The CIA-USAF talks dragged on for several months, with wining determined that SAC should have full control once the aircraft was deployed. Eventually President Eisenhower settled the dispute. "I want this whole thing to be a civilian operation," the President wrote. "If uniformed personnel of the armed services of the United States fly over Russia, it is an act of war—legally—and I don't want any part of it."[28]

With the issue of control over the program settled, the two agencies soon worked out the remaining details. On 3 August 1955, Dulles and Twining met at SAC headquarters in Omaha to sign the basic agreement, titled "Organization and Delineation of Responsibilities—Project OILSTONE" (OILSTONE was the Air Force codename for the project). This pact gave the Air Force responsibility for pilot selection and training, weather information, mission plotting, and operational support. The Agency was responsible for cameras, security, contracting, film processing, and arrangements for foreign bases, and it also had a voice in the selection of pilots. All aeronautical aspects of the project—the construction and testing of the aircraft—remained the exclusive province of Lockheed.[29]

As a result of this agreement, CIA remained in control of the program, but the Air Force played a very important role as well. As Richard Bissell later remarked about the U-2 project, "The Air Force wasn't just in on this as a supporting element, and to a major degree it wasn't in on it just supplying about half the government personnel, but the Air Force held, if you want to be precise, 49 percent of the common stock."[30]

One of the first Air Force officers assigned to Project OILSTONE was Col. Osmund J. Ritland. He began coordinating Air Force activities in the U-2 program with Richard Bissell in December 1954. On 27 June 1955, Ritland became Bissell's deputy, although Air Force Chief of Staff Twining did not officially approve this assignment until 4 August, the day after the signing of the CIA-Air Force agreement. In March 1956, Colonel Ritland returned to the Air Force and was followed as deputy project director by Col. Jack A. Gibbs.

Another Air Force officer, Lt. Col. Leo P. Geary, joined the program in June 1955 and remained with it until August 1966, longer than any of the other project managers. Using the Air Force Inspector General's office as cover with the title of Project Officer, AFCIG-5, Geary served as the focal point for all Defense Department support to the U-2 and OXCART programs. His 11 years with the overhead reconnaissance projects provided a high degree of Air Force continuity.[31]

TECHNICAL CHALLENGES TO HIGH-ALTITUDE FLIGHT

To get the U-2 aircraft ready to fly, Lockheed engineers had to solve problems never before encountered. Among these problems was the need for a fuel that would not boil off and evaporate at the very high altitudes for which the aircraft was designed. Gen. James H. Doolittle (USAF, Ret.), a vice president of the Shell Oil Company who had long been involved in overhead reconnaissance (most recently as a member of the Technological Capabilities Panel), arranged for Shell to develop a special low-volatility, low-vapor-pressure kerosene fuel for the craft. The result was a dense mixture, known as LF-IA, JP-TS (thermally stable), or JP-7, with a boiling point of 300°F at sea level. Manufacturing this special fuel required petroleum byproducts that Shell normally used to make its "Flit" fly and bug spray. In order to produce several hundred thousand gallons of LF-IA for the U-2 project in the spring and summer of 1955, Shell had to limit the production of Flit, causing a nationwide shortage. Because of the new fuel's density, it required special tanks and modifications to the aircraft's fuel-control and ignition systems.[32]

Even more important than the problem of boiling fuel was the problem of boiling blood, namely the pilot's. At altitudes above 65,000 feet, fluids in the human body will vaporize unless the body can be kept under pressure. Furthermore, the reduced atmospheric pressure placed considerable stress on the pilot's cardiovascular system and did not provide adequate oxygenation of the blood. Keeping the pilot alive at the extreme altitudes required for overflights therefore called for a totally different approach to environmental equipment; it required a system that could maintain pressure over much of the pilot's body. The technology that enabled U-2 pilots to operate for extended periods in reduced atmospheric pressure would later play a major role in the manned space program.

Advising the Agency on high-altitude survival were two highly experienced Air Force doctors, Col. Donald D. Flickinger and Col. W. Randolph Lovelace, II. Dr. Lovelace had begun his research on high-altitude flight before World War II and was a coinventor of the standard Air Force oxygen mask. In the early 1950s, he and Flickinger made daring parachute jumps from B47 bombers to test pilot-survival gear under extreme conditions. Flickinger served as the medical adviser to Project AQUATONE for almost a decade.[33]

Flickinger and Lovelace suggested that the Agency ask the David Clark Company of Worcester, Massachusetts, manufacturer of environmental suits for Air Force pilots, to submit designs for more advanced gear for the U-2 pilots. David Clark expert Joseph Ruseckas then developed a complex life-support system, which was the first partially pressurized "spacesuit" for keeping humans alive for lengthy periods at ultrahigh altitudes. The effort to provide a safe environment for pilots at high altitudes also involved the Firewel Company of Buffalo, New York, which pressurized the U-2 cockpit to create an interior environment equivalent to the air pressure at an altitude of 28,000 feet. The system was designed so that, if the interior cockpit pressure fell below the 28,000-feet level, the pilot's suit would automatically inflate. In either case, he could obtain oxygen only through his helmet.[34]

The early models of these MC-2 and MC-3 partial-pressure suits were very uncomfortable for the pilots. To prevent loss of pressure, the heavy coverall had to fit tightly at the wrists and ankles (in the early models of these suits, the feet were not included in the pressurization scheme). The pilot had to wear gloves and a heavy helmet that tended to chafe his neck and shoulders and was prone to fogging. Problems with the pilot life-support system were believed to have been the cause of several early crashes of the U-2.

Having gotten a pilot into this bulky suit and shoehorned him into his seat in the cockpit, the next problem was how to get him out in an emergency. The U-2 cockpit was very small, and the early models did not have an ejection seat. Even after an ejection seat was installed, pilots were reluctant to use it because they were afraid they would lose their legs below the knees when they were blown out of the cockpit. To save weight, the first pilot's seat was extremely simple with no height adjustment mechanism. Designed for pilots of above-average height, the seat could be adjusted for shorter pilots by inserting wooden blocks beneath the seat to raise it. In later versions of the aircraft, Kelly Johnson added a fully adjustable seat.[35]

The Air Force undertook bailout experiments at high altitudes from balloons in the autumn of 1955 to determine if the suit designed for the U-2 pilot would also protect him during his parachute descent once he was separated from the life-support mechanism inside the aircraft. To avoid getting the "bends" during such descents or during the long flights, pilots had to don their pressure suits and begin breathing oxygen at least 90 minutes before takeoff so that their bodies would have time to dissipate nitrogen. This procedure was known as prebreathing. Once the pilots were in their suits, eating and drinking became a major problem, as did urination. The first model of the pressure suit, used by Lockheed test pilots, made no provision for urination. A subsequent model required the pilot to be catheterized before donning his flying suit. This method of permitting urination during flight proved very uncomfortable and, by the autumn of 1955, was replaced with an external bladder arrangement that made the catheter unnecessary. To reduce elimination, pilots ate a low-bulk, high-protein diet on the day before and the morning of each mission.

To prevent pilots from becoming dessicated during

the long missions—a condition aggravated by their having to breathe pure oxygen—provision was made for them to drink sweetened water. This was accomplished by providing a small self-sealing hole in the face mask through which the pilot could push a straw-like tube attached to the water supply. Project personnel also pioneered in the development of ready-to-eat foods in squeezable containers. These were primarily bacon- or cheese-flavored mixtures that the pilot could squeeze into his mouth using the self-sealing hole in the face mask. Despite all these precautions, U-2 pilots normally lost 3 to 6 pounds of body weight during an eight-hour mission.[36]

Food and water were not the only items provided to pilots on overflight missions, they also received a suicide pill. During the early 1950s, tales of Soviet secret police torture of captured foreign agents led Bissell and Cunningham to approach Dr. Alex Batlin of Technical Services Division in the Directorate of Plans[37] for ideas to help "captured" U-2 pilots avoid such suffering. Batlin suggested the method used by Nazi war criminal Hermann Goering, a thin glass ampule containing liquid potassium cyanide. He said a pilot had only to put the ampule in his mouth and bite down on the glass, death would follow in 10 to 15 seconds. Project AQUATONE ordered six of the poison ampules, called L-pills, and offered one to each pilot just before a mission. It was up to each pilot to decide if he wanted to take an L-pill with him. Some did, most did not.[36]

DELIVERY OF THE FIRST U-2

On 25 July, less than eight months after the go-ahead call from Trevor Gardner, Kelly Johnson was ready to deliver the first aircraft, known as article

341, to the [deleted] site. With its long, slender wings and tail assembly removed, the aircraft was wrapped in tarpaulins, loaded aboard a C-124, and flown to [deleted] where Lockheed mechanics spent the next six days readying the craft for its maiden flight.

Before "Kelly's Angel" could actually take to the air, however, it needed an Air Force designator. Col. Allman T. Culbertson from the Air Force's Office of the Director of Research and Development pointed this out to Lieutenant Colonel Geary in July 1955, and the two officers then looked through the aircraft designator handbook to see what the options were. They decided that they could not call the project aircraft a bomber, fighter, or transport plane, and they did not want anyone to know that the new plane was for reconnaissance, so Geary and Culbertson decided that it should come under the utility aircraft category. At the time, there were only two utility aircraft on the books, a U-1 and a U-3. Geary told Culbertson that the Lockheed CL-282 was going to be known officially as the U-2.[39]

Johnson had designed the U-2 to use the Pratt & Whitney (P&W) J57/P-31 engine, which developed 13,000 pounds of thrust and weighed 3,820 pounds, giving it a power-to-weight ratio of 3.4 1. When the U-2 first took to the air, however, these engines were not available because the entire production was needed to power specially configured Canberra RB-57Ds for the Air Force. The first U-2s therefore used P&W J57/P-37 engines, which were 276 pounds heavier and delivered only 10,200 pounds of thrust at sea level, the resulting power-to-weight ratio of 27.1 was almost 20 percent less efficient than the preferred P-31 version.[40]

To conduct lengthy missions over hostile territory, the U-2 needed to carry a large amount of fuel. Kelly

Johnson used a "wet-wing" design for the U-2, which meant that fuel was not stored in separate fuel tanks but rather in the wing itself. Each wing was divided into two leak-proof compartments, and fuel was pumped into all the cavities within these areas, only the outer 6 feet of the wings were not used for fuel storage. The U-2 also had a 100-gallon reserve tank in its nose. Later, in 1957, Johnson increased the fuel capacity of the U-2 by adding 100-gallon "slipper" tanks under each wing, projecting slightly ahead of the leading edge.

One of the most important considerations in the U-2's fuel system was the need to maintain aircraft trim as the fuel was consumed. The aircraft therefore contained a complex system of feed lines and valves draining to a central sump, which made it impossible to provide the pilot with an empty/full type of fuel gauge. None of the first 50 U-2s had normal fuel gauges. Instead there were mechanical fuel totalizer/counters. Before the start of a mission, the ground crew set the counters to indicate the total amount of fuel in the wings, and then a flow meter subtracted the gallons of fuel actually consumed during the flight. The pilot kept a log of the fuel consumption shown by the counters and compared it with estimates made by mission planners for each leg of the flight. As a double check, U-2 pilots also kept track of their fuel consumption by monitoring airspeed and time in the air. Most pilots became quite expert at this. Several who did not came up short of their home base during the 20 years these planes were flown.[41]

INITIAL TESTING OF THE U-2

Preliminary taxi trials began on 27 July 1955, when the first run down the newly completed runway took the plane to 50 knots Lockheed's chief test pilot, Tony LeVier, was at the controls. A second taxi trial followed on 1 August. LeVier accelerated to 70 knots and began to try the ailerons. "It was at this point that I became aware of being airborne," LeVier noted afterward, "which left me with utter amazement, as I had no intentions whatsoever of flying. I immediately started back toward the ground, but had difficulty determining my height because the lakebed had no markings to judge distance or height I made contact with the ground in a left bank of approximately 10 degrees." The U-2 bounced back into the air, but LeVier was able to bring it back down for a second landing. He then applied the brakes with little effect, and the aircraft rolled for a long distance before coming to a stop.[42]

BisselJ, Cunningham, and Johnson saw the aircraft fall and bounce. Leaping into a jeep, they roared off toward the plane. They signaled to LeVier to climb out and then used fire extinguishers to put out a fire in the brakes. At a debriefing session that followed, LeVier complained about the poor performance of the brakes and the absence of markings on the runway. Damage to the prototype U-2 was very minor blown tires, a leaking oleostrut on the undercarriage, and damaged brakes. This unplanned flight was but a foretaste of the airworthiness of the U-2. New pilots all had difficulty in getting the U-2's wheels on the ground because at low speeds it would remain in ground effect and glide effortlessly above the runway for great distances.

Taxi trials continued for one more day and were followed by the first planned flight on 4 August 1955. LeVier was again at the controls and had been instructed by Kelly Johnson to land the U-2 by making initial contact with the main or forward landing gear and letting the plane settle back on the rear wheel. LeVier had disagreed with this approach, believing that the U-2 would bounce if he tried to touch down on the forward gear first. After flying the aircraft up to 8,000 feet, LeVier leveled off and began cycling the landing gear up and down, then he tested the flaps and the plane's stability and control systems. Finally, LeVier made his first landing approach. As the U-2 settled down, the forward landing gear touched the runway and the plane skipped and bounced into the air. LeVier made a second attempt to land front wheels first, and again the plane bounded into the air.

With Kelly Johnson watching from a chase plane and giving a constant stream of instructions, LeVier made three more unsuccessful landing attempts. With the light fading and a thunderstorm fast approaching from the mountains to the west, LeVier made one last approach using the method he had advocated letting the aircraft touch on its rear wheel first. This time the U-2 made a near-perfect landing, which came just in the nick of time. Ten minutes later, the thunderstorm began dumping an unheard-of 2 inches of rain, flooding the dry lakebed and making the airstrip unusable.[43]

Now that the first problems in flying and landing the U-2 had been worked out, Kelly Johnson scheduled the "official" first flight for 8 August 1955. This time outsiders were present, including Richard Bissell, Col. Osmond Ritland, Richard Horner, and Garrison Norton. The U-2 flew to 32,000 feet and performed very well. Kelly Johnson had met his eight-month deadline.[44]

LeVier made an additional 19 flights in article 341

before moving on to other Lockheed flight test programs in early September. This first phase of U-2 testing explored the craft's stall envelope, took the aircraft to its maximum stress limit (2.5 g's), and explored its speed potential. LeVier soon flew the aircraft at its maximum speed of Mach 0 85. Flight tests continued, with the U-2 ascending to altitudes never before attained in sustained flight. On 16 August LeYier took the aircraft up to 52,000 feet. In preparation for this flight, the 42-year-old test pilot completed the Air Force partial-pressure suit training program, becoming the oldest pilot to do so. Testing at even higher altitudes continued, and on 8 September the U-2 reached its initial design altitude of 65,600 feet.[45]

On 22 September 1955, the U-2 experienced its first flameout at 64,000 feet—more than 12 miles up After a brief restart, the J57/P-37 engine again flamed out at 60,000 feet, and the aircraft descended to 35,000 feet before the engine could be relit. Engineers from Pratt & Whitney immediately set to work on this problem. The P-37 model engine had significantly poorer combustion characteristics than the preferred but unavailable P-3 I version and therefore tended to flame out at high altitudes. Combustion problems usually became apparent as the U-2 began the final part of its climb from 57,000 to 65,000 feet, causing pilots to refer to this area as the "badlands" or the "chimney." Flameouts bedeviled the U-2 project until sufficient numbers of the more powerful P-31 engines became available in the spring of 1956.[46]

Meanwhile, with the airworthiness of the U-2 airframe proven, Lockheed set up a production line in the Skunk Works, but delivery of even the second-choice J57/P-37 engines became a major problem.

Pratt & Whitney's full production capacity for these engines for the next year was contracted to the Air Force for use in F-100 fighters and KC-135 tankers. Colonel Geary, with the help of a colleague in the Air Force Materiel Command, managed to arrange the diversion of a number of these engines from a shipment destined for Boeing's KC-135 production line, making it possible to continue building the U-2s.[47]

As the deliveries of U-2 airframes to the testing site increased, a major logistic problem arose: how to transfer Lockheed employees from Burbank to [location deleted] without arousing a great deal of curiosity. The project staff decided that the simplest approach would be to fly the essential personnel to the site on Monday morning and return them to Burbank on Friday evening. Frequent flights were also necessary to bring in supplies and visitors from contractors and headquarters. Therefore, a regularly scheduled Military Air Transport Service (MATS) flight using a USAF C-54 aircraft began on 3 October 1955. James Cunningham promptly dubbed this activity "Bissell's Narrow-Gauge Airline." Less than seven weeks after it started, a MATS aircraft bound for [location deleted] crashed on 17 November, killing all 14 persons aboard the plane, including the Project Security Officer, CIA's [name deleted] four members of his staff, and personnel from Lockheed and Hycon. This crash represented the greatest single loss of life in the entire U-2 program.[48]

U-2s, UFOs, AND OPERATION BLUE BOOK

High-altitude testing of the U-2 soon led to an unexpected side effect—a tremendous increase in reports of unidentified flying objects (UFOs). In the mid-1950s, most commercial airliners flew at altitudes between 10,000 and 20,000 feet and military aircraft like the B-47s and B-57s operated at altitudes below 40,000 feet. Consequently, once U-2s started flying at altitudes above 60,000 feet, air-traffic controllers began receiving increasing numbers of UFO reports.

Such reports were most prevalent in the early evening hours from pilots of airliners flying from east to west. When the sun dropped below the horizon of an airliner flying at 20,000 feet, the plane was in darkness. But, if a U-2 was airborne in the vicinity of the airliner at the same time, its horizon from an altitude of 60,000 feet was considerably more distant, and, being so high in the sky, its silver wings would catch and reflect the rays of the sun and appear to the airliner pilot, 40,000 feet below, to be fiery objects. Even during daylight hours, the silver bodies of the high-flying U-2s could catch the sun and cause reflections or glints that could be seen at lower altitudes and even on the ground. At this time, no one believed manned flight was possible above 60,000 feet, so no one expected to see an object so high in the sky.

Not only did the airline pilots report their sightings to air-traffic controllers, but they and ground-based observers also wrote letters to the Air Force unit at Wright Air Development Command in Dayton charged with investigating such phenomena. This, in turn, led to the Air Force's Operation BLUE BOOK. Based at Wright-Patterson, the operation collected all reports of UFO sightings. Air Force investigators then attempted to explain such sightings by linking them to natural phenomena. BLUE BOOK investigators regularly called on the Agency's Project Staff in Washington to check reported UFO sightings against U-2 flight logs. This enabled the investigators to eliminate the majority of the UFO reports, although they could not reveal to the letter writers the true cause of the UFO sightings. U-2 and later OXCART flights accounted for more than one-half of all UFO reports during the late 1950s and most of the 1960s.[49]

HIRING U-2 PILOTS

In authorizing the U-2 project, President Eisenhower told DCI Dulles that he wanted the pilots of these planes to be non-US citizens. It was his belief that, should a U-2 come down in hostile territory, it would be much easier for the United States to deny any responsibility for the activity if the pilot was not an American.

[one major paragraph deleted]

In theory the use of foreign pilots seemed quite logical, in practice it did not work out. The [deleted] could only fly light aircraft. Language was also a barrier for the [deleted] although several were good fliers. Because Lieutenant Colonel Geary had taken a class of [deleted] through flying school at [deleted] he got the job of training the [deleted] arranged for an Air Force officer of [deleted] to stay with the group during a preliminary training program a [deleted]. The plan to use foreign pilots soon ran into trouble when only [deleted] passed the school and reported [deleted]. They made only a few flights in the U-2, and by the autumn of 1955 they were out of the program.[50]

Even before the elimination of the [deleted] it was clear that there would not be enough trained foreign pilots available in time for deployment. Bissell therefore had to start the search for U-2 pilots all over again. Lt. Gen. Emmett (Rosy) O'Donnell, the Air Force's Deputy Chief of Staff for Personnel, authorized the use of Air Force pilots and provided considerable assistance in the search for pilots who met the high standards established by the Agency and the Air Force. The search included only SAC fighter pilots who held reserve commissions. The use of regular Air Force pilots was not considered because of the complexities involved in having them resign from the Air Force, a procedure that was necessary in order to hire them as civilians for the AQUATONE project.

SAC pilots interested in the U-2 project had to be willing to resign from the Air Force and assume civilian status—a process known as sheep-dipping—in order to conduct the overflights. Although Air Force pilots were attracted by the challenge of flying U-2s over hostile territory, they were reluctant to leave the service and give up their seniority. To overcome pilots' reluctance, the Agency offered handsome salaries, and the Air Force promised each pilot that, upon satisfactory conclusion of his employment with the Agency, he could return to his unit. In the meantime, he would be considered for promotion along with his contemporaries who had continued their Air Force careers.[51]

The selection process for Agency U-2 pilots was very rigorous. Because of the strain involved in flying at extreme altitudes for long periods of time, painstaking efforts were made to exclude all pilots who might be nervous or unstable in any way. The physical and psychological screening of potential U-2 pilots was conducted by the Lovelace Foundation for Medical Education and Research in Albuquerque, New Mexico, under a contract signed with the CIA on 28 November 1955. The CIA's insistence on more stringent physical and mental examinations than those used by the Air Force to select pilots for its U-2 fleet resulted in a higher rejection rate of candidates. The Agency's selection criteria remained high throughout its manned overflight program and resulted in a much lower accident rate for CIA U-2 pilots than for their counterparts in the Air Force program.[52]

PILOT TRAINING

Even before the recruiting effort got under way, the Air Force and CIA began to develop a pilot training program. Under the terms of the OILSTONE agreement between the Agency and the Air Force, responsibility for pilot training lay with SAC. This essential activity was carried out under the supervision of Col. William F. Yancey, who was assigned to March AFB and flew to [location deleted] each day. Colonel Yancey was in charge of six SAC pilots who were to be trained by Lockheed test pilots to fly the U-2. Once they became qualified, these SAC pilots would become the trainers for the "sheep-dipped" former Reserve SAC pilots, who would fly U-2 missions for the CIA.

The original U-2 test pilot, Tony LeVier, trained several other Lockheed test pilots in the difficult art of flying the U-2. Eventually there were enough trained Lockheed pilots available to test the aircraft coming off the assembly line and also train the SAC pilots. Training was difficult because there was no two-seat model of the U-2. All instruction had to be given on the ground before takeoff and then over the radio once the craft was airborne. Almost 15 years elapsed before a two-seat U-2 was available for training new pilots. Despite the difficulties involved in training U-2 pilots, Colonel Yancey had a cadre of six qualified Air Force U-2 pilots by September 1955. These six were now ready to train the Agency's pilots.[53]

Training pilots was not easy because the U-2 was a mixture of glider and jet. Although those chosen for the overflight program were all qualified fighter pilots, they now had to learn to fly the delicate U-2. Its large wings had tremendous lift but were also very fragile and could not survive the stresses of loops and barrel rolls. Moreover, the original U-2s were placarded, which meant that they could not be flown at sea level faster than 190 knots in smooth air or 150 knots in rough air. At operational altitude, where the air was much less dense, they could not exceed Mach 0 8 (394 knots). Speeds in excess of these limits could cause the wings or tail section to fall off.

Airspeed was a very critical factor for the U-2. At maximum altitude only 6 knots separated the speeds at which low-speed stall and high-speed buffet occurred. Pilots called this narrow range of acceptable airspeeds at maximum altitude the "coffin corner" because at this point the U-2 was always on the brink of falling out of the sky. If the aircraft slowed beyond the low-speed stall limit, it would lose lift and begin to fall, causing stresses that would tear the wings and tail off. A little too much speed would lead to buffeting which would also cause the loss of the wings or tail. Flying conditions such as these required a U-2 pilot's full attention when he was not using the autopilot. Airspeed was such a critical factor that Kelly Johnson added a vernier adjustment to the throttle to allow the pilot to make minute alterations to the fuel supply.[54]

Among the unique devices developed for the U-2 was a small sextant for making celestial "fixes" during the long overflights. Because cloud cover often prevented U-2 pilots from locating navigational points on the earth through the periscope, the sextant turned out to be the pilots' principal navigational instrument during the first three years of deployment. When clouds were not a factor, however, the periscope proved highly accurate for navigation.

During the final tests before the aircraft became operational, U-2 pilots found they could navigate by dead reckoning with an error of less than 1 nautical mile over a 1,000-nm course.[55]

FINAL TESTS OF THE U-2

Flight-testing of the U-2 continued throughout the fall and winter of 1955-56 in order to test all the various systems. By mid-January 1956, SAC officials were so impressed that they also wanted to purchase a fleet of these planes. On 30 January, DCI Dulles agreed to have CIA act as executive agent for this transaction, which the Air Force called Project DRAGON LADY. To maintain secrecy, the Air Force transferred funds to the CIA, which then placed an order with Lockheed for 29 U-2s in configurations to be determined by the Air Force. The Air Force later bought two more U-2s, for a total of 31. The aircraft purchased for the Air Force were known as the Follow-On Group, which was soon shortened to FOG.[56]

Once enough pilots had been trained, Project AQUATONE managers concentrated on checking out the complete U-2 system planes, pilots, navigation systems, life-support systems, and cameras. From 10 through 14 April 1956, U-2s equipped with A-2 cameras took off [location deleted] and made eight overflights of the United States in order to test the various flight and camera systems as part of the standard Air Force Operational Readiness Inspection. Colonel Yancey and his detachment served as observers during this weeklong exercise.

Colonel Yancey's group carefully examined all aspects of the U-2 unit from flight crews to camera technicians and mission programmers. When the exercise was over, Yancey reported that the detachment was ready for deployment. He then briefed a high-level Pentagon panel that included the Secretary of the Air Force and the Chief of Air Staff. These officials concurred with Yancey's determination that the U-2 was ready for deployment.[57]

During these final tests in the spring of 1956, the U-2 once again demonstrated its unique airworthiness. On 14 April 1956, James Cunningham was sitting his office in Washington when he received a call [name deleted] informing him that a westward-bound U-2 had experienced a flameout over the Mississippi River at the western border of Tennessee. Aftet restarting his engine, the pilot reported a second flameout and engine vibrations so violent that he was unable to get the power plant to start again. Early in the program Bissell and Ritland had foreseen such an emergency and, with the cooperation of the Air Force, had arranged for sealed orders to be delivered to every airbase in the continental United States giving instructions about what to do if a U-2 needed to make an emergency landing.

Cunningham had the project office ask the pilot how far he could glide so they could determine which SAC base should be alerted. The pilot, who by this time was over Arkansas, radioed back that, given the prevailing winds and the U-2's 21 1 glide ratio, he thought he could reach Albuquerque, New Mexico. Within minutes Cunningham was on the phone to Colonel Geary in the Pentagon, who then had the Air Force's Assistant Director of Operations, Brig. Gen. Ralph E. Koon, call the commander of Kirtland AYB near Albuquerque. General Koon told the base commander about the sealed orders and explained that an unusual aircraft would make a deadstick landing at Kirtland within the next half hour. The general then instructed the base commander to have air police keep everyone away from the craft and get it inside a hanger as quickly as possible.

After a half hour passed, the base commander called the Pentagon to ask where the crippled aircraft was. As he was speaking, the officer saw the U-2 touch down on the runway and remarked, “It’s not a plane, it’s a glider!” Even more surprised were the air police who surrounded the craft when it came to a halt. As the pilot climbed from the cockpit in his “space” suit, one air policeman remarked that the pilot looked like a man from Mars. The pilot, [name deleted] later reported to Cunningham that, from the beginning of the first flameout until the landing at Albuquerque, the U-2 had covered over 900 miles, including more than 300 by gliding.[58]

Aside from this extraordinary gliding ability, however, the U-2 was a very difficult aircraft to fly. Its very light weight, which enabled it to achieve extreme altitude, also made it very fragile. The aircraft was also very sleek, and it sliced through the air with little drag. This feature was dangerous, however, because the U-2 was not built to withstand the G-forces of high speed. Pilots had to be extremely careful to keep the craft in a slightly nose-up attitude when flying at operational altitude. If the nose dropped only a degree or two into the nose-down position, the plane would gain speed at a dramatic rate, exceeding the placarded speed limit in less than a minute, at which point the aircraft would begin to come apart. Pilots, therefore, had to pay close attention to the aircraft’s speed indicator because at 65,000 feet there was no physical sensation of speed, without objects close at hand for the eye to use as a reference.[59]

THREE FATAL CRASHES IN 1956

The first fatality directly connected with flying the U-2 occurred on 15 May 1956, when test pilot [name deleted] flying article 345A, had trouble dropping his pogos, the outrigger wheels that keep the wings parallel to the ground during takeoff. Once airborne [name deleted] made a low-level pass over the airstrip and shook loose the remaining pogo [name deleted] stalled the U-2 and it plunged to earth, disintegrating over a wide area. Three months later, on 31 August 1956, a second fatal crash occurred during a night-flying exercise [name deleted] stalled article 354 at an altitude of about 50 feet when he tried to climb too steeply at takeoff. The craft fell, cartwheeled on its left wing, and struck a power pole near the runway. More experienced U-2 pilots always cut back abruptly on the throttle as soon as the Pogo sticks fell away in order to avoid such stalls.

Before the year was out, two more U-2s were destroyed in crashes, one of them fatal. On 17 September 1956, article 346 lost part of its right wing while on its takeoff ascent from Lindsey Air Force Base in Wiesbaden, Germany. The aircraft disintegrated in midair, killing pilot [name deleted]. The loss of article 357 on 19 December 1956 resulted from pilot hypoxia. A small leak prematurely depleted the oxygen supply and impaired[name deleted] judgment as he flew over Arizona. Because of his inability to act quickly and keep track of his aircraft's speed, the U-2 exceeded the placarded speed of 190 knots and literally disintegrated when it reached 270 knots. [name deleted] managed to jettison the canopy and was sucked out of the aircraft at 28,000 feet. His chute opened automatically at 25,000 feet, and he landed without injury. The aircraft was a total loss.[60]

COORDINATION OF COLLECTION REQUIREMENTS

From the very beginning of the U-2 program, it was apparent that some sort of an interagency task force or office would be needed to develop and coordinate collection requirements for the covert overhead reconnaissance effort. In a three-page memorandum to DCI Dulles on 5 November 1954 setting forth the ideas of the Technological Capabilities Panel's Project 3 on this subject, Edwin Land wrote

> *It is recommended that. . . a permanent task-force, including Air Force supporting elements, be set up under suitable cover to provide guidance on procurement, to consolidate requirements and plan missions in view of priority and feasibility, to maintain the operation on a continuing basis, and to carry out the dissemination of the resulting information in a manner consistent with its special security requirements.*[61]

When the U-2's development and testing approached completion, Land's recommendation was put into effect. Following a meeting with Deputy Secretary of Defense Donald Quarles and Trevor Gardner (who had been promoted from his special assistant post to become Assistant Secretary of the Air Force for Research and, Development), Richard Bissell established an Ad Hoc Requirements Committee (ARC) on 1 December 1955. He then named James Q. Reber to be Intelligence Requirements Officer for the U-2 project and chairman of the ARC. Reber was already experienced in coordination with other intelligence agencies, for he had headed the Directorate of Intelligence DI Office of Intelligence Coordination for four years. The first full-scale ARC meeting took place on 1 February 1956 with representatives from the Army, Navy, and Air Force present. Attending for the CIA were representatives from the Office of Research and Reports (ORR) and the Office of Scientific Intelligence (OSI). The CIA membership later expanded to include the Office of Current Intelligence (OCI) and a representative from the Directorate of Plans. In 1957 the National Security Agency (NSA) also began sending a representative. The State Department followed suit in 1960, although it had been receiving reports from the committee all along.[62]

ARC's main task was to draw up lists of collection requirements, primarily for the U-2, but also for other means of collection. These lists prioritized targets according to their ability to meet the three major national intelligence objectives concerning the Soviet Union in the mid-1950s long-range bombers, guided missiles, and nuclear energy. The committee issued its list of targets for the use of the entire intelligence community using all available means of collection, not just for the CIA with the U-2.[63]

ARC gave the top priority target list to the Project Director, and the project staff's operations section then used the list to plan the flightpaths for U-2 missions. Although the requirements committee was not responsible for developing flight plans, it assisted the planners with detailed target information as required. When a flight plan was ready for submission to the President for approval, the committee drew up a detailed justification for the selection of the targets. This paper accompanied the flight plan.[64]

In developing and prioritizing lists of targets, thee committee members had to take into account the varying needs and interests of their parent organizations. Thus, the CIA representatives generally emphasized strategic intelligence, aircraft and munitions factories, power-generating complexes, nuclear establishments, roads, bridges, inland waterways. In contrast, the military services usually placed a heavier emphasis on order-of-battle data. The Air Force, in particular, had a strong interest in gathering intelligence on the location of Soviet and East European airfields and radars.

Although the committee members kept the interests of their services or agencies in mind, their awareness of the vital nature of their mission kept the level of cooperation high. The group always attempted to reach a consensus before issuing its recommendations, although occasionally this was not possible and one or more agencies would add a dissent to the recommendation of the committee as a whole.[65]

PREPARATIONS TO HANDLE THE PRODUCT OF U-2 MISSIONS

On 13 December 1954, DCI Allen Dulles and his assistant, Richard Bissell, briefed Arthur C. Lundahl, the chief of CIA's Photo-Intelligence Division (PID), on Project AQUATONE. At DCI Dulles's direction, Lundahl immediately set in motion within his division a compartmented effort, known as Project EQUINE, to plan for the exploitation of overhead photography from the U-2 project. With only 13 members, the PID staff was too small to handle the expected flood of photographs that the U-2 would bring back, so in May 1955 the Directorate of Support (DS) authorized expanding PID to [number deleted] persons. Soon afterward the division moved from its room in M Building to larger quarters in Que Building.

The Photo-Intelligence Division continued to expand in anticipation of large quantities of U-2 photography. Its authorized strength doubled in January

1956 when a new project known as HTAUTOMAT came into existence to exploit U-2 photography. All of the products from this project would be placed in the new control system. By the summer of 1956, the PID had moved to larger quarters in the Steuart Building at 5th Street and New York Avenue, NW PID photointerpreters had already begun to work with U-2 photography following a series of missions in April 1956, when U-2s photographed a number of US installations that were considered analogous to high-priority Soviet installations. As a result of these preparations, PID was ready for the mass of photography that began coming when U-2 operations commenced in the summer of 1956.[66]

THE IMPACT OF THE AIR FORCE PROJECT GENETRIX BALLOONS

While the Agency was making its final preparations for U-2 overflights, the Air Force started a reconnaissance project that would cause considerable protest around the world and threaten the existence of the U-2 overflight program before it even began. Project GENETRIX involved the use of camera-carrying balloons to obtain high-altitude photography of Eastern Europe, the Soviet Union, and the People's Republic of China. This project had its origins in a RAND Corporation study from 1951. By the end of 1955, the Air Force had overcome a number of technical problems in camera design and recovery techniques and had manufactured a large number of balloons for use in the project. President Eisenhower gave his approval on 27 December 1955, and two weeks later the launches from bases in Western Europe began. By the end of February 1956, the Air Force had launched a total of 516 balloons.[67]

Project GENETRIX was much less successful than

its sponsors had hoped. Once launched, the balloons were at the mercy of the prevailing winds, and many tended to drift toward southern Europe and then across the Black Sea and the desert areas of China. These balloons therefore missed the prime target areas, which lay in the higher latitudes. Large numbers of balloons did not succeed in crossing the Soviet Union and China, some because they were shot down by hostile aircraft, others because they prematurely expended their ballast supplies and descended too soon. Only 46 payloads were eventually recovered (one more than a year later and the last not until 1958) from the 516 balloons that had been launched. In four of these payloads the camera had malfunctioned, and in another eight the photography was of no intelligence value. Thus, only 34 balloons succeeded in obtaining useful photographs.[68]

The low success rate of the Project GENETRIX balloons was not the only problem encountered; far more serious was the storm of protest and unfavorable publicity that the balloon overflights provoked. Although the Air Force had issued a cover story that the balloons were being used for weather research connected with the International Geophysical Year, East European nations protested strongly to the United States and to international aviation authorities, claiming that the balloons endangered civilian aircraft. The Soviet Union sent strongly worded protest notes to the United States and the nations from which the balloons had been launched. The Soviets also collected numerous polyethelene gasbags, camera payloads, and transmitters from GENETRIX balloons and put them on display in Moscow for the world press.[69]

All of this publicity and protest led President Eisenhower to conclude that “the balloons gave more legitimate grounds for irritation than could be matched by the good obtained from them," and he ordered the project halted. On 7 February 1956 Secretary of State Dulles informed the Soviet Union that no more "weather research" balloons would be released, but he did not offer an apology for the overflights.[70]

Despite the furor caused by GENETRIX, Air Force Chief of Staff Twining proposed yet another balloon project only five weeks later, in mid-March 1956. This project would employ even higher flying balloons than GENETRIX and would be ready in 18 months. President Eisenhower informed the Air Force, however, that he was "not interested in any more balloons."[71]

Although the photo intelligence gained from Project GENETRIX was limited in quantity, it was still some of the best and most complete photography obtained of the Soviet Union since World War II. It was referred to as "pioneer" photography because it provided a baseline for all future overhead photography. Even innocuous photos of such things as forests and streams proved valuable in later years when U-2 and satellite photography revealed construction activity.

Of still greater importance to the U-2 program, however, was the data that US and NATO radars obtained as they tracked the paths of the balloons whose average altitude was 45,800 feet—over the Soviet Bloc. This data provided the most accurate record to date of high-altitude wind currents, knowledge that meteorologists were later able to put to use to determine optimum flightpaths for U-2 flights.

One completely, fortuitous development from Project GENETRIX had nothing to do with the cameras but involved a steel bar. This bar served a dual purpose the rigging of the huge polyethylene gasbag was secured to the top of the bar and the camera-payload and automatic-ballasting equipment was attached to the bottom. By sheer chance, the length of the bar—1 centimeters—corresponded to the wavelength of the radio frequency used by a Soviet radar known by its NATO designator as TOKEN. This was an S-band radar used by Soviet forces for early warming and ground-controlled intercept. The bar on the GENETRIX balloons resonated when struck by TOKEN radar pulses, making it possible for radar operators at US and NAIO installations an the periphery of the Soviet Union to locate a number of previously unknown TOKEN radars.

These radar findings, coupled with other intercepts made during the balloon flights, provided extensive data on Warsaw Pact radar networks, radar sets, and ground-controlled interception techniques. Analysis of these intercepts revealed the altitude capabilities and tracking accuracy of radars, the methods used by Warsaw Pact nations to notify each other of the balloons' passage (handing off), and the altitudes at which Soviet aircraft could intercept the balloons. All of this information could be directly applied to future U-2 missions.[72]

These positive results from Project GENETRIX did not outweigh the political liabilities of the international protests. CIA officials became concerned that the ill will generated by balloon overflights could sour the Eisenhower administration on all overflights, including those by the U-2, which was just about ready for deployment. Therefore, DDCI Cabell wrote to Air Force Chief of Staff Twining in February 1956 to warn against further balloon flights because of the "additional political pressures being generated against all balloon operations and overflights, thus increasing the difficulties policy decisions which would permit such operations in the future."[73]

In addition to its concern for the future of the U-2 program, the Agency feared that President Eisenhower's anger at balloon overflights might result in the curtailment of the balloon program that the Free Europe Committee—a covert Agency operation based in West Germany—used to release propaganda pamphlets over Eastern Europe.

AQUATONE BRIEFINGS FOR SELECTED MEMBERS OF CONGRESS

Although knowledge of the U-2 project was a closely guarded secret within both the Agency and the Eisenhower administration, DCI Dulles decided that a few key members of Congress should be told about the project. On 24 February 1956, Dulles met with Senators Leverett Saltonstall and Richard B. Russell, the ranking members of the Senate Armed Services Committee and its subcommittee on the CIA. He shared with them the details of Project AQUATONE and then asked their opinion on whether some members of the House of Representatives should also be informed. As a result of the senators' recommendation that the senior members of the House Appropriations Committee should be briefed, Dulles later met with its ranking members, Representatives John Taber and Clarence Cannon. Official Congressional knowledge of the U-2 project remained confined to this small group for the next four years. The House Armed Services Committee and its CIA subcommittee did not receive a CIA briefing on the U-2 project until after the loss of Francis Gary Powers's U-2 over the Soviet Union in May 1960.[74]

THE U-2 COVER STORY

In February 1956, while the controversy over balloon flights was still raging and the U-2 was completing its final airworthiness tests, Richard Bissell and his staff began working on a cover story for overseas operations. It was important to have a plausible reason for deploying such an unusual looking plane, whose glider wings and odd landing gear were certain to arouse curiosity.

Bissell decided that the best cover for the deployment of the U-2 was an ostensible mission of high-altitude weather research by the National Advisory Committee on Aeronautics (NACA). Such a cover story, however, needed the approval of all concerned. Air Force intelligence, the Air Weather Service, the Third Air Force, the Seventh Air Division, the SAC U-2 project officer, the Air Force Headquarters project officer, and NACA's top official, Dr. Hugh Dryden. Moreover, the CIA Scientific Advisory Committee was also consulted about the cover plan.

Senior CIA officials and the other agencies involved in providing cover for the U-2 approved the final version of the overall cover story at the end of March 1956. The project staff then began working on contingency plans for the loss of a U-2 over hostile territory. Bissell advised the project's cover officer to "produce a document which sets forth all actions to be taken, not only press releases and the public line to be taken, but also the suspension of operations and at least an indication of the diplomatic action . . . We should at least make the attempt in this case to be prepared for the worst in a really orderly fashion." The cover officer then prepared emergency procedures based on the overall weather research cover story, and Bissell approved these plans. There was one final high-level look at the cover story on 21 June 1956, the day after the first U-2 mission over Eastern Europe, when Bissell met with General Goodpaster, James Killian, and Edwin Land to discuss the pending overflights of the Soviet Union, including the proposed emergency procedures. Killian and Land disagreed with Bissell's concept and made a much bolder and more forthright proposal in the event of the loss of a U-2 over hostile territory, the United States should not try to deny responsibility but should state that overflights were being conducted "to guard against surprise attack." This proposal was put aside for further thought (which it never received), and Bissell's weather research cover remained the basis for statements to be made after a loss. The project staff then went on to prepare a number of different statements to be used in various scenarios, including one in which the pilot was captured. Even in such a case, however, the proposed policy was for the United States to stick to the weather research cover story, a course of action that would prove disastrous in May 1960.[75]

[1]Although the Lockheed CL-282 was not designated as the U-2 until July 1955, this study will use the more widely known designator to avoid confusion.

[2]Bissell Interview (S); *OSA History*, chap. 3, p. 1 (TS Codeword)

[3]*OSA History*, chap 3, p 2 (TS Codeword), Bissell interview, 8 November 1984 (S); Beschloss, *Mayday*, p 89.

[4]*OSA History*, chap 3, pp. 6–7. Chap. 4. Pp. 1–2. Chap. 5, pp. 27–29 (TS Codeword); Chro*nology of the Office of Special Activities, 1954–1968,* (CIA: DS&T. 1969), p. 2-4 (TS Codeword) (hereafter cited as *OSA Chronology*).

[5]*OSA History*, chap. 3, pp. 5–7 (TS Codeword).

[6]Project AQUATONE Table of Organization, 28 April 1955 in *OSA History*, chap. 3, annex 15 (TS Codeword).

[7]*OSA History*, chap. 18, pp. 7– (TS Codeword), *OSA Chronology*, pp. 4, 7, 10, 45 (TS Codeword)

[8]Johnson, "Log for Project X," 29 November-3 December 1954 (U)

[9]John S. Warner, Office of the General Counsel, interview by Donald E.

Welzenback, Washington, DC, tape rcording 5 Aug. 1983 (S); *OSA History*, chap. 5, pp. 1–2 and annex 42 (TS Codeword); Johnson, "Log for Project X," 21 February 1955.

[10]The Lockheed "Skunk Works" was named after the Kickapoo Joy Juice factory known as the "Skonk Works" in Al Capp's comic strip *Li'l Abner*.

[11]Ben A. Rich (current head of the "Skunk Works"), interview by Donald E. Welzenbach and Gregory W. Pedlow, Burbank, California, 26 August 1988.

[12]Kelly Johnson, "A High-Altitude Reconnaissance Aircraft," 9 December 1954, Lockheed Contract Piles. OSA Records (S).

[13]For the design features of the U-2 in early 1955, see R F Boehme, *Summary Report Reconnaissance Aircraft*, Lockheed Aircraft Corporationeport 10420, 28 January 1955, pp. 7–9, OSA Records, [deleted] (S)

[14]Baker interview (S)

[15]*Ibid.*

[16]*OSA History*, chap. 1 annex 3, pp. 1–3 (TS Codeword).

[17]Ibid., chap 1, pp. 7–8 (TS Codeword).

[18]"Basic Configuration and Camera Data," 24 January 1956, OSA Records (TS Codeword); *OSA History*, chap. 5, annex 44 (TS Codeword).

[19]Ibid; Baker interview (S).

[20]Baker interview (S).

[21]Ibid

[22]Information supplied by James Baker to Donald E. Welzenbach, 12 May 1986 (U).

[23]*OSA History*, chap. 8, pp. 1–2 (TS Codeword); Miller, *Lockheed U-2*, pp. 19–20.

[24]*OSA History*, chap. 8, pp. 2–6 (TS Codeword); Johnson, Log for Project X, 25–29 April 1955; Clarence L. "Kelly" Johnson with Maggie Smith *Kelly More Than My Share of It All* (Washington, DC: Smithsonian Institute Press, 1985), p. 123.

[25]*OSI History*, chap. 7, pp. 4–6 (TS Codeword).

[26]Information supplied by James Cunningham to Donald W. Welzenbach (S).

[27]Ibid.

[28]*OSA History*, chap. 3, pp. 8–15 (TS Codeword); Beschloss, *Mayday*, pp. 105–107.

[29]*OSA History*, chap. 3, p. 15 and annex 14 (TS Codeword).

[30]Speech given by Richard Bissell at CIA Headquarters, 12 October 1965 (TS Codeword).

[31]Brig. Gen. Leo A. Geary (USAF-Ret.), interview by Donald E. Welzenbach, tape recording, 3 April 1986 (S): *OSA History*, chap. 3, p. 3 (TS Codeword).

[32]Land interview (TS Codeword); Bissell interview (S): James A Cunningham. Jr., interviee by Donald E. Weizenbach, Washington. DC, tape recording, 4 October 1983 (TS Codeword).

[33]OSA History, chap. 10, pp. 29–34 (TS Codeword).

[34]Ibid, chap. 5, p. 19 (TS Codeword).

[35]Lecture by Maj. Gen. Patrick J. Halloran (former Air Force U-2 pilot) at the National Air & Space Museum, 24 April 1986 (U).
[36]Information supplied by James Cunningham and former U-2 pilots [deleted] Donald E. Welzenbach, May 1980.
[37]At the time this Directorate was known as the Deputy Directorate/Plans, with the slash interpreted to mean either for or "of" Terminology for the major subdivisions of the CIA and their directors has varied over the past four decades. For the sake of consistency, all titles of Directorates and Deputy Directors have been placed in the current Agency format: the organization is known as the "Directorate of X" and the head is known as the "Deputy Director for X."
[38]Information supplied by James Cunningham to Donald E. Welzenbach; Sayre Stevens, Memorandum for the Record, "Discussion with Dr. Alex Batlin Re Project MKNAOMI," July 1975 (S).
[39]Geary interview (S).
[40]*OSA History*, chap. 8, p. 13 (TS Codeword).
[41]Informationsupplied by Norman Nelson, former director of Lockheed's Skunk Works, to Donald E. Welzenbach, 14 March 1986 (U); Miller, *Lockheed U-2*, pp. 77, 96.
[42]Transcripts of the test pilots and observers' comments on the initial U-2 test flights have been published in "Secret First Flight of Article 001" *Spyplanes* vol. 2, 1988, pp. 64–71, 82–85.
[43]Ibid, pp. 21–22; Johnson, "Log for Project X," 4 August 1955.
[44]Johnson, "Log for Project X," 8 August 1955.
[45]*OSA Chronology*, p. 7 (TS Codeword), Miller, *Lockheed U-2*, p. 22.
[46]*OSA History*, chap. 8, pp. 12–14 (TS Codeword).
[47]Geary interview (S).
[48]*OSA History*, chap. 7, pp. 17–19 (TS Codeword).
[49]Information supplied by James Cunningham to Donald E. Welzenbach (U).
[50]*OSA History*, chap. 10, pp. 1–10 (TS Codeword); Geary interview (S).
[51]*OSA History*, chap. 10, pp. 5–6 (TS Codeword); Geary interview (S): Francis Gary powers with Curt Gentry, *Operation Overflight* (New York: Holt, Rinehart, and Wilson, 1970), pp. 25–27.
[52]*OSA History*, chap. 10, pp. 5–6; chap. 5, p. 18 (TS Codeword).
[53]*OSA History*, chap. 11, pp. 1–7 (TS Codeword).
[54]Cunningham interview (TS Codeword); John Parangosky, interview by Donald E. Welzenbach, tape recording 6 March 1986 (S); information supplied by [name deleted] to Donald E. Welzenbach (S).
[55]Cunningham interview (TS Codeword).
[56]*OSA History*, chap. 5, pp. 25–26 (TS Codeword).
[57]Bissell interview (S); *OSA History*, chap. 11 pp. 15–16 (TS Codeword).
[58]Bissell interview (S); Cunningham interview (TS Codeword); Brig. En. Leo A. Geary, interview by Gregory W. Pedlow, Colorado Springs, Colorado, 12 October 1988 (S).
[59][name deleted] (former U-2 pilots), interview by Donald E. Welzenbach, Washington, DC, May 1986 (S).

[60]U-2 Accident Reports, folders 4, 10, and 14, OSA records [deleted] (S).
[61]*OSA History*, chap. 1, annex 1 (TS Codeword).
[62]Minutes of the Ad Hoc Requirements Committee of 1 February 1956, intelligence Community (IC) Staff records, COMIREX, [deleted] "ARC Minutes, 1956–1957;" Memorandum for the Joint Study Group from James Q. Reber, "Handling of Requirements for the U-2," 15 August 1960, IC Staff records, [deleted] "CHALICE (General)" (TS Codeword).
[63]Memorandum for the Joint Study Group from James Q. Reber, "Handling of Requirements for the U-2," 15 August 1960, IC Staff records, [deleted] "CHALICE (General)" (TS Codeword).
[64]Ibid; James Q. Reber, interview by Donald E. Welzenbach and Gregory W. Pedlow, Washington, DC, 21 May 1987 (S).
[65]Reber interview (S).
[66]For a more detailed history of photointerpretation in the CIA, see [deleted] *The National Photographic Interpretation Center,* vol. 1, *Antecdents and Early Years,* Directorate of Science and Technology Historical Series NPIC-2. December 1972, pp. 171–194 (S).
[67]P G Strong, Attachment to Memorandum for DCI Dulles, "Project GENETRIX Summary," 15 February 1956 (S).
[68]Final Report, Project 119L, 1st Air Division (Meterological Survey) Strategic Air Command, 5 March 1956, D-582, General Summary (S, declassified 1979).
[69]*New York Times,* 10 February 1956, p. 1; *Omaha World Herald,* 11 February 1956, p. 1.
[70]Andrew J. Goodpaster, Memorandum for the Record, "10 February 1956 Conference of Joint Chiefs of Staff with the President," WHOSS, Alpha, DDEL (TS, declassified 1980), Stephen E. Ambrose, *Eisenhower. The President* vol. 2 (New York: Simon and Schuster, 1984), p. 310.
[71]Quoted in Ambrose, *Eisenhower: The President*, p. 310.
[72]Final Report, Project 119L, 1st Air Division (Meterological Survey) Strategic Air Command, 5 March 1956, D-582, General Summary (TS, declassified 1979).
[73]Philip C. Strong, Attachment to Memorandum for DCI Dulles, "Project GENETRIX Summary." 15 February 1956, OSI records (S).
[74]John S. Warner, Legislative Counsel, Memorandum for the Record, "AQUATONE Briefings,"18 November 1957, Office of Congressional Affairs records, [deleted] (S); Warner interview (S).
[75]*OSA History*, chap. 8, pp. 30–35; chap. 11, annex 73 (TS Codeword).

3

U-2 Operations in the Soviet Bloc and Middle East, 1956–1968

By January 1956, everyone working on Project AQUATONE could see that the U-2 was nearing the time for operational deployment. During tests the aircraft had met all the criteria established in late 1954. Its range of 9,250 miles was sufficient to overly continents, its altitude of 72,000 feet was beyond the reach of all known antiaircraft weapons and interceptor aircraft, and its camera lenses were the finest available.

[about one-third page deleted]

THE DEPLOYMENT OF DETACHMENT A [deleted]

The first Agency U-2 detachment, consisting of [number deleted] aircraft and pilots, was known publicly as the 1st Weather Reconnaissance Squadron, Provisional (WRSP-I). The "provisional" designation gave the U-2 detachments greater security because provisional Air Force units did not have to report to higher headquarters. WRSP-1, known within the Agency as Detachment A, began deploying [deleted] on 29 April 1956. By 4 May, all of the detachment's personnel and equipment, including [number deleted] aircraft, had arrived at [location deleted].

Shortly after deployment, on 7 May, the National Advisory Committee on Aeronautics (NACA) released an unclassified U-2 cover story stating that a Lockheed-developed aircraft would be flown by the USAF Air Weather Service to study such high-altitude phenomena as the jet stream, convective clouds, temperature and wind structures at jet-stream levels, and cosmic-ray effects up to 55,000 feet.[3]

[one-half page deleted]

THE MOVE TO WIESBADEN

To avoid arousing further reaction in the United Kingdom and to begin the program of U-2 overflights beyond the Iron Curtain without further delay, Bissell moved Detachment A on 11 June 1956 to Wiesbaden, one of the busiest airfields in West Germany, without notifying West German authorities. The detachment commander, Col. Frederick McCoy, was disappointed in his hope that the redeployment of the U-2s could be accomplished without drawing undue attention. The strange-looking planes, with bicycle-type wheels and wings so long they touched the ground after landing, aroused considerable interest. Wiesbaden was to be only a temporary home for Detachment A, the Air Force began preparing [deleted] near the East German border for use by the U-2s [deleted] was an old World War II airbase that had been one of the launching sites for the GENETRIX balloons.[5]

Soon after the [number deleted] U-2s arrived in Wiesbaden, they were refitted with the more powerful J57/P-31 engines. The new engines were better suited for operations behind the Iron Curtain because they were less likely to suffer flameouts than the earlier model. Once the new engines were installed, the aircraft received the designation U-2B.[6]

Bissell was anxious to get the overflights started by late June because SAC weather experts had predicted that the best weather for photographing the Soviet Union would be between 20 June and 10 July. Bissell, however, had not yet received final authorization from President Eisenhower to begin overflights of the Soviet Union. On 28 May 1956, when DCI Allen Dulles met with the President to discuss the U-2's readiness for operations, Eisenhower still made no decision on overflights. Three days later Dulles and Air Force Chief of Staff Nathan Twining prepared a paper for the President outlining "AQUATONE Operational Plans." In the meantime, President Eisenhower had entered Walter Reed Hospital for tests for an abdominal ailment that turned out to be ileitis, requiring an operation. During his recovery from surgery, Eisenhower would make his final decision on the overflight program.[7]

PRESIDENT EISENHOWER'S ATTITUDE TOWARD OVERFLIGHTS

The President had mixed feelings about overflights of the Soviet Union. Aware that they could provide extremely valuable intelligence about Soviet capabilities, he, nevertheless, remained deeply concerned that such flights brought with them the risk of starting a war. From the very beginning of the U-2 program, President Eisenhower had worked to minimize the possibility that overflights could lead to hostilities. He had always insisted that overflights by military aircraft were too provocative, and in 1954 he had therefore supported the Land committee's proposal for an unarmed civilian aircraft instead of the military reconnaissance planes favored by the Air Force. For the same reason, Eisenhower had resisted attempts by the Air Force to take the U-2 program away from the CIA in 1955.

In fact, the President's desire to avoid secret reconnaissance missions over the Soviet Union, with all their risks, led him to make his famous "Open Skies" proposal in the summer of 1955, when the U-2 was still under development but making good progress. At the Geneva summit conference on 21 July 1955, President Eisenhower offered to provide airfields and other facilities in the United States for the Soviet Union to conduct aerial photography of all US military installations if the Soviet Union would provide the United States with similar facilities in Russia. Not surprisingly, Soviet leader Nikita Khrushchev almost immediately rejected Eisenhower's offer. Although the President had hoped that the Soviet Union would accept his proposal, he was prepared for rejection. While Open Skies was still being considered, Eisenhower had stated, "I'll give it one shot. Then if they don't accept it, we'll fly the U-2."[8]

Even though President Eisenhower had approved every stage of the U-2's development, knowing full well that the aircraft was being built to fly over the Soviet Union, the actual decision to authorize such flights was very difficult for him. He remained concerned that overflights could poison relations with the Soviet Union and might even lead to hostilities. One argument that helped overcome the President's reluctance was the CIA's longstanding contention that U-2 flights might actually go undetected because Soviet radars would not be able to track aircraft at such high altitudes. This belief was based on a 1952 study of Soviet World War II-vintage radars and on 1955 tests using US radars, which—unknown to US officials—were not as effective as Soviet radars against high-altitude targets. Shortly before U-2 operations began, however, the CIA's Office of Scientific Intelligence (OSI) conducted a vulnerability study of the U-2 that was published on 28 May 1956. The study's conclusion was that "Maximum Soviet radar detection ranges against the Project aircraft at elevation in excess of 55,000 feet would vary from 20 to 150 miles. In our opinion, detection can therefore be assumed." The OSI study added, however, "It is doubtful that the Soviets can achieve consistent tracking of the Project vehicle."[9] Completed just three weeks before the initiation of overflights, this study seems to have had little impact on the thinking of the top project officials. They continued to believe that the Soviets would not be able to track the U-2 and might even fail to detect it, except for possible vague indications.[10]

Soviet radars were not President Eisenhower's only concern. Also fearing that a malfunction might cause a U-2 to crash inside the Soviet Union, he asked Allen Dulles what the consequences would be. The President's staff secretary, Col. Andrew J. Goodpaster, who was present at virtually all White House meetings on the U-2 project and served as the President's intermediary to the CIA on this issue, later recalled.

> *Allen's approach was that we were unlikely to lose one. If we did lose one, the pilot would not survive . . . We were told—and it was part of our understanding of the situation—that it was almost certain that the plane would disintegrate and that we could take it as a certainty that no pilot would survive and that although they would know where the plane came from, it would be difficult to prove it in any convincing way.*[11]

CIA assurances that the U-2 would probably not be detected, and that a crashed U-2 could not be traced back to the United States, helped overcome the President's worries about overflights. The most important reason why President Eisenhower decided to send reconnaissance aircraft over the Soviet Union, however, was the urgent need for accurate intelligence to confirm or disprove claims of Soviet advances in long-range bombers and missiles. The initial sighting of the new Soviet Bison bomber in the spring of 1954 had been followed by reported sightings of more than 30 of these bombers in the spring and summer of 1955 (in reality these were sightings of the same group of 10 aircraft that circled around out of sight and made several passes during a Soviet air show). Soon members of Congress were calling for investigations into the relative strength of the US and Soviet Air Forces.[12] Early in 1956, concern about a possible Soviet advantage in long-range bombers grew as Air Force Chief of Staff Twining informed the Senate Armed Services Committee that the Soviet Union already had more Bisons than the United States had B-52s and that the Soviets would be able to "maintain this advantage for some time if they keep on the production curve we are now predicting."[13] By May 1956, reporting on the growing Soviet air strength was no longer confined to aviation journals; *US News and World Report,* for example, featured articles headlined "Can Soviets Take the Air Lead?" and "Is U.S. Really Losing in the Air?"[14]

Alongside fear of possible Soviet superiority in long-range bombers came a new potential threat Soviet progress in guided missile research. Trevor Gardner, Air Force Assistant Secretary for Research and Development, warned in September 1955 that "the most complex and baffling technological mystery today is not the Russian capability in aircraft and nuclear weapons but rather what the Soviet progress has been in the field of guided missiles."[15] On 30 January 1956, *Time* magazine made the guided missile its cover story. The article began by describing a hypothetical crisis set in 1962 in which the United States suffered a humiliating defeat because it had lagged behind the Soviet Union in guided missile development.[16] Just two weeks after this story appeared, the Soviets successfully tested a missile with a range of 900 miles, and President Eisenhower admitted at a press conference that the Soviet Union might be ahead of the United States in some areas of the missile field. Administration critic Senator Stuart Symington then claimed, "The facts are that our missile development may be ahead in the short-range area, but their missile development is ahead in the area that counts by far the most—the long-range area."[17] Fears of Soviet missile progress increased when Nikita Krushchev stated on 23 April 1956, "I am quite sure that we shall have very soon a guided missile with a hydrogen-bomb warhead which could hit any point in the world."[18]

Faced with growing Congressional and public anxiety over Soviet offensive capabilities, President Eisenhower approved the proposed overflight program Colonel Goodpaster relayed this decision to Bissell, Land, and Killian at a meeting on 21 June. The President nevertheless maintained tight control over the progress and authorized only 10 days of overflights when operations over the Soviet Union were ready to start in early July 1956.[19]

FIRST OVERFLIGHTS OF EASTERN EUROPE

The CIA initiated U-2 flights over hostile territory even before the President granted final approval for overflights of the Soviet Union. After consulting with the Commander of US Air Force Europe, Richard Bissell used existing Presidential permission for Air Force overflights of the Soviet Union's East European satellites as his authority to plan a mission over Poland and East Germany. Bissell had informed the President of his intention to conduct such missions in the "AQUATONE Operational Plan" submitted on 31 May.

The first operational use of a U-2 took place on Wednesday, 20 June 1956. [name deleted] flew a U-2 equipped with an A-2 camera over Poland and East Germany. At the end of the mission, Detachment A immediately rushed the exposed film to the United States for processing. The developed film arrived at the Photo-Intelligence Division (PID) on 22 June 1956. PID personnel considered the pictures obtained by mission 2003 to be of good quality.[20]

Following the success of this first mission, Bissell was eager to begin overflights of the Soviet Union. But even after the President granted his approval on 21 June, such missions could not yet take place for two reasons. First, President Eisenhower had agreed with a CIA and State Department recommendation that West German Chancellor Konrad Adenauer be informed in advance of US plans to overfly the Soviet Union from bases in Germany (in keeping with existing policies Adenauer was not informed about overflights of Eastern Europe). Second, Soviet party chief Nikita Khrushchev had invited representatives of the US Air Force to the Moscow Air Show, which opened on 23 June 1956. Led by Air Force Chief of Staff Nathan F. Twining, the delegation would be in the Soviet Union for a week, and General Twining requested that no overflights of the Soviet Union be staged until the Air Force delegation had left.[21]

Both of these restrictions on overflights of the Soviet Union were cleared up by the end of June. [approximately five and one-half lines deleted]

A few days later the Air Force delegation returned from Moscow, but now unfavorable weather prevented the start of operations against the Soviet Union.

While waiting for the clouds over the Soviet Union to clear, Detachment A carried out two more overflights of Eastern Europe on 2 July 1956: mission 2009 over Czechoslovakia, Hungary, and Bulgaria; and mission 2010 over East Germany, Poland, Hungary, and Romania. That afternoon Bissell and DDCI Cabell gave President Eisenhower a detailed briefing on the first U-2 overflight, which the President found "very interesting, very positive." Eisenhower was anxious to know, however, whether radars had tracked the aircraft. Bissell replied that, although East European radars had picked up the 20 June flight, radar operators had misread the altitude as only 42,000 feet. He added that the Agency was awaiting reports on that morning's flights to see if they, too, had been detected. Noting that the U-2 detachment had four aircraft working and could average up to two flights per day, Bissell told the President that the crews were "ready and eager to go in beyond the satellites" and overfly the center of the Soviet Union.[23]

Eisenhower replied that he thought it "urgent" to know whether the recent flights had been tracked by hostile radars. The President was obviously concerned that CIA estimates that the U-2 could fly virtually undetected were proving false. One of the reasons why he had approved the overflight program was the CIA's assurance that the Soviet Union would remain unaware of the flights or at the very worst—receive only occasional, vague indications.

FIRST U-2 FLIGHTS OVER THE SOVIET UNION

The question of how well the Soviets could track U-2 flights had not yet been settled when the first overflights of the Soviet Union took place. On Wednesday, 4 July 1956, the U-2 known as Article 347 began the first flight over the Soviet Union. Final authorization for mission 2013 had come shortly before takeoff. Late on the evening of 3 July, Bissell went to project headquarters in the Matomic Building to give the "Go" or "No go" decision. Although the President had approved the overflight, the final decision to start a mission depended on a number of factors, especially the weather over the target area and at the takeoff and landing sites. Bissell made the decision just before midnight Washington time, which was six o'clock in the morning in Wiesbaden. This pattern of last-minute approvals continued for the duration of the U-2 overflight program.[24]

When Wiesbaden received the "Go" signal, a U-2, equipped with an A-2 camera and flown by pilot [name deleted] took off on a course that took it over Poznan, Polana, where riots had occurred on 28–30 June. After Poznan, [name deleted] headed for Belorussia, where he turned north to Leningrad. The last leg of the mission took the U-2 over the Soviet Baltic states before returning to Wiesbaden. The main target of this mission was the naval shipyards in Leningrad, center of the Soviet Union's submarine construction program. Mission 2013's route also overflew a number of major military airfields to make an inventory of the new Bison jet-engine heavy bomber.[25]

The second overflight, on the following day, continued the search for Bison bombers. Pilot [name deleted] route was similar but somewhat to the south of [location deleted] and also flew farther east, more than 200 kilometers past Moscow. Although the Soviet capital was almost completely hidden by clouds, the A-2 camera with haze filters took some usable photographs of the city. These turned out to be the only U-2 photographs of Moscow because no other mission was sent over the Soviet capital. Among the key targets photographed during mission 2014 were the Fili airframe plant, where the Bison was being built, the bomber arsenal at Ramenskoye, where the Bisons were tested, the Kaliningrad missile plant, and the Khimki rocket-engine plant.[26]

When Allen Dulles returned to work on Thursday, 5 July 1956, he asked Bissell if any overflights had taken place during the Independence Day holiday. One had been made on the fourth and another just that morning, Bissell replied. (Because of the six-hour time difference, the 5 July flight was safely back in Wiesbaden by the time Dulles spoke to Bissell.) When Dulles asked the routes of these missions, Bissell told him that they had overflown both Moscow and Leningrad. "Oh my Lord," Dulles exclaimed, "do you think that was wise the first time?" "Allen," Bissell replied, "the first is the safest."[27]

President Eisenhower also wanted to know the results of the 4 and 5 July flights, but his principal concern was whether there had been any indication that either flight had been discovered or tracked by radar. Eisenhower told Colonel Goodpaster "to advise Mr. Allen Dulles that if we obtain any information or warning that any of the flights has been discovered or tracked, the operation should be suspended."

Additional Overflights, 9-10 July 1956
Mission 2020 9 July 1956
Mission 2021 9 July 1956
Mission 2023 10 July 1956
Norway
Sweden
Finland
OSLO
STOCKHOLM
HELSINKI
North Sea
Denmark
COPENHAGEN
Baltic Sea
MOSCOW
R. S. F. S. R.
U. S. S. R.
Minsk
Belorussian S S R.
WARSAW
Poland
WEST
EAST GERMANY
BONN
AMSTERDAM
BRUSSELS
PRAGUE
Czechoslovakia
GERMANY
France
Kiev
Ukranian S S R
Lvov
VIENNA
Austria
BUDAPEST
Hungary
Romania
BELGRADE
Yugoslavia
BUCHAREST
Danube
Bulgaria
SOFIA
Black Sea
Sevastopol
Simferopol
Kerch
Sea of Azov
Italy
ROME
Corsica
Sardinia
TIRANE
Greece
ATHENS
ANKARA
Turkey
Sicily
Mediterranean Sea
TUNIS
Tunisia
NICOSIA
Cyprus
Secret NOFORN

Goodpaster called both Dulles and Bissell and was told that reports on tracking or attempted interception of the U-2s would not be available for another 36 hours. Later that day the two CIA officials met with Goodpaster to ask if flights could continue in the meantime. Goodpaster replied that his understanding of the President's directive was that the operation should continue "at the maximum rate until the first evidence of tracking was received."[28]

Although President Eisenhower had originally spoken of suspending the overflights if they were "discovered or tracked," his main concern was to learn if the Soviets could track U-2 missions, meaning that they could follow the flight on their radar screens for most or all of the missions and thus have numerous opportunities to attempt interception. Certainly the President hoped that U-2 flights could not even be detected, but reports received on the 20 June overflight of Eastern Europe had already indicated that this goal was unrealistic. The President's emphasis therefore shifted to tracking. If the Soviets could successfully track U-2 missions, he wanted the overflights halted.[29] Reports on Soviet radar coverage of the first two overflights of the Soviet Union became available on 6 July. These reports showed that, although the Soviets did detect the aircraft and made several very unsuccessful attempts at interception, they could not track U-2s consistently. Interestingly, the Soviet radar coverage was weakest around the most important targets, Moscow and Leningrad, and the Soviets did not realize that U-2s had overflown these two cities.[30]

Detachment A carried out three more overflights of the Soviet Union during the 10-day period authorized by the President. Two of the missions (2020 and

2021) took place on a single day, 9 July 1945. They covered much of Eastern Europe, and the Ukraine and Belorussia in the Soviet Union. Unfortunately, a broken camera shutter ruined much of the photography of one of the flights. The third mission (2023), on the following day, included the Crimean Peninsula.[31]

The film from the first overflight (4 July) was flown to the United States immediately after the U-2 landed at Wiesbaden. Several members of the Photo Intelligence Division were on hand when the film was developed to check on the results. Also present was James Baker, who had accepted an offer by project officials to get a firsthand look at how the new A-2 lenses were working.[32]

The photos from July overflights were generally good, despite occasional problems caused by cloud cover. The huge amount of film taken by these missions provided more information about the Soviet Union's ability to track and intercept U-2s Photointerpreters examining the films eventually discovered the tiny images of MiG-15s and MiG-17s beneath the U-2s in various pursuit and attack attitudes climbing, flipping over, and falling toward Earth. It was even possible to determine their approximate altitudes. These photographs showed that the Soviet air defense system was able to track U-2s well enough to attempt interception, but they also provided proof that the fighter aircraft available to the Soviet Union in 1956 could not bring down a U-2 at operational altitude.[33]

One problem with early U-2 photography became apparent only after the first films were developed. If there was surface water on the runway at Wiesbaden when the U-2 took off, the camera windows became begrimed. Although the water dried during the flight, the oily scum it left behind degraded the photographic image. To combat this problem, AQUATONE ground crews took brooms and spent several hours before takeoff sweeping puddles of water from the runway to be used by the U-2. Kelly Johnson eventually designed a jettisonable cover for the camera windows, which was released at the same time as the pogos so that it could be recovered and reused.[34]

SOVIET PROTEST NOTE

The 4 and 5 July overflights brought a strong protest from the Soviet Union on 10 July in the form of a note handed to the US Embassy in Moscow. The note said that the overfights had been made by a "twin-engine medium bomber of the United States Air Force" and gave details of the routes flown by the first two missions. The note did not mention Moscow or Leningrad, however, because the Soviets had not been able to track these portions of the overflights. The Soviet note stated that the flights could only be evaluated as "intentional and conducted for the purposes of intelligence." As soon as the note arrived at the White House on the evening of 10 July 1956, Colonel Goodpaster called Bissel and told him to stop all U-2 overflights until further notice. The next morning Goodpaster met with Bissell to review the U-2 situation. Bissell said three additional flights had taken place since the missions mentioned in the Soviet note but added that no more were planned.[35]

Later Eisenhower told Goodpaster that he "didn't like a thing" about the Soviet note and was going to discuss the matter with Secretary of State Dulles. With the strong approval of President Eisenhower, Goodpaster informed DCI Dulles that "there is to be no mention of the existence of this project or of operations incident to it, outside the Executive Branch, and no mention within the Executive Branch to others than those who directly need to know of the operation, as distinguished from output deriving from it."[36]

During these initial overflights, the U-2 flew above 69,000 feet and could be seen only fleetingly by pilots of the Soviet interceptor aircraft. Thus, it appears that the Soviet claim that the intruder was a twin-engine bomber was probably based on the assumption that this was another overflight by a reconnaissance version of the twin-engine Canberra bomber, similar to the RAF overflight of Kapustin Yar in 1953. The US reply, sent to the Soviets on 19 July, truthfully denied that any US "military planes" had overflown the Soviet Union on the days in question. Meanwhile, on 16 July the Polish Ambassador to the United States delivered an oral protest concerning overflights of Poland on 20 June and 2 July. This was followed by a protest note from the Czechoslovak Government on 21 July. No formal reply was sent to the two Soviet satellite states.[37]

The details of the flightpaths listed in the Soviet and Polish protests, along with the subsequent photographic evidence of Soviet interception attempts, made it clear that U-2s could not fly undetected over the Soviet Union or Eastern Europe and could even be tracked for extended periods of time. This news greatly disturbed President Eisenhower. In a meeting, with Allen Dulles on 19 July 1956, the President recalled how he had been told that "not over a very minor percentage of these (flights) would be picked up." He went on to question "how far this should now be pushed, knowing that detection is not likely to be avoided." After discussing the possibility of basing U-2s in the Far East, President Eisenhower went on to say that he had "lost enthusiasm" for the U-2 activity. He noted that, if the United States were on the receiving end of a Soviet overflight operation, "the reaction would be drastic." The President was also concerned that the American public might learn of the overflights and be shocked that their country had violated international law. He stated, "Soviet protests were one thing, any loss of confidence by our own people would be quite another."[38]

The President's rapid disenchantment with the project was not lost on Richard Bissell. Fearing for the U-2 program's survival, he met with the Land committee in early August 1956 to urge them to help make the U-2 less vulnerable to radar pulses. His goal was to reduce the aircraft's radar cross section so that it would be less susceptible to detection. Edward Purcell had some ideas on this and suggested that he supervise a new project in the Boston area to explore them. At the direction of the Land committee, Bissell set in motion a project known as [deleted] to establish a [deleted] several MIT scholars who conducted studies and experiments into radar-absorbing materials and techniques proposed by Purcell. The effort, known as Project RAINBOW, got under way by the end of the year.[39]

THE END OF THE BOMBER GAP

During the three-week period of 20 June to 10 July 1956, U-2s had made eight overflights beyond the Iron Curtain, including five over the Soviet Union. PID's photointerpreters were busy until the end of August with their initial evaluation of the photography obtained by these flights. Their efforts were complicated by the division's move on 9 July from Que Building to the Steuart Building, but, when the photointerpreters were finished, they were able to write "finis" to the controversy over Soviet bomber strength.

Although the Air Force had claimed that the Soviet Union possessed almost 100 of the new Myasishchev-4 (Bison) heavy bombers, U-2 photography proved this assertion wrong. There were no Bison bombers at any of the nine long-range bomber bases photographed by the July missions. DCI Allen Dulles was particularly impressed by the photographs of the Soviet bomber bases, which in later years he called "million-dollar" photography. The actual value of the U-2 photos was probably even greater because, on the strength of their evidence, the White House was able to deny Air Force requests for additional B-52 bombers to "catch up" to the Soviets.[40]

Because of the need to protect the source of the information about Soviet bomber strength, the controversy surrounding this issue did not immediately die down. In November 1956, when the CIA began providing new Bison production figures based on U-2 photography without identifying the source, some members of Congress—unaware of the existence of the U-2—questioned the motivation behind the reduced estimates. They suggested that either the earlier estimates of Soviet bomber strength had been inflated to increase Air Force appropriations or the new estimates had been reduced by White House direction in order to hold down military expenditures. No one in the White House, the CIA, or the Air Force could reveal that U-2 photographs had actually provided the primary evidence for this change in the estimates.[41]

The need to keep the existence of the U-2 program secret caused problems even within the CIA itself .The Office of Security sharply restricted the number of persons who could be cleared for access to U-2 photography. The special clearance was granted on a "slot" basis, and only the person assigned to a particular position or "slot" could have the clearance. The U-2 photographs were kept in a secure room, and only those with special clearances were admitted to the room. In addition, the Office of Security considered U-2 information too sensitive to use in CIA publications. As a result, many analysts did not have access to information that would have greatly aided the production of intelligence estimates.[42]

TACTICAL INTELLIGENCE FROM U-2S DURING THE SUEZ CRISIS

Although U-2s had ceased flying over the Soviet Bloc because of President Eisenhower's standdown order, they could still be used elsewhere in the world. The Middle East would be the next area for U-2 operations. On 26 July 1956, Egyptian President Gamal Abdel Nasser nationalized the Suez Canal Company in retaliation for the decision by the United States and the United Kingdom to withdraw financial support for the Aswan Dam project. Nasser's action provoked an international crisis that would have a permanent effect on the U-2 program.

Long before the Suez Crsis developed, the CIA had planned to deploy U-2s in Turkey for use in the Soviet overflight program. On 1 May 1956, US Charge d'Affaires Foy D. Kohler approached Turkish Prime Minister Adnan Menderes on this matter. He told the Prime Minister that the effort was a continuation of the GENETRIX program, during which balloons had been released from Turkey, and involved aircraft that could fly 10,000 feet higher than any Soviet plane. Menderes gave his approval immediately. At the time of the Suez takeover, however, the second contingent of U-2 aircraft and pilots was still being trained in [location deleted]. This unit would not be ready for redeployment before the end of August and would not become established at Incirlik airbase near Adana, Turkey, until early September 1956. The Agency referred to the AQUATONE detachment at Adana as Detachment B, cryptonym [deleted]. By whatever name, the Adana detachment became the mainstay of U-2 activity for the next three and a half years.[43]

The fast-moving events of the Suez Crisis would not wait for Detachment B pilots to complete their training. With tension growing between Egypt and the Suez Canal Company's former owners, the United Kingdom and France, as well as between Egypt and Israel, US military and foreign policy planners needed immediate information about developments in the eastern Mediterranean. Detachment A was, therefore, assigned the first Middle Bast overflights. On 29 August, U-2 missions 1104 and 1105 left Wiesbaden and overflew the eastern Mediterranean littoral, [deleted]. Because these target areas were beyond the round trip range of the Wiesbanden-based U-2s, the planes landed at Adana for refueling. The next day, the same two planes, with different pilots, took off from Adana and overflew the same Middle East territory, this time including [deleted] before returning to Wiesbaden. The film contained evidence of large numbers of British troops on Malta and Cyprus and more new [deleted] than had previously been reported.[44]

As the situation around Suez grew more tense, the Eisenhower administration decided to release some of the U-2 photos to the British Government. On 7 September, James Reber, chairman of the Ad Hoc Requirements Committee, and Arthur Lundahl, chief of the Photo Intelligence Division, flew to London, taking with them photos of the eastern Mediterranean area, including the Suez Canal, taken on 30 August. These were the first and the only photos of the Middle East that the President authorized to be given to the British during the 1956 crisis.[45]

The Eisenhower administration viewed the developments in the eastern Mediterranean with great concern. To keep the President and Secretary of State abreast of developments in the area, Deputy Director for Intelligence Robert Amory established on 12 September a multiagency group known as the PARAMOUNT Committee to monitor the situation on a round-the-clock basis. The PARAMOUNT Committee worked inside PID headquarters in the Steuart Building. Composed of members from CIA, State, NSA, Army, Navy, and Air Force, this committee met daily—frequently several times a day to produce reports based on information obtained from U-2 photography, communications and electronic intelligence, and agents. The photointerpreters working for the PARMOUNT committee also came from several agencies the CIA, the Army, and the Navy.[46]

The Suez Crisis was a major turning point in the use of the U-2 airplane. Before this crisis, the U-2 had been seen solely as a collector of strategic intelligence, with high-quality results considered more important than speed. U-2 film had, therefore, been returned to the manufacturer for optimum development and then interpreted in Washington using the most up-to-date devices. Now, because of the Middle East crisis, Project AQUATONE was expected to perform like a tactical reconnaissance unit, developing film immediately after landing for instant interpretation or "readout." Photo-intelligence Division personnel assigned to Project HTAUTOMAT (U-2 film exploitation), therefore, had to arrange for forward processing of the U-2 film to avoid unacceptable delays in providing intelligence on tactical developments around Suez.

PID acted quickly to carry out its new assignment. Lundahl and Reber flew from the United Kingdom to US Air Force Europe headquarters in Wiesbaden on 12 September to make arrangements for processing and interpreting U-2 film in [deleted]. They had been preceded by [name deleted], chief of PID's Special Projects Branch. Following detailed discussions with Air Force photo-intelligence personnel, the CIA representatives arranged to use a portion of a nearby Air Force photo laboratory for developing U-2 film. With the assistance of [name deleted] chief of the HTAUTOMAT photo laboratory, and Air Force personnel, [name deleted] had the lab ready for processing on the following day, when the next U-2 mission returned from the Middle East. After quickly developing the film, [name deleted] and his joint staff of CIA and armed forces personnel studied it for indications of British and French preparations for hostilities and sent their first report to Washington on 15 September.

Although the Air Force provided considerable assistance in establishing [deleted] photo laboratory, Air Force officials did not like the idea of CIA personnel controlling overseas photo processing and interpretation centers, which were normally under Air Force control. Further negotiations led to a CIA-Air Force agreement at the end of October, under which the Air Force would name the commanding officer for such installations and the CIA would designate the deputy, who was responsible for technical and intelligence matters.[47]

PID soon added two photointerpreters and a lab technician to the [deleted] operation, which continued to develop and interpret U-2 photography of the

Middle East throughout September and October 1956. This unit's timely and accurate information enabled the PARAMOUNT Committee to predict the joint Israeli-British-French attack on Egypt three days before it took place.

[paragraph beginning deleted] During the rest of the month, Detachment A pilots flew another eight missions over the Middle East. By this time, the new Detachment B in Turkey was ready for operations, and it was better positioned to provide coverage of the Middle East. Detachment B began flying missions in September and soon became the primary detachment for Middle East overflights, conducting nine out of the 10 such missions flown in October.[48]

Detachment B's first U-2 flight, on 11 September 1956, made passes over [location deleted]. The next flight, more than two weeks later, covered much the same ground but flew as far west as [deleted]. Both were "special" missions aimed at [one-half page deleted].

[deleted] Other U-2 photographs revealed the presence [deleted]. The Anglo-French military buildup greatly irritated President Eisenhower, who considered these activities a violation of the 1950 Tripartite Declaration, in which the United States, the United Kingdom, and France had agreed to maintain the status quo in armaments and borders in the Middle East.

U-2 photography continued to keep the President and other key officials well informed about the progress of the crisis [deleted]. Secretary of State John Foster Dulles told the President on 28 October that he believed an Israeli attack on Jordan was imminent, adding that he thought the British and French would take advantage of such an attack to occupy the Suez Canal. [51]

The 10-day Middle East war began on the afternoon of 29 October 1956 with Israeli paratroop drops in the Sinai peninsula, followed by mobile columns striking deep into Egyptian territory [deleted] where he photographed black puffs of smoke from the fighting between Israel and Egypt. Adana-based U-2s were in the air for the next two days filming the Suez Canal area [deleted].

The United Kingdom and France entered the fray on the evening of 31 October with bombing raids against major Egyptian airfields. The Anglo-French bombing campaign continued for the next 48 hours. Early on the morning of 1 November, an Adana-based U-2, piloted by [deleted] flew south [deleted] where he made several passes to obtain complete coverage of the Israeli-Egyptian fighting there. He then headed west to Cairo, passing directly over the main Egyptian airbase at Almaza, where he filmed neatly arranged rows of Egyptian military aircraft. Continuing past Cairo to film another airfield, [deleted] turned southeast and then north to fly along the Nile, again crossing directly over Almaza. The photography from this leg of the mission revealed the burning wreckage of the Egyptian aircraft. During the short period of time that had passed between [deleted] passes, a combined Anglo-French air armada had attacked the airbase. When shown the before and after photos of Almaza, President Eisenhower told Arthur Lundahl. "Ten-minute reconnaissance, now that's a goal to shoot for!"[54] Eisenhower was pleased with the aerial photography but angered by what it depicted an Anglo-French attack on Egypt. He quickly called for a cease-fire [deleted].

The 1 November mission over Cyprus and Egypt also photographed Anglo-French preparations to invade Egypt. President Eisenhower was informed of this impending invasion on Sunday, 4 November. On the following day, British and French paratroopers dropped near Port Said at the north end of the Suez Canal. This action prompted Soviet Premier Nikolai Bulganin to send messages to France, Britain, and Israel warning that the Soviet Union was ready to use force to crush the aggressors.[55]

Early on the morning of election day, 6 November, the Anglo-French invasion armada arrived at Port Said and began landing troops. Back in Washington President Eisenhower met with Allen Dulles to discuss the deepening international crisis. Worried that the Soviet Union might be poised to intervene in the war, the President ordered Dulles to have the Adana-based U-2s fly over Syria to see whether the Soviets were moving planes to Syrian airbases in preparation for a strike against the forces attacking Egypt. The answer to Eisenhower's question came much sooner than expected because on the previous day a U-2 had already overflown Syria before making a run across northern Egypt. The film from this flight had reached Wiesbaden for processing and readout during the night. The results were in the hands of the PARAMOUNT Committee by midmorning on 6 November, while the President was motoring to Gettysburg to cast his ballot. By the time the President returned to the White House by helicopter at noon, Colonel Goodpaster was waiting for him with an answer there were no Soviet aircraft in Syria. Because of the President's concern about possible Soviet moves, Syria was the target of 14 additional U-2 flights between 7 November and 18 December 1956.[56]

The increasing reliance on Adana-based U-2s for coverage of the Middle East during the Suez Crisis made it difficult for the photointerpreters to supply timely information. When Detachment B aircraft returned to their base at Adana, there were no film-processing facilities available, and the film had to be flown to [deleted] adding a 10- to 15-hour delay. During the gradual buildup of the crisis, this delay had been tolerated, but, once actual hostilities broke out, US decisionmakers needed a more rapid response. On 29 October, Richard Bissell ordered Lundahl to establish a film-processing facility [deleted]. Two PID employees went to [deleted] on 13 November to set up the facility, and two photointerpreters moved from [deleted] to [deleted] to help in the effort. Forward processing was, however, hampered by the location of the [deleted] very end of a long supply line.

The PID team obtained and outfitted a trailer for film processing, but many problems had to be overcome. The first major problem was obtaining enough clean water. Detachment B personnel, therefore, purchased large amounts of borax locally for use in purifying water. In fact, they bought so much borax on the local market that one of them was arrested [deleted] who believed be was using the chemical to make drugs. It was also difficult to obtain a constant source of developers and fixers for processing the U-2 film, since the large Air Force supply facility at Wheelus AFB in Libya refused to provide the needed photographic chemicals. When PID personnel accompanied processed film from [deleted] to the United States, they returned to [deleted] sitting atop cartons of chemicals for the next day's processing. At first, film was developed in improvised tanks using flimsy wooden spools and hand-turned cranks to move the film through the solutions. Later, the [deleted] facility moved from its trailer to a building and received more up-to-date processing equipment. As was the case with the photo lab [deleted] personnel came from the Agency and the armed forces.[57]

The need to produce very timely intelligence diminished after the British and French agreed to a cease-fire on 7 November 1956. By the end of the month, foreign troops began evacuating Egyptian territory, and the pressure on [deleted] photointerpretation unit eased. The facility remained in existence, however, and was used twice in December 1956 and 11 times in the first half of 1957. It was then placed in caretaker status, for emergency use only.

RENEWED OVERFLIGHTS OF THE SOVIET UNION

Throughout the fall of 1956, U-2s provided valuable coverage of the Middle East crisis, but they were not conducting their original mission of strategic reconnaissance of the Soviet Union. President Eisenhower had halted all such overflights by his order of 10 July, and, in the months that followed, he remained unconvinced by CIA arguments in favor of a resumption of overflights. On 17 September 1956, DDCI Cabell and Richard Bissell went to the White House to ask President Eisenhower to authorize more flights over the Soviet Union. Adm. Arthur W. Radford, Chairman of the Joint Chiefs of Staff, also attended the meeting. Bissell and Defense Department representatives reviewed the valuable intelligence from the July U-2 flights, and Bissell then informed Eisenhower that many important intelligence requirements remained unfilled. To fill these requirements, Bissell noted, would require photography of approximately 15 separate areas of the Soviet Union. Pleading for the authority to resume overflights, Bissell stressed that conditions for photography were becoming less favorable as the days grew shorter. While the U-2 was then still safe from interception, he added, it might not be in the future.[58]

President Eisenhower acknowledged the value of the U-2 but emphasized that the international political aspects of overflights remained his overriding concern. He said he would talk further with John Foster Dulles about the matter, noting that the Secretary of State had at first seemed to belittle the political risk but had later found it increasingly worrisome.

A little more than two weeks later, on 3 October, when the President again met with Bissell, Cabell, and Radford, John Foster Dulles was also present. In opening the meeting, Eisenhower said he had become discouraged regarding Project AQUATONE. Although he had been assured that "there would be a good chance of not being discovered on most, if not all, operations, just the opposite had proved true." The President observed that arguments in favor of resuming U-2 operations did not take world opinion into consideration. He added that great efforts had been made for many years "to create an opinion in the world that we are not truculent and do not want war," and, if knowledge of the U-2 overflights got out, world opinion would view them as "provocative and unjustified."[59]

Secretary of State Dulles said that, although he essentially agreed with the President's comments, he thought that "really important results" might be obtained by a seven to 10-day operation. He, nevertheless, questioned the long-term value of the results DDCI. Cabell replied that U-2 photographs would be useful much longer than the Secretary of State had implied because they would establish a reference bank of geographic and manmade features. Siding with Cabell, Admiral Radford pointed out the need for more intelligence to make estimates better.

President Eisenhower was not convinced by these arguments. Although willing to consider extensions of the radar-seeking ferret flights he had authorized along the Soviet borders, he remained opposed to penetration flights over the Soviet Union.

Events in Eastern Europe in the fall of 1956 helped to change the President's mind. In October the Soviet Union backed away from a confrontation with nationalist Communist leaders in Poland only to find itself facing a similar situation in Hungary, where mass demonstrations led to the formation of a new government under Imre Nagy on 23 October 1956. Soviet troops and tanks temporarily withdrew from Budapest while awaiting reinforcements. By early November, however, the Kremlin leadership decided that events in Hungary were getting out of hand—particularly when Premier Nagy announced his nation's withdrawal from the Warsaw Pact—and ordered Soviet troops to suppress the Hungarian uprising. Although President Eisenhower deplored the Soviet intervention, he turned down CIA requests for permission to airdrop arms and supplies to the Hungarian rebels. In fact, the President forbid all overflights of that nation, including those by U-2 aircraft, and none was made.[60]

Although President Eisenhower had not been willing to allow overflights during the Hungarian crisis, the Soviet Union's actions in Hungary convinced him to authorize renewed overflights of the Soviet Bloc, a decision that was made easier by his reelection by a large margin in early November. Initially, however, the President only authorized overflights of Eastern Europe and Soviet border regions, not the deep penetration overflights that had been requested by CIA. At a 15 November 1956 meeting with Acting Secretary of State Herbert Hoover, Jr. (John Foster Dulles was recovering from cancer surgery), JCS Chairman Adm. Arthur Radford, DCI Allen Dulles, and Richard Bissell, Eisenhower explained why he refused to allow overflights of the Soviet Union. "Everyone in the world says that, in the last six weeks, the United States has gained a place it hasn't held since World War II. To make trips now would cost more than we would gain in form of solid information." Hoover agreed and noted, "If we lost a plane at this stage, it would be almost catastrophic." Torn between his desire to maintain a "correct and moral" position and his wish to know what the Soviet Union was up to, the President finally authorized several overflights of Eastern Europe and the Soviet border, "but not the deep one," adding that the aircraft should "stay as close to the border as possible."[61]

The first of these flights, mission 4016 on 20 November 1956, was the first overflight of Soviet territory since 10 July. This mission left Adana and flew east over Iran, then reversed and flew west along the Soviet-Iranian border to Soviet Armenia, where it crossed into the Soviet Union and photographed Yerevan. An electrical malfunction then forced the pilot, Francis Gary Powers, to return to Adana. Soviet interceptor aircraft made several unsuccessful attempts to reach this U-2, and the Soviet Government sent a secret protest note to Washington.[62]

On 10 December, Bulgaria was the target of two U-2 missions, one (4018) from Detachment B at Adana and another (2029) from Detachment A [deleted] Bulgarian fighter aircraft made 10 different attempts to intercept the first mission, but the flight proceeded without difficulty.[63]

The second flight came close to crashing but not

through the efforts of interceptors. The pilot of mission 2029 was [deleted] who had flown the first U-2 mission over Moscow on 5 July. He was known to his colleagues as the Lemon-Drop Kid because he always carried these hard candies in the knee pocket of his flight suit. Despite warnings to all pilots about the danger of opening the helmet faceplate at high altitudes, several pilots were known to do so. Some ate candy bars, [deleted] favored lemon drops. On the morning of 10 December, [deleted] was undergoing prebreathing, the Air Force enlisted man who oversaw his preflight regimen placed an L-pill in the righthand knee pocket of [deleted] flight suit, unaware that this pocket also contained [deleted] supply of lemon drops. After he took off, [deleted] began indulging in his habit of sucking lemon drops. About midway into the mission, he opened his faceplate and popped into his mouth what he thought was another lemon drop. After closing the faceplate, he began sucking on the object and thought it strange that it had no flavor and was much smoother than the previous lemon drops. Although tempted to bite down, [deleted] decided instead to reopen his faceplate and see what it was he had in his mouth. Spitting the object into his hand, he saw that he had been sucking on the L-pill with its lethal contents of potassium cyanide. Just a thin layer of glass had stood between him and death. The loss of his aircraft over Bulgaria would have exposed the U-2 program to worldwide publicity and would probably have resulted in an early end to overflights.[64]

Detachment A's security officer overheard [deleted] relating the L-pill story to a fellow pilot several days later and promptly reported the conversation to headquarters. When details of [deleted] close call reached Washington, James Cunningham immediately ordered

L-pills placed in boxes so that there would be no chance of mistaking them for anything else. The L-pill continued to be available for another three years. Then in January 1960, the commander of Detachment B, [deleted] raised an important question that had never been considered what would happen if an L-pill with its volatile contents accidentally broke inside the cockpit of a U-2? Realizing that such an accident would result in the death of the pilot, James Cunningham ordered the destruction of all L-pills and then turned to [deleted] for a better idea. By this time the state of the art in lethal devices was a needle poisoned with algal, an extremely deadly shellfish toxin. The needle was hidden in a tiny hole in a silver dollar supplied by Cunningham. Only one poison-needle coin was made because Cunningham decided that, if any pilot had to use it because of capture, there would probably not be any more overflights.[65]

Although the U-2 overflights of Eastern Europe in late 1956 caused renewed Soviet protests, the sharpest protest came on 15 December 1956, after three specially modified USAF RB-57D bombers photographed the city of Vladivostok in a high-speed dash over the Far Eastern coast of the Soviet Union (as part of the Air Force's Operation BLACK KNIGHT). President Eisenhower had approved the mission after being told by the Air Force that the high-speed RB-57Ds would probably not be detected.[66]

Reacting strongly to the Soviet protest, the President told Secretary of State Dulles on 18 December that he was going to "order complete stoppage of this entire business." As for a reply to the Soviet protest, Dulles said, "I think we will have to admit this was done and say we are sorry. We cannot deny it." Dulles noted that "our relations with Russia are pretty tense at the moment." Eisenhower agreed, noting that this was no tune to be provocative. He then instructed Colonel Goodpaster to call Secretary of Defense Wilson, Joint Chiefs of Staff Chairman Radford, and DCI Dulles to order. "Effective immediately, there are to be no flights by US reconnaissance aircraft over *Iron Curtain* countries."[67]

Flights along the borders of Iron Curtain countries continued, however, and, on 22 December 1956, Detachment B flew the first mission (4019) by a U-2 equipped for electronic intercept. The electronic-detection equipment known as the System-V unit (see appendix C — deleted, Ed.) was installed in the bay normally used by the main camera, and the plane flew along the Soviet border from the Black Sea to the Caspian Sea and on to Afghanistan. The System-V unit worked well.[68]

Early in 1957, a mission along the Soviet border accidentally turned into an overflight. On 18 March 1957, a U-2 collecting electronic intelligence along the Soviet southern border entered Soviet airspace because of compass error compounded by a slight error in the pilot's dead reckoning. Because of heavy cloud cover, the pilot, [name deleted] did not realize he was over the Soviet Union until he saw Soviet fighters attempting to intercept him. These attempts at interception once again demonstrated the Soviets' ability to track the U-2 and their inability to harm it. [69]

At this point in early 1957, the U-2 program was in limbo. Although the President would not allow U-2s to fly their primary mission of reconnaissance of the Soviet Union, he did not cancel the program and continued to authorize flights along Soviet borders. The CIA's overhead reconnaissance program also faced a renewed bid by the Air Force, which now had its own growing U-2 fleet, to gain control of the overflight program in the spring of 1957. The uncertainty surrounding the future of the project made planning and budgeting extremely difficult. In April t957, Richard Bissell asked the DCI and DDCI to push for a decision on whether the U-2 program was to continue in civilian hands and what its scope was to be. In briefing papers prepared for the DCI, Bissell argued for maintaining a nonmilitary overflight capability, which could "maintain greater security, employ deeper cover, use civilian pilots, keep the aircraft outside military control, and, therefore, make possible more plausible denial of US military responsibility in the face of any Soviet charges. " In urging the resumption of overflights, Bissell stated that four U-2 missions over border regions of the Soviet Union or Eastern Europe had been detected by the Soviets without causing any diplomatic protest. He also noted that the President's Board of Consultants on Foreign Intelligence Activities had unanimously recommended the resumption of overflights.[70]

All of these issues were discussed on 6 May 1957, when President Eisenhower met with Deputy Secretary of Defense Donald Quarles, Air Force Chief of Staff Nathan Twining, Acting Secretary of State Christian Herter, and three CIA officials—DCI Dulles, DDCI Cabell, and Richard Bissell. The President expressed concern about the impact of overflights on US-Soviet relations and about possible Soviet responses such as closing off access to Berlin. Although remaining opposed to flights over most of the Soviet Union, Eisenhower finally agreed to permit some flights over peripheral areas such as Kamchatka Peninsula and Lake Baikal, as well as the Soviet Union's atomic testing area at Semipalatinsk. Such overflights could be staged from [deleted]. The President rejected the Air Force's request to take over the U-2 program, stating that he preferred to have the aircraft manned by civilians "during operations of this kind."[71]

The President had once again agreed to allow overflights of the Soviet Union, although only over certain areas, because the need to learn more about the capabilities and intentions of the Soviet Union was too compelling. In particular, the President and top administration officials wanted to gather more data on the Soviet Union's missile program, a subject for which considerable Soviet boasting—but no hard data—was available.

Even after he had authorized the resumption of overnights, President Eisenhower maintained tight control over the program. He personally authorized each overflight, which meant that Richard Bissell would bring maps to the White House with the proposed routes marked on them for the President to examine. More than once, according to Bissell, Eisenhower spread the map out on his Oval Office desk for detailed study, usually with his son John (an Army officer serving as a White House aide) and Colonel Goodpaster looking over his shoulder. On occasion, the President would pick up a pencil and eliminate a flight leg or make some other correction to the flight plan.[72]

RADAR-DECEPTIVE "DIRTY BIRDS"

One additional reason why President Eisenhower had again authorized overflights of the Soviet Union was renewed CIA promises that Soviet detection or tracking of the U-2 was unlikely. At the 6 May 1957 meeting with the President, Richard Bissell reported on the progress that had been made in developing radar camouflage and absorption devices for the U-2. Once these devices were installed on the operational U-2s, he explained, the "majority of incidents would be undetected."[73]

Work on methods of reducing the U-2's vulnerability to radar detection had begun in the fall of 1956 as the result of President Eisenhower's disenchantment with the overflight program following Soviet detection and tracking of the first series of U-2 missions [deleted] was conducting this research under a project codenamed RAINBOW [name deleted] formerly of M1T, converted the theories of Harvard physicist Edward Purcell into systems that could be used on aircraft [deleted] radar-deception system consisted of a series of attachments to the U-2. First bamboo poles and later fiberglass rods were attached to the wings, where they would not interfere with the control surfaces. At the ends of these poles, completely circling the aircraft, was a small-gauge wire with precisely spaced ferrite beads. The wire and beads were supposed to capture incoming 70-MHz radar pulses and either trap them in the loop or weaken them so much that they would not register as a valid radar return. This configuration was called the trapeze and was not very successful.

A second approach, tested in early 1958, involved the use of plastic material containing a printed circuit designed to absorb radar pulses in the 65- to 85-MHz range. Nicknamed "wallpaper," this material was glued to parts of the U-2's fuselage, nose, and tail. Although the "trapeze" and "wallpaper" systems provided protection against some Soviet radars, the systems proved ineffective against radars operating below 65-MHz or above 85-MHz. Furthermore, both of these additions degraded the U-2's performance. The weight and drag of "trapeze" reduced the aircraft's operating ceiling by 1,500 feet, and "wallpaper" sometimes caused engines to overheat.[74]

[deleted] research results were tested by another firm known as Edgerton, Germeshausen & Grier (EG&G), which was also composed of MIT faculty members. Under an Air Force contract to evaluate radars, EG&G operated a small testing facility [deleted] not far from [deleted]. Although Kelly Johnson had been closely involved with the radar deception project since its early days, he cooperated reluctantly because he disliked adding attachments that made his aircraft less airworthy (Johnson's dislike of the antiradar attachments was reflected in the unofficial nickname for aircraft that had been so modified—"dirty birds"). After Lockheed mechanics had mounted the various RAINBOW devices on the prototype U-2, a Lockheed test pilot would fly the plane over EG&G's [deleted] installation. This was little more than a series of radar sets and a trailer containing instrumentation. EG&G technicians could thus record and evaluate the U-2's radar returns as it traversed a specified course over their facility.[75]

This method of testing radar-deceptive modifications proved both time consuming and dangerous. During a test flight on 2 April 1957, the "wallpaper" modification acted as insulation around the engine of the U-2 known as article 341, causing it to overheat and flameout. Unable to restart the power plant, Lockheed test pilot Robert Sieker bailed out but was struck and killed in midair by the U-2's tailplane. The aircraft crashed in an area [deleted] so remote [deleted] search teams needed four days to locate the wreckage. The extensive search attracted the attention of the press, and a 12 April 1957 article in the *Chicago Daily Tribune* was headlined, "Secrecy Veils High-Altitude Research Jet, Lockheed U-2 Called *Super Snooper*."[76]

Because of its large wingspan, an out-of-control U2 tended to enter a classical flat spin before ground contact. This slowed descent and actually lessened the impact. If there was no fire after impact, the remains of crashed U-2s were often salvageable, as was the case with the wreckage of article 341. Kelly Johnson's crew at the Skunk Works used the wreckage, along with spares and salvaged parts of other crashed U-2s, to produce another flyable airframe for about [deleted]. The U-2's ability to survive a crash in fairly good condition should have been noted by the Development Projects Staff for consideration in its contingency plans for a loss over hostile territory because the equipment on board the aircraft could easily compromise the weather research cover story.

The loss of one of Lockheed's best test pilots, as well as the prototype "dirty bird" U-2, led Kelly Johnson to suggest that Lockheed install a large boom at the [deleted] radar test facility. Using boom, which could lift entire airframes 50 feet in the air, technicians could change the airframe's attitude and run radar tests almost continuously without having to fuel and fly the plane.[78]

By the summer of 1957, testing of the radar-deception system was complete, and in July the first "dirty bird" (DB) arrived at Detachment B. The first operational use of this aircraft occurred on 21 July 1957 in mission 4030 over [deleted]. On 31 July, the same aircraft made a run over the Black Sea. There were a total of nine DB missions over the USSR. The antiradar system did not prove very effective, and its use was curtailed in May 1958.[79]

THE NEW DETACHMENT C

On 8 June 1957, a U-2 took off from Eielson Air Force Base in Alaska to conduct the first intentional overflight of the Soviet Union since December 1956. This mission broke new ground in two respects it was the first overflight conducted from American soil and the first by the new Detachment C.

Detachment C (known officially as Weather Reconnaissance Squadron, Provisional 3) was composed of the third group of pilots to complete their training [deleted] in the autumn of 1956, this third detachment needed a new base because [deleted] was about to become the training site for a large number of Air Force pilots who would fly the 29 U-2s purchased by the Air Force. The Agency decided that the best location for Detachment C would be the [deleted] and began looking for bases there.

Even without the arrival of the Air Force pilots, Detachment C could not have stayed [deleted] much longer. In June 1957, the entire facility had to be evacuated [approximately three lines deleted]. All remaining CIA personnel, materiel, and aircraft were transferred to Edwards AFB, California, and became known as Detachment G.

[deleted] The Agency then turned to the Navy, which granted permission for Detachment C to use the Naval Air Station at Atsugi, Japan. The Japanese Government received no notification of the proposed deployment because at that time it had no control over activities involving US military bases in Japan. Deployment of Detachment C began in early 1957 but was complicated by a recent decision to permit the families of Project AQUATONE employees to accompany them on overseas tours. As a result, program managers had to find housing facilities on the base or in

nearby communities, not an easy task in crowded Japan.[80]

Detachment C began conducting missions in June 1957 after several aircraft and pilots flew to Eielson Air Force Base near Fairbanks, Alaska. Air Force radar order-of-battle reports and NSA studies had revealed that the radar network in the Soviet Far East, with antiquated radar sets and personnel of a lower caliber than those in the western Soviet Union, was relatively ineffective. To take advantage of these weaknesses, Detachment C staged three missions from Alaska into the Soviet Far East. The first, on 7/8 June (the aircraft crossed the international date line during the flight), was unable to photograph its target, the ICBM impact area near Klyuchi on the Kamchatka Peninsula, because of bad weather and, therefore, never entered Soviet airspace. A second attempt to photograph Klyuchi on 19/20 June was marred by a camera malfunction that ruined every third frame of photography. This flight was tracked by Soviet radars, but there was no attempt at interception. After a pause of almost three months during which Detachment C received a dirty-bird U-2, the detachment's third mission over Klyuchi on 15/16 September 1957 achieved excellent results. The radar-deception devices proved ineffective, however, as the U-2 was tracked by Soviet radar and trailed by five fighters.[81]

DETACHMENT B FLIGHTS [DELETED]

The most important series of overflights in the summer of 1957 were those that Detachment B staged to gather intelligence on the Soviet Union's guided missile and nuclear programs. President Eisenhower had approved these overflights at the meeting on 6

May 1957, [approximately 10-12 lines deleted]. A C-124 brought in eight pilots and ground crews to prepare for missions over the Soviet Union and the People's Republic of China (PRC) beginning on 4 August (Operation SOFT TOUCH). During a 23-day period, these aircraft made nine flights, seven over the USSR and two over the PRC. Although one of the seven flights over the USSR was a failure because the camera malfunctioned after taking only 125 exposures, the remaining missions over Central Asia were a complete success, producing a bonanza of information that kept scores of photointerpreters busy for more than a year.[82]

The 5 August flight, a dirty bird piloted by [name deleted] was the first to photograph the major Soviet space launch facility east of the Aral Sea in Kazakhstan. None of the mission planners was certain just where the range was located, so the U-2 pilot followed the rail lines in the area. As a result, the plane did not pass directly over the rangehead and obtained only oblique photography.

Although known in the West today as Tyuratam, this missile installation had no name when it was first photographed in August 1957. In preparation for a briefing to President Eisenhower on the SOFT TOUCH photography, Dino Brugioni, an assistant to PID chief Arthur Lundahl, examined all the existing maps of the area to see if he could find a place name for the missile base. Only one map, made by the Germans during World War II, showed a community in the vicinity of the missile facility. The settlement's name was Tyuratam, which means "arrow burial ground" in the Kazakh language, and this was the name Brugioni gave the missile base. Official Soviet releases concerning this base have always referred to it as Baykonur, but the community of Baykonur is actually more than 200 miles north of Tyuratam.[83]

While PID was still analyzing the SOFT TOUCH photography, the Soviet Union announced the successful launch of an intercontinental ballistic missile (ICBM) from Baykonyr (Tyuratam). On 26 August 1957, the Soviet news agency TASS stated that a "super-long-range multistage intercontinental ballistic rocket" had been successfully tested, adding "it is now possible to send missiles to any part of the world."[84] The Soviet announcement made the intelligence community want even more information on Tyuratam, and a second U-2 piloted by [name deleted] flew over the area on 28 August 1957, just one week after the Soviet ICBM launch. This mission obtained excellent vertical photographs of the main launch complex, and photointerpreters soon determined that the Soviets had only one launchpad at Tyuratam. The base was not photographed again until 9 July 1959, at which time it still had only one launch pad, although two more were under construction.[85]

On 20 and 21 August 1957, U-2s conducted the first overflights of the Soviet nuclear testing grounds at Semipalatinsk, north-northwest of Lake Balkhash. The first mission, piloted by [name deleted] passed over part of the proving grounds, flew on to Novokuznetsk, and then proceeded to Tomsk, where it began its return leg that included coverage of a very large uranium-processing facility at the new city of Berezovskiy. In the second mission, [name deleted] flew directly over the Semipalatinsk proving grounds only four hours before a half-megaton device was detonated. In fact, the U-2 unknowingly photographed the aircraft that was to drop the nuclear device. These photographs also revealed evidence of a recent, low-yield, above-ground nuclear test [one and one-half lines deleted].

On its way to Semipalatinsk, the 21 August mission flew a search pattern over the western end of Lake Balkash looking for another Soviet missile-related installation and made the first photographs of what was later determined to be the new missile test center at Saryshagan. This facility was used to test radars against incoming missiles fired from Kapustin Yar, 1,400 miles to the west. Saryshagan later became the center for the development of the Soviet Union's advanced and ballistic missile (ABM) weapon system.

On 23 August 1957, DDCI Cabell, Richard Bissell, and Air Force Chief of Staff Twining with President Eisenhower to report on the results of Operation SOFT TOUCH. They showed the President some of the photographic results of the earlier missions and reported on the effects of the antiradar measures. Although the antiradar measures had not proved successful, the photographic yield from the missions was extremely valuable. Bissell then informed the President that the SOFT TOUCH operation was just about to conclude with the transfer of the aircraft back to Adana. He asked permission for one of the U-2s to make another overflight of the Soviet Union on this return trip, but the President denied the request, not wishing to conduct any more overflights than were necessary.[87]

THE DECLINE OF DETACHMENT A

During the summer of 1957, all overflights of the Soviet Union were conducted by either Detachment B or Detachment C. Detachment A in Germany was a less desirable starting point for overflights of the Soviet Union because such missions had to cross Eastern Europe first, increasing the likelihood of detection and diplomatic protests. Furthermore, the Soviet Union's air defense and radar networks were strongest along its western borders, so Detachment B missions over the southern portion of the Soviet Union and Detachment C missions in the Far East were less risky than those conducted by Detachment A. Finally, the main target of U-2 photography after the bomber issue receded was Soviet missile and nuclear progress. The testing areas for these weapons were located in the vast open spaces of the south-central and eastern portions of the Soviet Union, which lay beyond the range of Detachment A's aircraft.

The decline in importance of Detachment A had begun with the President's standdown order of 10 July 1956. During the next three months, the detachment conducted only 11 missions, all over the Mediterranean region rather than the original target of the Soviet Union, and the slow pace of activity and change in mission adversely affected pilot morale. One of the detachment's aircraft was lost in a crash on 17 September, killing pilot [name deleted] and garnering unwanted publicity. Conditions improved when the detachment moved to the newly renovated facility at [location deleted] early October 1956, but security now became a problem there. Detachment A personnel discovered that a long, black Soviet-Bloc limousine was parked at the end of the [location deleted] runway whenever the U-2s took off.[88]

During the next year, Detachment A mounted only four overflights. The first two were over Eastern Europe: one over Bulgaria on 10 December 1956 and the other over Albania on 25 April 1957. Then a long period of inactivity followed, ending with a third mission on 11 October 1957, which conducted electronic surveillance of Soviet naval maneuvers in the Barents

Sea. [approximately four lines deleted]

Although the final missions of Detachment A achieved excellent results, project headquarters had already decided that Western Europe was not a satisfactory location for overflights of the Soviet Union and had notified Detachment A on 20 September 1957 that its operations would cease in November. By 15 November 1957, all of the detachment's personnel and aircraft had returned to the United States. During Detachment A's 17-month period of operations, seven pilots had flown a total of 23 missions: six over the Soviet Union, five over Eastern Europe, and most of the remaining 12 missions over the Mediterranean area.[90]

[almost the entire page and a footnote reference deleted]

DECLINING OVERFLIGHT ACTIVITY

Operation SOFT TOUCH (427 August 1957) proved to be the high water mark of U-2 operations against the Soviet Union. Detachment B staged one more overflight on 10 September 1957, when a U-2 piloted by [name deleted] flew from Adana to photograph the Kapustin Yar Missile Test Range [deleted] obtaining photographs of a large medium-range ballistic missile (MRBM) on the launchpad. Six days later Detachment C conducted its successful overflight of the ICBM impact site at Klyuchi, and October saw the final two overflights of Detachment A. After these missions, penetration overflights became a rarity. There would be only six more during the next 32 months: one, in 1958, two, in 1959, and three, in 1960 (one of which was unsuccessful). During this period, President Eisenhower did authorize a number of flights along

Soviet border areas that occasionally penetrated short distances inside the border, but the Chief Executive had become extremely wary of authorizing "deep penetration" overflights, which invariably brought protests from Moscow.

The border flights took place under tight controls. Beginning in the fall of 1957, all messages from Washington to Adana giving coordinates for flights along the Soviet border contained the statement "This is not a penetration overflight" and warned about flying too close to Soviet borders. The Soviets even attempted to shoot down U-2s flying well within international airspace above the Black Sea, as was the case on 27 October 1937, when electronic intelligence equipment on a U-2 flight over the Black Sea that never violated Soviet airspace revealed 12 attempts at interception by Soviet fighters.[93]

The sole U-2 overflight of 1958 was conducted by a dirty bird From Detachment C. On 1 March 1958, mission 6011 overflew the Soviet Far East and photographed the Trans-Siberian Railroad, Sovetskayn Gavan', the Tatar Strait, and a strange installation at Malaya Sazanka, which was eventually determined to be a structure for mating nuclear devices with their detonators. This was the first and only U-2 overflight of the Soviet Union staged [deleted].

On 5 March 1958, the Soviet Union delivered a vigorous protest concerning this mission, prompting President Eisenhower to tell Colonel Goodpaster on 7 March to inform the CIA that U-2 flights were to be "discontinued, effective at once."[95] This standdown was to last more than 16 months, until July 1959. The Soviets had not been fooled by the antirader devices carried by mission 6011, as was demonstrated by the detailed information about the mission contained. In a Soviet aide-memoire delivered on 21 April 1958. It was clear that dirty bird aircraft were not effective and that Soviet radar operators had little difficulty in tracking them At this point, the Agency abandoned the use of the antiradar devices on the U-2. As a substitute, Lockheed began working to develop a paint with radar-suppressant qualities, but this project also proved unsuccessful.

The U-2s were not the only cause for the Soviet protests that so vexed the President. [approximately four lines deleted] Ten days later the Air Force began launching balloons designed to fly across the Soviet Union and Eastern Europe. This new balloon project (known as WS-461L) had been authorized by President Eisenhower on 25 June after Deputy Secretary of Defense Donald Quarles argued that a small number of balloons should be launched to take advantage of a newly discovered change in the west-to-east jet stream. Normally, this fast-moving air current stayed at an altitude of 55,000 feet, but, during June and July, it turned abruptly upward over the Bering Sea just west of Alaska, climbed to 110,000 feet, and then reversed direction. One of the key arguments that convinced the President to approve the project was Quarles's claim that the balloons' "chance of being detected is rather small and their identification or shootdown practically nil."[96]

Release of the balloons took place from an aircraft carrier in the Bering Sea on 7 July 1958. Nothing was heard about them until 28 July, when Poland sent a note protesting the overflight of a US-made, camera-carrying balloon that had fallen to earth in central Poland. The loss of this balloon was because of human error. Each balloon was equipped with a timing device that would cause it to drop its camera and film payload after crossing the target areas. An Air Force technician aboard the aircraft carrier had calculated that the balloons should cross the Eurasian landmass in about 16 days. Thus, he adjusted regulators aboard the balloons to cause automatic descent after 400 hours aloft. When bad weather delayed the launch for three successive days, however, the technician forgot to reset the timing devices. As a result, one payload fell into Poland. None of the three WS-461L balloon payloads was recovered.[97]

The Polish protest was quickly followed by a Soviet note protesting the balloons' violation of the Soviet Union's airspace. Several months later, the Soviets placed the US balloon and photographic equipment on display in Moscow for the world's press. President Eisenhower was angry that the Defense Department's assurances that the balloons would not be detected had proved false. Even worse, one of the balloons had been recovered by the Poles because the Air Force had disobeyed his instructions for the balloon project. When the Air Force had proposed the use of timers to bring down the balloons at the end of the mission, Eisenhower had said no, fearing that a malfunction could cause the balloons to come down prematurely. Furious at the Air Force's insubordination, the President ordered General Goodpaster on 29 July 1958 to tell the Air Force that "the project is to be discontinued at once and every cent that bas been made available as part of any project involving crossing the Iron Curtain is to be impounded and no further expenditures are to be made."[98]

Two days later Eisenhower followed up this order with a formal memorandum to Secretary of Defense Neil McElroy telling him that "there is disturbing evidence of a deterioration in the processes of discipline and responsibility within the armed forces." He cited, in particular, "unauthorized decisions which have apparently resulted in certain balloons falling within the territory of the Communist Bloc" and overflights over routes "that contravened my standing orders." [99]

On 2 September 1958, there was another violation of Soviet airspace when an unarmed Air Force BC-130 on an electronic intelligence collection mission crossed from Turkey into Soviet Armenia and was shot down by Soviet fighter aircraft. Six of the men on board were killed and the remaining 11 were never heard from again, despite State Department attempts to get the Soviet Union to reveal their fate. [100]

President Eisenhower was disturbed by the increased superpower tension that had resulted from violations of Soviet airspace by US balloons and aircraft because he still hoped to enter into arms limitation negotiations with the Soviets. On 8 September 1958, the United States sent a note to the Soviet Union calling for a Soviet answer to US proposals for a "study of the technical aspects of safeguards against the possibility of surprise attack." One week later the Soviets agreed to participate and suggested that the talks begin in Geneva on 10 November 1958. President Eisenhower was also attempting to persuade the Soviet Union to begin talks aimed at eliminating the atmospheric testing of nuclear weapons. These efforts began with a 22 August 1958 offer to suspend US nuclear tests for one year on the condition that the Soviet Union also refrain from further tests and join in negotiations. On 30 August, Soviet Premier Nikita Khrushchev accepted the proposal and agreed to start talks on 31 October 1958 in Geneva. When the talks began, however, the Soviets refused to agree to a test ban and carried out nuclear tests at

Semipalatinsk on 1 and 3 November. Nevertheless, during the late summer and early autumn of 1958, President Eisenhower, determined to reduce to a minimum any aggravation of the Soviets, kept the U-2 overflight program in limbo.[101]

In November 1958, relations with the Soviet Union worsened after Khrushchev precipitated a new crisis over West Berlin by announcing plans to sign a peace treaty with East Germany by May 1959. He stated that such a treaty would terminate Allied rights in West Berlin. Four days later, Soviet troops began harassing US Army truck convoys on the highways leading from West Germany to West Berlin. Although this new Berlin crisis never became as threatening as the blockade of 1948–49, President Eisenhower wished to avoid any actions that would provoke the Soviets. Tension over West Berlin was, therefore, an additional reason for continuing to keep the U-2 away from the Soviet Bloc.[102]

CONCERNS ABOUT SOVIET COUNTERMEASURES AGAINST THE U-2

Another reason for President Eisenhower's growing reluctance to authorize flights over the Soviet Union may have been concern that the Soviets were developing countermeasures that would enable them to shoot down a U-2. Before the program started, Richard Bissell had estimated that the U-2 would be able to fly over the Soviet Union with impunity for only about two years. This period was already over, and the Soviets were working frantically to devise a means to stop U-2 overflights. From the very beginning, Soviet air defense units had not only tracked U-2s with radars, but had also made repeated efforts to shoot them down with antiaircraft weapons and interceptor aircraft. In 1956 such attempted interceptions had involved primarily MiG-15s and MiG-17s, which could barely reach 55,000 feet. The advent of MiG-19s and MiG-21s, which could climb even higher, provided a greater threat for U-2 pilots.

Realistic training for pilots learning to intercept the U-2 became possible after the Soviets developed a new high-altitude aircraft, the Mandrake, which was actually an improved version of the Yakovlev-25 all-weather interceptor. The Mandrake used a high-lift, low-drag wing design similar to that employed by the U-2, but its twin engines made it heavier. The Mandrake's operating altitude was 55,000 to 65,000 feet, and its maximum altitude was 69,000, far less than the 75,000 feet reached by the U-2. Like the U-2, the Mandrake's wings would not tolerate great stresses, so it could not be used as an attack aircraft at the high altitudes at which both planes operated. Between 1957 and 1959, Yakovlev built 15 to 20 of these aircraft in two versions the Mandrake-R or YAK-25RM and the Mandrake-T, sometimes called the YAK-26. These high-altitude aircraft were used to overfly the Middle East, India, China, and Pakistan, as well as border regions of NATO nations in Europe during the late 1950s and early 1960s. It is not believed that Mandrakes ever attempted to overfly the continental United States.[103]

Beginning in late 1957, the Mandrake served as a practice target for pilots of high-performance Soviet MiG-19 and MiG-21 interceptors. The Soviet technique that most concerned U-2 pilots was the "snap up" or power dive and zoom climb. In this maneuver, ground-based radar operators would direct the interceptor aircraft along the same flight path as the U-2. When the MiG pilot achieved the same compass heading as the U-2 flying more than 10,000 feet above him, he would put his aircraft into a shallow dive to pick up speed, apply full throttle to the engine, then pull back on the stick and zoom as high as he could. In this manner the Soviet pilot hoped to come up directly beneath the U-2 so he could use his guns and missiles against the shiny U-2 etched in silver against the dark blue-black of space. Using this maneuver, some MiGs were able to climb as high as the U-2 but seldom got very close. At this height the MiGs were completely out of control, their small, swept-back wings provided insufficient lift; and their control surfaces were too small to maintain aircraft stability. U-2 pilots often spotted MiGs that reached the apex of their zoom climbs and then fell away toward the earth. The US pilots' greatest fear was that one of the MiGs would actually collide with a U-2 during a zoom climb.[104]

U-2 pilots complained that they felt like ducks in a shooting gallery under these circumstances and suggested that the underside of the silvery aircraft be camouflaged in some manner. Kelly Johnson had originally believed the U-2 would fly so high that it would be invisible, thus eliminating the need to paint the aircraft and thereby avoiding the added weight and drag that paint produced. The paint penalty was calculated to be a foot of altitude for every pound of paint. A full coat of paint cost the U-2 250 feet of altitude, substantially less than the 1,500-foot penalty paid for the addition of dirty bird devices.

By late 1957, Johnson agreed that something had to be done. After a series of tests over Edwards AFB, Lockheed began coating the U-2s with a standard blue-black military specification paint on top and a lighter cloud-blue paint below. Subsequent tests [deleted] revealed that the U-2s were less conspicuous when painted all over with a matte-finish blue-black color, which helped them blend with the dark canopy of space.[105]

MORE POWERFUL ENGINES FOR THE U-2

Less conspicuous paints were not the only answer to the growing threat of Soviet interceptors, A more powerful engine would increase the U-2's maximum altitude, which was the surest way to protect the aircraft from all Soviet threats. During late 1958 and early 1959, Lockheed began refitting the Agency's 13 remaining U2s—originally the Agency had taken delivery of 20 planes and the Air Force of 31—with the more powerful Pratt & Whitney J75-P13 jet engine. This new power plant generated 4,200 pounds more thrust while adding only 2,050 pounds more weight. With its greater power, the engine permitted the U-2 to reach operational altitude more quickly, thereby reducing the telltale contrails that the U-2 produced as it passed through the tropopause at 45,000 to 55,000 feet. With the new engine, U-2 passed through this portion of the atmosphere faster and did so before entering hostile airspace, thus reducing the chance of visual detection. The J75 power plant also made it possible for the U-2 to carry a larger payload and gain another 2,500 feet in altitude, permitting it to cruise at 74,600 feet. The new engines were in very short supply because of the needs of the Air Force's F-105 construction program, but Colonel Geary used his Air Force contacts to obtain an initial supply of 12 engines. The Air Force never equipped its original U-2s with the J75 engines.[106]

Detachment C in Japan received the first of these re-engined aircraft, known as U-2Cs, in July 1959, and two more arrived in Turkey for Detachment B in

August. All Agency U-2s had the new engines by the summer of 1962, but by then only seven CIA U-2s remained in service.

INTERVENTION IN LEBANON, 1958

Although the U-2 was used less and less for its original role of gathering strategic intelligence on the Soviet Bloc, it had acquired the new mission of providing US decisionmakers with up-to-date information on crisis situations all around the world. The first use of the U-2 to gather tactical intelligence occurred during the 1956 Suez Crisis. Afterward, U-2s from the Turkish-based Detachment B conducted periodic overflights to monitor the situation in the troubled Middle East, and they became especially active during the summer of 1958.

On 15 July 1958, President Eisenhower ordered US troops to land in Lebanon in response to a request for assistance by Lebanese President Camille Chamoun. Three months earlier, Eisenhower had turned down a similar request because the rioting that had led President Chamoun to ask for American aid had died down before intervention became necessary. In July, however, President Eisenhower saw the overall situation in the Middle East as much more threatening. On 14 July forces aligned toward Egyptian President Gamal Abdel Nasser overthrew the Government of Iraq and assassinated the royal family. Long concerned by the growing influence of Nasser, who had close ties to the Soviet Union and now headed both Egypt and Syria in the new United Arab Republic, President Eisenhower decided that US intervention was necessary to stabilize the situation in Lebanon and to show Nasser that the United States was willing to use force to defend its vital interests in the region. Before intervening in Lebanon, the United States consulted with the United Kingdom. which also decided to intervene in the Middle East by sending paratroopers to assist the Government of Jordan on 17 July.

With US Marines and Army troops deployed in a potentially hostile situation in Lebanon. US military commanders and intelligence community analysts immediately requested tactical reconnaissance flights to look for threats to the US units and evidence that other Middle Eastern countries or the Soviet Union might be preparing to intervene. The U-2s of Detachment B in Turkey carried out these missions.

Because tactical reconnaissance required an immediate readout of the films taken, the Photographic Intelligence Center (the new name for the Photo-Intelligence Division from August 1958) quickly reopened the film-developing unit at Adana and staffed it with lab technicians and photointerpreters. Throughout the summer of 1958, Detachment B U-9s brought back photography of military camps, airfields, and ports of those Mediterranean countries receiving Soviet arms. The detachment also kept a close watch on Egyptian-based Soviet submarines, which posed a threat to US 6th Fleet ships in the Mediterranean. In addition, U-2s flew occasional electronic intelligence collection missions along the Soviet border and over the Black Sea without centering Soviet airspace. In late August, as the crisis in the Middle East eased, the United States began withdrawing its 14,300 troops. It was not until 25 October, however, that the last American soldier left Lebanon.[107]

[one paragraph of approximately eight-ten lines deleted]

[2 full pages deleted]

THE U-2 PROJECT AT THE BEGINNING OF 1959

Early 1959 saw Detachment B aircraft active primarily over Middle Eastern countries, with occasional overflights of Albania to check for reported Soviet missile installations. Detachment C mainly collected high-altitude weather data, although it also flew two missions [location deleted] and Southwest China (see chapter 5). The overflight program against the Soviet Union seemed to be at a standstill, but pressures within the government were building to resume deep-penetration flights to resolve the growing "missile-gap" controversy.

Organizationally, the U-2 project underwent a major change after Richard Bissell became CIA's Deputy Director for Plans on 1 January 1959. At first glance, Bissell's selection seems unusual because he had spent most of his Agency career heading the U-2 project, but his first major assignment had been coordinating support for the operation that overthrew the leftist Government of Guatemala in 1954. Furthermore, Bissell's U-2 project was the major covert collector of intelligence against the CIA's primary target, the Soviet Union.

During his years as head of the Development Projects Staff (DPS), Bissell had opposed proposals to bring all Agency air activities together into a single office, fearing that he would lose control of the U-2 project. Once he became Deputy Director for Plans, his viewpoint changed; he was now in a position to consolidate all air activities under his own control. On 16 February 1959, the DPS became the Development Projects Division (DPD) of the Directorate of Plans (at the time known as the Deputy Directorate/Plans or DDP). Despite the tremendous increase in the scope of his duties after assuming control of the DDP, Bissell retained personal control of his previous Development Projects Staff projects the U-2 program, another project to develop a photosatellite, and a third project to design a follow-on aircraft for the U-2 (OXCART). Although the amalgamation of all Agency air operations and the transfer of the U-2 project to the DDP made sense, the question remained as to whether one individual could effectively control all these different activities.

[1]*OSA History*, chap. 11, pp. 10–15 (TS Codeword)
[2]Ibid, pp. 17–18 (TS Codeword).
[3]Press Release of 7 May 1956 (U) in *OSA History*, chap. 7, annex 60 (TS Codeword).
[4][approximately three lines of footnote material deleted]
[5]*OSA History*, chap. 11, pp. 21–23 (TS Codeword)
[6]IBID, pp. 23, 26 (TS Codeword).
[7]Ibid., pp. 23–25 and annex 73, "AQUATONE Operational Plans," 31 May 1956 (TS Codeword).
[8]Quoted in Beschloss, *Mayday*, p. 105.
[9]*OSA History*, chap. 11, p. 31 (TS Codeword). For the belief that the U-2 might go undetected see the Leghorn interview and Dwight D. Eisenhower, *Waging Peace, 1956–1961* (New York, 1965), p. 41.
[10]Richard M. Bissell, Jr., interview by Gregory W. Pedlow, tape record, Farmington, Connecticut, 28 October 1988 (S).
[11]Quoted in Beschloss, *Mayday,* p 118.
[12]Robert Holtz, "Russian Jet Airpower Gains Fast on US," *Aviation Week,* 23 May 1955, pp. 12–15; "Aviation Week Story Spurs Debate on US, Red Airpower Positions," *Aviation Week*, 30 May 1955, pp. 13–14.
[13]Claude Witze, "Russians Outpacing US in Air Quality, Twining Warns Congress," *Aviation Week,* 27 February 1956, pp. 26–28; Robert Hotz, "Russian Air Force Now Gaining in Quality," *Aviation Week,* 12 March 1956, p. 286.
[14]"Can Soviets Take the Air Lead? What LeMay, Wilson, Ike Say," *US News and World Report*, 11 May 1956, pp. 108–114, "Is US Really Losing in the Air?" *US News and World Report*, 18 May 1956, pp. 25–27.
[15]William Coughlin, "Gardner Defends Greater R&D Spending," *Aviation Week*, 26 September 1955, p. 14.
[16]"Missiles Away," *Time*, 30 January 1956, pp. 52–55.

[17]Robert Hotz, "Firing of 900-Mile Russian Missile Spurs US Changes," *Aviation Week*, 20 February 1956, p. 27.
[18]"Is Russia Really Ahead in Missile Race?," *US News and World Report*, 4 May 1956, p. 34.
[19]*OSA History,* chap. 11, pp. 27–29 (TS Codeword); A. J. Goodpaster, memorandum for the Record, 21 June 1956, WHOSS, Alpha, DDEL (TS).
[20]*OSA History,* chap. 11, p. 27 (TS Codeword); Mission folder 2003 (20 June 1956), OSA records, [deleted] (TS Codeword).
[21]Nathan F. Twining, *Neither Liberty nor Safety* (New York: Holt, Rinehart & Winston, 1966), pp. 259–260; *OSA History*, chap. 11, p. 27 (TS Codeword).
[22]*OSA History*, chap. 11, p. 28 (TS Codeword).
[23]Andrew J. Goodpaster's handwritten notes on 2 July 1956 meeting, WHOSS, Alpha, DDEL (TS).
[24]Bissell interview by Welzenbach (S); Cunningham interview (TS Codeword).
[25][deleted] *National Photographic Interpretation Center: The Years of Project HTAUTOMAT, 1956–1958*, Directorate of Science and Technology Historical Series NPIC-3, December 1974, 6 vols (hereafter cited as *NPIC History*), vol. 1, p. 20 (S); Mission folder 2013 (4 July 1956), OSA records, [deleted] (TS Codeword). Note on mission numbers: each proposed mission received a number, but not all of these missions were flown.
[26]*NPIC History*, vol. 1, p. 21 (S); Mission folder 2014 (5 July 1956), OSA records, [deleted] TS Codeword)
[27]Bissell interview by Welzenbach (S).
[28]Andrew J. Goodpaster, Memorandum for the Record, 5 July 1956, WHOSS, Alpha, DDEL (TS).
[29]Gen. Andrew J. Goodpastre, interview by Donald E. Welzenbach and Gregory W. Pedlow, Washington, DC, 8 July 1987 (S).
[30]Mission folders 20134 (4 July 1956) and 2014 (5 July 1956), OSA records [deleted] (TS Codeword).
[31]Mission folders 2020 (9 July 1956), 2021 (9 July 1956) and 2023 (10 July 1956), OSA records. [deleted] (TS Codeword).
[32]Cunningham interview (TS Codeword).
[33]Lundahl and Brugioni interview (TS Codeword).
[34]Baker interview (S).
[35]"Alleged Violations of Soviet Territory: Soviet Note of July 10, 1956 with U.S. Reply," *US Department of State Bulletin*, 30 July 1956, pp. 191–192; Andrew J. Goodpaster, Memorandum for the Record, 11 July 1956, WHOSS, Alpha, DDEL (TS).
[36]Andrew J. Goodpaster, Memorandum for the Record, 11 July 1956, WHOSS, Alpha, DDEL (TS).
[37]"Alleged Violations of Soviet Territory: Soviet Note of July 10, 1956 with U.S. Reply," *US Department of State Bulletin*, 30 July 1956, pp. 191–192; *OSA History*, chap. 11, pp. 32–33 (TS Codeword).
[38]Andrew J. Goodpaster, Memorandum for the Record, 19 July 1956, WHOSS, Alpha, DDEL (TS).

[39]Records of [footnote material deleted] (TS Codeword).
[40]*NPIC History*, vol. 1, p. 23(S).
[41]John Prados, *The Soviet Estimate: U.S. Intelligence Analysis and Russian Military Strength* (New York: Dial Press, 1982), pp. 45–47.
[42]Lundahl and Brugioni interview (TS Codeword).
[43]*OSA History*, chap. 11, pp. 9, 39–40; chap. 12, pp. 5, 12 (TS Codeword).
[44]Mission folders 1104 (29 August 1956)and 1105 (29 August 1956), OSA records, [deleted] TS Codeword).
[45]Lundahl and Brugioni interview (TS Codeword); *NPIC History*, vol. 1, pp. 56–58 (S).
[46]*NPIC History*, vol. 1, pp. 47–49, 54–56 (S).
[47]Ibid, pp. 49–52 (S).
[48]*OSA History*, chap. 19, annex 120, "CIA U-2 Missions Flown, 1956–1968," pp. 1–2 (TS Codeword).
[49]Lundahl and Brugioni interview (TS Codeword).
[50]Dwight D. Eisenhower [footnote material deleted].
[51]Lundahl and Brugioni interview (TS Codeword).
[52]Telephone calls, 28 October 1956, DDE Diary, DDEL
[53][footnote deleted] Mission folder 1314 (30 October 1956). OSA records, [deleted] (TS Codeword).
[54]Lundahl and Brugioni interview (TS Codeword); [deleted].
[55]Donald Neff, *Warriors at Suez: Eisenhower Takes America into the Middle East* (New York: Simon and Schuster, 1981), p. 403.
[56]Memorandum of Conference, 6 November 1956, Eisenhower Diary, Whitman File, DDEL (U): *OSA History*, chap. 19, annex 120, p. 3 (TS Codeword).
[57]*NPIC History*, vol. 1, pp. 53–54 (S); Lundahl and Brugioni interview (TS Codeword).
[58]Andrew J. Goospaster, Memorandum of Conference, 17 September 1956, WHOSS, Alpha, DDEL (TS).
[59]Andrew J. Goodpaster, Memorandum for the Record, 3 October 1956, WHOSS, Alpha, DDEL (TS).
[60]Cunningham interview (TS Codeword).
[61]Andrew J. Goodpaster, Memorandum of Conference with the President, November 15, 1956, WHOSS, Alpha, DDEL (TS); Ambrose, *Eisenhower: The President*,p. 374.
[62]Mission folder 4016, 20 November 1956, OSA records, [deleted] (TS Codeword).
[63]Mission folders 2029 (10 December 1956) and 4018 (10 December 1956), OSA records, [deleted] (TS Codeword).
[64]Cunningham interview (TS Codeword); [deleted] interview by Donald E. Welzenbach Washington, DC, 7 May 1986 (S).
[65]Cable from Detachment B to Development [deleted] 4 January 1960; cable from [deleted] to Detachment B, 7 January 1960, OSA records, [deleted] "Operation KNIFE EDGE" (TS Codeword).
[66]Goodpaster interview (S).
[67]Telephone calls 18 December 1956, DDE Diary, DDEL, (U); Andrew

J. Goodpaster, Memorandum for the Record, 18 December 1956, WHOSS, Alpha, DDEL (TS, downgraded to S); the Soviet protest note of 15 December 1956 and the US reply of 11 January 1957 are contained in "Alleged Overflight of Soviet Area by American Planes," *US Department of State Bulletin,* vol. 36, 28 January 1957, p. 135. Although Dulles's initial inclination had been to offer an apology, the US reply stated that the "only authorized United States Air Force flights in the general area of the Sea of Japan were normal training activities."

68Mission folder 4019 (22 December 1956), OSA records, [deleted] (TS Codeword).

69Information supplied by [deleted] to Donald E. Welzenbach (S), Mission folder 4020 (18 March 1957), OSA records, [deleted] (TS Codeword).

70*OSA History*, chap. 4, pp. 15–16; annex 22 (TS Codeword).

71Andrew J. Goodpastere, Memorandum of Conference with the President, 6 May 1957 (TS); "Record of Action—Meeting of May 6, 1957," WHOSS, Alpha, DDEL (TS).

72Bissell interview by Welzenbach (S); Beschloss, *Mayday*, p. 140.

73Andrew J. Goodpaster, Memorandum of Conference with the President, 6 May 1957 (TS); "Record of Action—Meeting of May 6, 1957," WHOSS, Alpha, DDEL (TSL).

74Records of [deleted] OSA records (TS Codeword).

75References to EG&G programs for the U-2 are contained in the later Convair contracts for Projects FISH and KINGFISH OSA records. (TS Codeword).

76Accident folder, crash of 2 April 1957, OSA records (S).

77Lockheed contracts, OSA Records (S).

78Ibid (S).

79Cunningham interview (TS Codeword).

80*OSA History*, chap. 15, pp. 2, 16–19; chap. 16, p. 1 (TS Codeword).

81Mission folders 6002 (8 June, 1957), 6005 (20 June 1957), and 6008 (16 September 1957), OSA records, [deleted] TS Codeword).

82*OSA History*, chap. 12, pp. 19–20 (TS Codeword); *NPIC History*, vol. 1, pp. 159–161 (S).

83Lundahl and Brugioni interview (TS Codeword).

84"Is Russia Ahead in Missile Race," *US News and World Report,* 6 September 1957, pp. 30–33.

85Mission folders 4058 (28 August 1957) and 4125 (9 July 1959), OSA records, [deleted] (TS Codeword).

86Mission folder 4045 (20 August 1957) and 4050 (21 August 1957), OSA records [deleted] (TS Codeword).

87Mission J. Goodpaster, Memorandum for the Record, 23 August 1957, WHOSS, Alpha, DDEL (TS).

88*OSA History*, chap. 11, pp. 41–42 (TS Codeword).

889[footnote deleted]

90*OSA History*, chap. 11, p. 44; chap. 19, annex 120 (TS Codeword).

91Ibid, chap. 11, pp. 44–45 (TS Codeword); *NPIC History*, vol. 3, pp.

447–8 (S).

[93]Mission folder 4061 (27 October 1957), OSA records, [footnote material deleted] (TS Codeword).

[94]Mission folder 6011 (1 March 1958) OSA records [footnote material deleted] (TS Codeword).

[95]Andrew J. Goodpaster, Memorandum for the Record, 7 March 1958 WHOSS, Alpha, DDEL (TS declassified).

[96]Andrew J. Goodpaster, Memorandum for the Record, 25 June 1958, WHOSS, Alpha, DDEL (TS).

[97]Donald E. Welzenbach, "Observation Balloons and Weather Satellites," *Studies in Intelligence* 30 (Spring 1986): pp. 26–28 (S).

[98]Andrew J. Goodpaster, Memorandum for the Record, 29 July 1958, WHOSS, Alpha, DDEL (S); Goodpaster interview (S).

[99]Quoted in Ambrose, *Eisenhower: The President*, pp. 475–476.

[100]"US Representations to the Soviet Government on C-130 Transport Shot Down by Soviet Fighter Aircraft," *US Department of State Bulletin*, 23 February 1959, pp. 262–271; Beschloss, *Mayday*, p. 159.

[101]Ambrose, *Eisenhower: The President,* pp. 489–491.

[102]Ibid., pp. 502–504.

[103]"Yakovlev Yak-25RM Mandrake," *Jane's Defense Weekly*, vol. 3, no. 7, 16 February 1985.

[104]Information supplied by [deleted] to Donald E. Welzenbach, May 1986.

[105]Lockheed contracts, OSA records (S).

[106]*OSA History*, chap. 16, p. 8 (TS Codeword); Geary interview (S).

[107]Ambrose Eis*enhower: The President* pp. 462–473.

4

The Final Overflights of the Soviet Union, 1959–1960

THE U-2 AND THE "MISSILE-GAP" DEBATE

Despite President Eisenhower's reluctance to send U-2s over the Soviet Bloc, he once again authorized overflights in the summer of 1959, after a pause of more than a year. The overriding factor in his decision was the growing "missile-gap" controversy, which had its roots in a series of dramatic Soviet announcements during the second half of 1957. The first announcement revealed the successful test of an intercontinental ballistic missile in August. Then in October, the Soviets announced the successful orbiting of the world's first artificial earth satellite, Sputnik. One month later the Soviets orbited a second satellite containing a dog and a television camera. To many Americans, including some influential members of Congress, the Soviet Union's space successes seemed to indicate that its missile program was ahead of that of the United States. By the spring of 1958, after the United States had successfully launched several satellites, fears of a space technology gap between the two superpowers had eased. By the end of the year, however, new concerns arose that the Soviet Union was producing a missile arsenal that would be much larger than that of the United States. This was the famous missile gap that received widespread publicity beginning in early 1959.[1]

The missile-gap controversy was fueled by Soviet boasts about the success of their missile program. On 4 December 1958, a Soviet delegate to the Geneva Conference on Surprise Attack stated "Soviet ICBMs are at present in mass production." Five days later, Soviet Premier Nikita Khrushchev asserted that the Soviet Union had an ICBM capable of carrying a 5-megaton nuclear warhead 8,000 miles. These statements seemed all the more ominous because, during this same month of December, the first attempt to launch the new US Titan ICBM failed. In reality, all of the Soviet statements were sheer propaganda; they had encountered difficulties with the SS-6 ICBM, and the program was at a standstill. As a result, there were no ICBM launches from Tyuratam between 29 May 1958 and 17 February 1959, a space of almost nine months.[2]

To conceal the difficulties in their missile program, Soviet leaders continued to praise its alleged successes. At the beginning of February 1959, Khrushchev opened the Soviet Communist Party Congress in Moscow by claiming that "serial production of intercontinental ballistic rockets has been organized." Several months later Soviet Defense Minister Rodion Malinovsky stated that these missiles were capable of hitting "precisely any point" and added, "Our army is equipped with a whole series of intercontinental, continental and other rockets of long, medium and short range." When asked at a press conference to comment on Malinovsky's statement, President Eisenhower replied, "They also said that they invented the flying machine and the automobile and the telephone and other things . . . Why should you be so respectful of this statement this morning, if you are not so respectful of the other three?"[3] Nevertheless, the Soviet statements were taken at face value by most Americans, including many members of the intelligence community.

As concern about Soviet missile progress increased, even the interruption in Soviet ICBM testing was seen as evidence of a Soviet advantage. Although the CIA correctly reasoned that the Soviets were experiencing difficulties in developing an operational ICBM, the Air Force assumed that the Soviets had halted testing because the missile was ready for deployment.[4]

The controversy intensified early in February 1959, when Secretary of Defense Neil H. McElroy testified before the Senate Preparedness Investigating Committee on Soviet missile capabilities for the next few years. McElroy told the Senators that in the early 1960s the Soviet Union might have a 3 to 1 advantage over the United States in operational ICBMs. McElroy stressed that the gap would be temporary and that at its end the United States would enjoy a technological advantage because it was concentrating on developing the more advanced solid-fueled missiles rather than increasing the number of obsolescent liquid-fueled missiles, but it was his mention of a 3 to 1 missile gap that made the headlines. Administration critics such as Senator Stuart Symington quickly charged that the actual gap would eventually be even larger.[5]

Faced with rising public and Congressional concern about the missile gap, Defense Department officials pressed President Eisenhower to authorize renewed overflights to gather up-to-date information about the status of the Soviet missile program. Following a National Security Council meeting on 12 February, Chairman of the Joint Chiefs of Staff Twining, Secretary of Defense McElroy, and Deputy Secretary of Defense Quarles stayed behind to talk to the President about overflights. They hoped that the need to refute criticism of the missile gap from Symington and other Democratic Senators would persuade the President to loosen his policy on the use of the U-2. McElroy pointed out that no matter how often Allen Dulles briefed these critics, they would not believe his reassurances about the absence of a missile gap without positive proof such as photographs. More overflights would be needed to obtain the kinds of photographs required.

The President was not swayed by these arguments. Noting that the reconnaissance satellite project was "coming along nicely," he stated that U-2 flights should be "held to a minimum pending the availability of this new equipment." Quarles objected that the satellites would not be ready for up to two years, but the President replied that this did not matter because the Soviets would not be able to build a first-strike force of ICBMs in the near future. President Eisenhower finally conceded that "one or two flights might possibly be permissible," but he ruled out "an extensive program." In light of the "crisis which is impending over Berlin" be did not want to be provocative.[6]

As the missile-gap controversy raged, President Eisenhower stuck to his refusal to permit overflights of the Soviet Union, although the Soviet Union's resumption of ICBM testing almost persuaded him to change his mind. On 10 April 1959, the President tentatively approved several overflights, but, on the following day, he called in McElroy and Bissell to inform them that he was withdrawing his authorization, explaining that "there seems no hope for the future unless we can make some progress in negotiation." Eisenhower remained worried by "the terrible propaganda impact that would be occasioned if a reconnaissance plane were to fail." Although he agreed that new information was necessary, especially in light of the "distortions several senators are making of our military position relative to the Soviets," Eisenhower believed that such information would not be worth "the political costs."[7]

The President remained willing to consider flights that did not overfly Soviet territory, and in June he authorized two electronic intelligence collection missions along the Soviet-Iranian border. The two missions of Operation HOT SHOP took place on 9 and 18 June 1959. The first of these missions was noteworthy because it involved both an Agency U-2 and an Air Force RB-57D Canberra. The two aircraft cruised along the Soviet border and made the first telemetry intercept ever from a Soviet ICBM during first-stage flight, 80 seconds after launch.[8]

Efforts to persuade the President to authorize penetration missions continued. On 7 July 1959, Allen Dulles and Richard Bissell met with Eisenhower to discuss the possibility of a penetration flight to gather intelligence on the Soviet missile program. Discussions continued the following day with the addition of Secretary of State Herter, who stated in support of the CIA proposal that "the intelligence objective outweighs the danger of getting trapped." The strong backing of the proposed overflight by both CIA and the State Department finally convinced President Eisenhower to approve the mission.[9]

On 9 July 1959, more than 16 months after the

previous overflight of the Soviet Union, a U-2 equipped with a B camera [deleted] flew over the Urals, and then crossed the missile test range at Tyratam. This mission, known as Operation TOUCHDOWN, produced excellent results. Its photography revealed that the Soviets were expanding the launch facilities at Tyuratam. While this overflight was under way, another U-2 flew a diversionary mission along the Soviet-Iranian border.[10]

Despite its success, this overflight remained an isolated incident. President Eisenhower was unwilling to authorize additional overflights of the Soviet Union, in part because he did not wish to increase tension before Premier Khrushchev's visit to the United States scheduled for 15-27 September 1959. Nevertheless, the President still wanted as much intelligence on the Soviet missile program as possible. Because the Soviets were conducting an extensive program of missile tests in mid-1959, Eisenhower authorized a steady stream of the less provocative electronic intelligence (ELINT)-gathering missions (14 in all) along the Soviet border during the remainder of the year.[11]

Within the United States, concern about the Soviet missile program continued to grow. On 12 September 1959 the Soviets scored another space success when their Luna 2 rocket reached the moon, and Khrushchev stressed this success when he arrived in the United States three days later. He also boasted of Soviet missile progress in private conversations with President Eisenhower, while making no mention of overflights by the United States. After the trip was over, Khrushchev and other leading Soviet officials continued to make exaggerated claims about the extent of their missile force, adding to the confusion and concern within the US intelligence community.

Thus in November 1959, Soviet Premier Khrushchev told a conference of journalists, "Now we have such a stock of rockets, such an amount of atomic and hydrogen weapons, that if they attack us, we could wipe our potential enemies off the face of the earth." He then added that "in one year, 250 rockets with hydrogen warheads came off the assembly line in the factory we visited."[12] Because the Soviet Union had been launching at least one missile per week since early fall, US policymakers placed great weight on his remarks.

Despite the intelligence community's intense interest in the Soviet Union's nuclear and missile programs, President Eisenhower did not authorize any more overflights of the Soviet Union during the remainder of the year. On the other hand, he raised no objections to (and probably welcomed) [one-third page deleted].

Because there had been so few overflights in 1958 and 1959, many questions about the Soviet missile program remained unanswered. Within the intelligence community there was still considerable disagreement over the size of the Soviet missile force. Thus, during testimony before the US Senate in January 1960, DCI Allen Dulles, Secretary of Defense Thomas Gates, and Air Force Chief of Staff Nathan Twining each gave different figures for the number of deployed Soviet missiles. Although the CIA figures were based on evidence gained from overflights, Dulles could not reveal this fact to the Senate and, therefore, faced very sharp questioning.[14]

As a result of these Senate hearings, Dulles was determined to obtain permission for more overflights in order to settle the missile-gap question once and for all and end the debate within the intelligence community. To accomplish this, Dulles proposed photographing the most likely areas for the deployment of Soviet missiles. At this time there was still no evidence of SS-6 ICBM deployment outside the Tyuratam missile test range. Because the SS-6 was extremely large and liquid fueled, analysts believed these missiles could only be deployed near railroads. Existing U-2 photography showed railroad tracks going right to the launching pad at the test site. Dulles, therefore argued that SS-6 installations could easily be located by flying along railroad lines. Dulles was supported by members of the President's Board of Consultants on Foreign Intelligence Activities. At a meeting of the board on 2 February 1960, Gen. James Doolittle urged President Eisenhower to use overflights of the Soviet Union to the maximum degree possible. The President's response, as summarized in General Goodpaster's notes of the meeting, showed that the upcoming summit meeting was already an important factor in his attitude toward U-2 flights. "The President said that he has one tremendous asset in a summit meeting, as regards effect in the free world. That is his reputation for honesty. If one of these aircraft were lost when we are engaged in apparently sincere deliberations, it could be put on display in Moscow and ruin the President's effectiveness."[15]

A few days later, another U-2 took to the sky on a mission over the Soviet Union [approximately six to eight lines deleted] The excellent photography from this mission did not reveal a single mission site, but analysts did discover a new Soviet bomber, dubbed the BACKFIN, at Kazan.[16]

Despite the outcome of this mission, the missile-gap debate continued. The Air Force still insisted that the Soviets had deployed as many as 100 missiles. The Army, Navy, and CIA, however, doubted that any had been deployed, because none could be found. Additional U-2 photography was needed to settle the debate. In mid-February, President Eisenhower reviewed plans for four additional U-2 missions. [deleted] made the President more willing to consider [deleted] and he agreed to allow one mission to be flown during the month of March. The President's continued restrictions upon the use of the U-2 disturbed DCI Dulles, who sent a memorandum to the National Security Council on 1 March 1960 asserting that the cardinal objective of obtaining information on Soviet missile deployment could be better achieved if the U-2 were given freer rein.[17]

In authorizing another overflight of the Soviet Union, President Eisenhower directed that it be conducted before 30 March. Because of complications in getting permission from Pakistan to use the airfield [deleted], however, the mission could not be staged in March, and the President agreed to extend his deadline until 10 April 1960. One day before the expiration of this deadline, a U-2 equipped with a B-camera took off [deleted] on the last successful overflight of the Soviet Union, Operation SQUARE DEAL. As had been the case during the previous two overflights, a second U-2 flew a diversionary mission along the Soviet-Iranian border [deleted] mission 4155 headed first for Saryshagan, where it obtained the first pictures of two new Soviet radars, the HEN HOUSE and HEN ROOST installations. The U-2 then flew to the nuclear testing site at Semipalatinsk. Returning to the Saryshagan area, it crisscrossed the railroad network there and then proceeded to Tyuratam, where it photographed a new two-pad, road-served launch area that suggested a new Soviet missile was in the offing.[18]

In his memoirs Nikita Khrushchev remarked that

this U-2 should have been shot down, "but our anti-aircraft batteries were caught napping and didn't open fire soon enough." Khrushchev explained that Soviet missile designers had developed a high-altitude antiairctaft missile and batteries of this missile had been deployed near known targets of the U-2.[19]

The CIA already had strong indications of improvements in the Soviet air defense system, and early in 1960 the Development Projects Division had asked Air Force experts at the Air Technical Intelligence Center (ATIC) for a frank assessment of Soviet capabilities against the U-2. On 14 March 1960, Col. William Burke, acting chief of the DPD, relayed the ATIC assessment to Richard Bissell.

> *The greatest threat to the U-2 is the Soviet SAM. Although the ATIC analysis concedes a remote possibility that the SAM may be less effective than estimated, their present evaluation is that the SAM (Guideline) has a high probability of successful intercept at 70,000 feet providing that detection is made in sufficient time to alert the site.*[20]

One of the reasons why Operation SQUARE DEAL had been selected for the 9 April flight was that mission planners believed that penetration from the [location deleted] area offered the greatest chance of escaping Soviet air defense system. [deleted] March letter recommending SQUARE DEAL as the preferred route for the next overflight had stated, "There is a reasonable chance of completing this operation without detection." Escaping detection had become important because, if the Soviet SAMs received sufficient advanced warning, they posed a major threat to the U-2.

CIA hopes that flights from [location deleted] might

go undetected proved false. On the 9 April overflight, the U-2's ELINT-collection unit (System VI) indicated Soviet tracking at a very early stage of the mission. Although the Soviets failed to intercept the U-2, their success at tracking it should have served as a warning against future overflights from [location deleted] (or anywhere else, for that matter). On 26 April 1960, [name deleted] informed Richard Bissell that "experience gained as a result of Operation SQUARE DEAL indicates that penetration without detection from the [location deleted] area may not be as easy in the future as heretofore."[21] Unfortunately, neither [name deleted] nor Richard Bissell took the logical step of recommending the cessation of overflights now that the risks had increased substantially. The lure of the prospective intelligence gain from each mission was too strong, and the Soviets' lack of success at interception to date had probably made the project staff overconfident. Furthermore, both DCI Allen Dulles and the President's Board of Consultants on Foreign Intelligence Activities were pressing for more photos of the Soviet Union in order to settle the missile-gap debate raging in the intelligence community and Congress.

THE LAST OVERFLIGHT OPERATION GRAND SLAM

Even before the 9 April overflight took place, President Eisenhower had consented on 28 March to an additional overflight during the month of April. His willingness to allow yet another overflight was strengthened when the Soviet Union did not protest the 9 April mission. As Presidential science adviser George Kistiakowsky later remarked about the lack of protest, "This was virtually inviting us to repeat the sortie."[22]

Although President Eisenhower had authorized another overflight for April, he left the designation of its targets up to the experts at the CIA. Of the three missions that remained under consideration, one—Operation SUN SPOT—would overfly southern targets, Tyuratam and Vladimirovka, while the other two would cover railroad networks in the north-central portion of the Soviet Union. The intelligence community had been interested in this area ever since late 1959, when there were indications that the Soviets were building an SS-6 launch facility there. This was the first indication that SS-6s might be located anywhere other than Tyuratam testing facility, where the missiles were launched from a general purpose launching pad. The intelligence community was anxious to obtain photography of a deployed SS-6 site because it could provide exemplars for photointerpreters to use in searching subsequent overhead photography for similar installations.[23]

The two proposed overflights that would cover the northern railroad lines received the strongest consideration. Both plans contained new features. Operation TIME STEP called for a U-2 to take off from the USAF base at Thule, Greenland, [deleted]. The aircraft would then fly over Novaya Zemlya on its way to cover the railroad lines from the Polyarnyy Ural Mountains to Kotlas [deleted]. The other proposed overflight, Operation GRAND SLAM, was the first U-2 mission planned to transit the Soviet Union, all previous missions had penetrated not more than halfway and then left in the general direction from which they came. GRAND SLAM proposed to fly across the Soviet Union from south to north, departing [end of paragraph deleted]

[approximately four lines deleted at new paragraph beginning] Bissell informed the White House that neither mission could be flown before 19 April. Once the maneuvers ended, bad weather over the Soviet Union kept the mission from taking place when it was originally scheduled. Richard Bissell, therefore, asked President Eisenhower for more time, and, on 25 April, General Goodpaster relayed the President's instructions to Bissell that "one additional operation may be undertaken, provided it is carried out prior to May 1. No operation is to be carried out after May 1."[24] The President did not want to fly missions any later than that because the Paris Summit was scheduled to begin on 16 May 1960.

By this time, CIA planners were concentrating on Operation GRAND SLAM as the most likely route for the proposed mission because it offered the best chance of photographing suspected locations of Soviet ICBM sites. The other proposed overflight, Operation TIME STEP out of Greenland, was more likely to run into bad weather (which would affect both navigation and photography) because the flightpath would remain above 60° north latitude during the entire mission. Furthermore, mission planners opposed this route because of its greater risk. In his letter to Richard Bissell on 14 March 1960, [name deleted] stated:

> *Operation "TIME STEP" is our last choice because we can assume, with a 90 percent probability of being correct, that we will be detected on entry, tracked accurately throughout the period in denied territory (approximately four hours), and will evoke a strong PVO [Soviet Air Defense] reaction. This flight plan would permit alerting of SAM sites, and pre-positioning of missile equipped fighters in the Murmansk area (point of exit)*

> *thus enhancing the possibility of successful intercept. In addition, we must assume that even were the Soviets unable to physically interfere with such an incursion, sufficient evidence will be available to permit them to document a diplomatic protest should they desire to do so?*[25]

The concerns raised by [name deleted] about TIME STEP should also have been raised about Operation GRAND SLAM, which would be the most adventuresome overflight to date because it proposed covering so much of the Soviet Union. If the Soviets could track the U-2 early in the mission, they would have plenty of time to prepare to intercept the aircraft.

The pilot selected for Operation GRAND SLAM was Francis Gary Powers, the most experienced U-2 pilot in the program. Powers had joined the project in May 1956 and had flown 27 operational missions in the U-2, including one each over the Soviet Union and China as well as six along the Soviet border.

To prevent the U-2 from being seen [deleted] project managers decided to ferry the aircraft from [deleted] the night before the scheduled flight. Once the plane was refueled and its camera was loaded, it would take off at daybreak, with little if any exposure to local residents because of darkness and its short stay—less than six hours on the ground. Originally scheduled for Thursday, 28 April, GRAND SLAM was canceled because of bad weather over the northern Soviet Union. This had been the case for the past several weeks. When this flight was canceled, the U-2 returned to Adana before sunrise. That evening the U-2 flew [location deleted] for another attempt to stage the mission early on the 29th, but bad weather again forced cancellation of the mission, and the U-2 returned to Adana. Because of continued bad weather over the target areas, no mission was planned for Saturday, 30 April.[26]

Meanwhile, the plane ferried to [location deleted] on 27 and 28 April had accumulated so many hours of flight time that it had to be removed from service for periodic maintenance. A different aircraft was, therefore, ferried [location deleted] Saturday night, 30 April. This aircraft, article 360, had made a crash landing in [deleted] during the previous September (see chapter 5). Although it had been refurbished by Lockheed and now had the more powerful J75 engine that would give it greater altitude, pilots did not completely trust this aircraft and considered it a "hangar queen." As Powers noted in his memoirs, "Its current idiosyncrasy was one of the fuel tanks, which wouldn't feed all its fuel."[27] The aircraft was equipped with a B-model camera, a System-VI electronic intelligence unit, [approximately four lines deleted].

Operation GRAND SLAM, mission 4154 and the 24th deep-penetration overflight of the Soviet Union, began almost 30 minutes late on Sunday, 1 May 1960, a delay due to difficulty in getting takeoff approval from Washington. This delay was caused by communications problems that are typical at sunrise and sunset during spring and autumn, when the ionosphere will not support reliable communications. In attempting to relay the authorization message, the radio operator in Adana was unable to reach [name or location deleted]. Realizing that neither the prearranged nighttime nor daytime frequencies were working, the operator began sending a message in the clear, using one of the guard frequencies in the transition area between the daytime and nighttime frequencies. The radio operators at [deleted] kept hearing the Morse [deleted] as they tuned from one prearranged frequency to the other.' Then one of the [deleted] operators decided to tune in the guard frequency where the Morse transmission was strongest. He was able to discern a break in the letters, making the message read [deleted] realized this [deleted]. The detachment chief, Col. William Shelton, who had been waiting anxiously inside the radio van for a "Go" or "No Go" message, leaped from the van and ran across the field to give the signal for takeoff to Powers, who was sitting in the U-2C at the end of the runway.[28]

Powers started his takeoff roll at 0159Z on 1 May1960. Once airborne, Powers guided his aircraft toward Afghanistan. Following standard operating procedure, Powers clicked his radio switch when he reached penetration altitude of 66,000 feet, which signaled the operations unit at [location deleted] that everything aboard the aircraft was working and the mission would proceed as planned. Aside from this simple signal, Powers and all U-2 pilots maintained strict radio silence during penetration missions.

Powers' first target was the Tyuratam Missile Test Range after which he headed for Chelyabinsk, just south of Sverdlovsk. The planned route would take him over Kyshtym, Sverdlovsk, northwest to Kirov, north over Yur'ya and Plesetsk, then to Severodvinsk, northwest to Kandalaksha, north to Murmansk, and, finally, [location deleted].

May Day turned out to be a bad time to overfly the Soviet Union. On this major holiday, there was much less soviet military air traffic than usual, so Soviet radars could easily identify and track Powers' U-2. In addition, the Soviets responded to the intrusion by ordering a ban on civilian air traffic in a large portion of the Soviet Union. Soviet radar began tracking the U-2 when it was still 15 miles south of the Soviet-

Afghan border and continued to do so as the aircraft flew across the Central Asian republics. When Powers reached the Tashkent area, as many as 13 Soviet interceptor aircraft scrambled in an unsuccessful attempt to intercept his plane.

Powers never made it past Sverdlovsk. Four and a half hours into the mission, an SA-2 surface-to-air missile detonated close to and just behind his aircraft and disabled it 70,500 feet above the Sverdlovsk area. The plane began spiraling down toward the ground and Powers looked for a way out. Unable to use the ejection seat because centrifugal force had thrown him against the canopy, he released the canopy and prepared to bail out, waiting to arm the destruction device at the last minute, so that it would not go off while he was still in the plane. When he released his seatbelt, however, he was immediately sucked out of the aircraft and found himself dangling by his oxygen hose, unable to reach the destruction switches. Finally, the hose broke and he flew away from the falling aircraft. After he fell several thousand feet, his parachute opened automatically, and he drifted to earth where he was quickly surrounded by farmers and then by Soviet officials.[29] His aircraft had not been destroyed by the crash, and the Soviets were able to identify much of its equipment when they put it on display 10 days later. Even if Powers had been able to activate the destruction device, however, it would not have destroyed the aircraft. The small explosive charge was only designed to wreck the camera.

How had the Soviets succeeded in downing the U-2? Although some CIA project officials initially wondered if Powers had been flying too low through an error or mechanical malfunction, he maintained that he had been flying at his assigned altitude and had been brought down by a near miss of a Soviet surface-to-air missile. This turned out to be the case, for in March 1963, the US air attache in Moscow learned that the Sverdlovsk SA-2 battery had fired a three-missile salvo that, in addition to disabling Powers' plane, also scored a direct hit on a Soviet fighter aircraft sent aloft to intercept the U-2.[30] Mission planners had not known about this SAM site before the mission because they always laid out flight plans to avoid known SAM sites.

THE AFTERMATH OF THE U-2 DOWNING

The first indication that something was wrong with Powers' mission came even before he was overdue at [location deleted]. The CIA Operations Center learned on 1 May at 0330 hours Washington time that the Soviets had discontinued radar tracking of the flight's progress two hours earlier (0529Z), southwest of Sverdlovsk. Although there was no word from the Soviet Union concerning the missing I-2, key project personnel assembled in the Agency control center that morning (with the exception of Bissell, who was out of town and did not arrive until 1530) to analyze the latest information and discuss courses of action. They quickly established a new project, known as Operation [deleted] to gather and evaluate all available information about the downed U-2.[31]

Bissell and the other project officials did not know whether Powers was dead or if the plane and camera had been destroyed, but they believed that there was no way that a pilot could survive a crash from an altitude above 70,000 feet. They, therefore, decided to stick with the standard cover story for U-2 flights that they were weather flights staged by the National Aeronautics and Space Administration (NASA)—originally the National Advisory Committee for Aeronautics, renamed in 1958. This cover story had been approved by the President in 1956.

By the end of the day, the Operation [deleted] officials had prepared a statement based on the standard cover story but modified to fit the available information on Powers' flight and to show Adana as the aircraft's base in order to conceal Pakistan's role in the mission. This revised cover story, along with a mission flight plan consistent with it, was sent to the field commander [deleted] to replace the cover story that had been prepared and distributed in advance of the mission. The first announcement of the new cover story came late on 2 May by the Adana base commander, but it did not appear in print until the following day. On Tuesday, 3 May, NASA released a statement about a high-altitude weather plane that was missing on a flight inside Turkey. The statement had been designed to provide an explanation for the presence of wreckage inside the Soviet Union by noting that "the pilot reported over the emergency frequency that he was experiencing oxygen difficulties."[32] Thus, if the Soviets protested and pointed to wreckage inside their borders, NASA could claim that the pilot had lost consciousness and the aircraft had then flown into the Soviet Union before crashing.

This statement had been prepared for a "best case" scenario, that is to say, one in which neither the pilot nor the plane and film survived. However, pilots had bailed out from extremely high altitudes and survived, and there was even evidence from previous U-2 crashes that much of the aircraft itself could be salvaged. The small destructive charge aboard the U-2 was not sufficient to destroy much more than the camera. The tightly rolled film, which could reveal the exact purpose of the mission even if the pilot and aircraft did not survive, was very hard to destroy. Kelly Johnson later conducted an experiment that revealed film taken out of a completely burned-out aircraft could still provide usable imagery.[33] After almost four years of successful U-2 missions, Richard Bissell and the rest of the Development Projects Division had become overconfident and were not prepared for the "worst case" scenario that actually occurred in May 1960. This failure played directly into the hands of Soviet Premier Nikita Khrushchev, who shrewdly decided to release information about the downed U-2 a little at a time, thereby encouraging the United States to stick with its vulnerable cover story too long. As he later wrote, "Our intention here was to confuse the government circles of the United States. As long as the Americans thought the pilot was dead, they would keep putting out the story that perhaps the plane had accidentally strayed off course and been shot down in the mountains on the Soviet side of the border."[34] The first word from the Soviet Union came on Thursday, 5 May, when Premier Khrushchev announced to a meeting of the Supreme Soviet that a US "spyplane" had been downed near Sverdlovsk. He made no mention of the fate of its pilot.

Khrushchev's announcement aroused considerable interest in the media in the United States, and that same day the State Department and NASA issued another statement that continued the "weather plane" cover story, adding that the pilot became lost during a routine mission near the Caucasus Mountains. Soon afterward, the US Ambassador to Moscow cabled a report to the State Department indicating that the pilot might be alive after all. Two days later, on 7 May 1960, Khrushchev confirmed this report by revealing that the U-2 pilot was alive and had admitted his mission of spying on the Soviet Union.

This revelation completely demolished the US cover story, and senior administration officials then debated what the appropriate course of action should be. Allen Dulles offered to take responsibility for the overflight and resign, but President Eisenhower did not want to give the world the impression that he was not in control of his administration. On Wednesday, 11 May, the President read a statement to the press in which he assumed full responsibility for the U-2 mission but left open the question of future overflights, even though four days earlier he had approved the recommendation of his key foreign policy advisers to terminate all provocative intelligence operations against the Soviet Union.[35]

The U-2 affair had its greatest consequences when the long-awaited summit meeting in Paris began less than a week later on 16 May. Soviet Premier Khrushchev insisted on being the first speaker and read a long protest about the overflight, ending with a demand for an apology from President Eisenhower. In his reply Eisenhower stated that overflights had been suspended and would not be resumed, but he refused to make a formal apology. At that point the summit ended, as did all hopes for a visit to the Soviet Union by President Eisenhower.

THE WITHDRAWAL OF THE OVERSEAS DETACHMENTS

The loss of Powers' U-2 ultimately resulted in the end of Detachment B in Turkey. As soon as the Development Projects Division learned that Powers was alive in Soviet hands, it immediately evacuated the [location deleted] to protect the secret of their involvement in the project. Project officials hoped that flights might eventually resume from Adana, but President Eisenhower's order ending overflights of the Soviet Union made this very unlikely. Less than four weeks later, a coup ousted the government of Turkish Premier Adnan Menderes on the night of 27 May 1960. Because the new government had not been briefed on the U-2, Project Headquarters refused to allow any U-2 flights from Adana, even those necessary for maintaining the aircraft's airworthiness. As a result, no more U-2s flew out of Adana. Instead of being ferried home, three of the four remaining U-2s were disassembled and loaded aboard C-124 cargo planes for the return trip to the United States.[36]

The fourth U-2 remained inside a hangar at Incirlik airbase for several years, looked after by a skeleton crew, in case the Adana installation needed to be reactivated. Finally the decision was made to close down the Adana U-2 facility. During Detachrnent B's 44 months of active existence, 21 pilots had flown its aircraft, including [deleted] and three pilots transferred from the deactivated Detactment A. Fourteen Detachment B pilots were later assigned to other U-2 detachments, but the closing down of Detachment B marked the [approximately four lines deleted].

The loss of Powers' U-2, the resultant failure of the Paris Summit, and the end of U-2 operations in Turkey were just the first in a series of setbacks for the U-2 program. On 8 July 1960, the Japanese Government, faced with growing anti-American sentiment and complaints in the press about the presence of "spyplanes" on Japanese territory, asked the United States to remove the U-2s. The very next day the CIA closed Detachment C; its U-2s were dismantled and returned to the United States aboard C-124s.[37]

In the midst of the furor in Japan, on 1 July 1960,

just six weeks after the Paris Summit, Soviet fighter aircraft shot down an Air Force RB-47 on an electronic intelligence collection mission over international waters near the Soviet Union's Kola Peninsula. Two survivors were captured. The Soviet Union claimed that the aircraft had violated its airspace, while the United Slates denounced the Soviets for downing the plane over international waters. The acrimony exacerbated an already tense international atmosphere.[38]

One additional blow to the U-7 program came in the summer of 1960. NASA, concerned about the damage to its reputation from its involvement in the U-2 affair and hoping to obtain international cooperation for its space program, decided to end its support of the cover story that U-2s were conducting weather research under its auspices.[39]

These developments resulted in a complete halt to all U-2 operations from overseas bases for more than six months. Pilots and aircraft from Detachments B and C were consolidated into Detachment G at Edwards Air Force Base California, [deleted]. Detachment G now comprised eight pilots from Detachment B and three pilots from Detachment C. Because Powers' capture had compromised Project CHALICE, the Agency assigned a new cryptonym to the U-2 effort, henceforth it was called Project IDEALIST.[40]

THE FATE OF FRANCIS GARY POWERS

Downed U-2 pilot Francis Gary Powers underwent extensive interrogation at the hands of the Soviets. His instructions from the CIA on what to do in the event of capture were meager, and he had been told that he might as well tell the Soviets whatever they wanted to know because they could get the information from his aircraft anyway. Nevertheless, Powers tried to conceal as much classified information as possible while giving the appearance of cooperating with his captors. To extract the maximum propaganda value from the U-2 Affair, the Soviets prepared an elaborate show trial for Powers, which began on 17 August 1960. Powers continued to conceal as much information as possible, but, on the advice of his Soviet defense counsel, he stated that he was sorry for his actions. The Soviet court sentenced him to 10 years' "deprivation of liberty," with the first three to be spent in prison.[41]

During the next 18 months, confidential negotiations to obtain the release of Powers took place as the United States explored the possibility of trading convicted Soviet master spy Rudolf Abel for Powers. These negotiations were conducted by Abel's court-appointed defense counsel, former OSS lawyer James Donovan, in correspondence with Abel's "wife" (probably his Soviet control) in East Germany. In November 1961, Acting DCI Pearre Cabell wrote to Secretary of State Dean Rusk supporting such a trade, and on 10 February 1962 the actual exchange took place in the middle of the Glienecke Bridge connecting East and West Berlin. As part of the deal, American graduate student Frederick Pryor, who had been jailed in East Germany for espionage, was released at another location.

After Powers returned to the United States, he underwent extensive debriefing, for many questions about his mission remained unanswered. To conduct the debriefing, the Agency immediately reconvened the Damage Assessment Team that had met for two months in the summer of 1960 to estimate what Powers knew about the overflight program and could have told Soviet interrogators. Given Powers' long involvement with the U-2 program, the team had concluded in 1960 that his knowledge was extensive and he had probably revealed most of it to the Soviets. After two weeks of debriefing Powers in February 1962, however, the team found that the damage was much less than had been estimated, and they were quite satisfied with Powers' behavior.[42] After reading the debriefing reports, Allen Dulles expressed support of Powers' actions and told Powers, "We are proud of what you have done," but Dulles had already resigned as DCI in November 1961.[43] The new DCI, John A. McCone, demanded a closer look at Powers' actions and set up a Board of Inquiry headed by retired Federal Judge E. Barrett Prettyman. After eight days of hearings and deliberation, the board reported on 27 February that Powers had acted in accordance with his instructions and had "complied with his obligations as an American citizen during this period." The board, therefore, recommended that he receive his back pay.

The Prettyman Board's finding was based on a large body of evidence indicating that Powers was telling the truth about the events of 1 May 1960. The testimony of the experts who had debriefed Powers after his return; a thorough investigation of Powers' background with testimony by doctors, psychiatrists, former Air Force colleagues, and his commander at Adana, Powers' own testimony before the board, the results of a polygraph examination that he had volunteered to undergo, and the evidence provided by photographs of the wreckage of his aircraft, which Kelly Johnson had analyzed and found consistent with Powers' story. Nevertheless, DCI McCone remained skeptical. He asked the Air Force to convene its own panel of experts to check Johnson's assessment of the photographs of the U-2. The Air Force quickly complied, and the panel supported Johnson's findings. McCone then seized upon the one piece of evidence that contradicted Powers' testimony—a report by the National Security Agency (NSA) that suggested that Powers may have descended to a lower altitude and turned back in a broad curve toward Sverdlovsk before being downed and ordered the Prettyman Board to reconvene on 1 March for another look at this evidence. The board remained unconvinced by NSA's thin evidence and stuck to its original findings. A few days later, on 6 March 1962, Powers appeared before the Senate Armed Services Committee, which commended his actions. The Senate Foreign Relations Committee also held brief hearings on the U-2 Affair, with DCI McCone representing the CIA.[44]

Although all of these inquiries found Powers to have acted properly, they did not release many of their favorable findings to the public, which had received a very negative image of Powers' behavior from sensational press reports and statements by public figures who were not aware of (or chose to ignore) the truth about Powers' actions while in captivity. One member of the Senate Foreign Relations Committee, Senator John J. Williams, expressed concern about the impact of this silence on Powers' reputation in a question to DCI McCone on 6 March 1962. "Don't you think he is being left with just a little bit of a cloud hanging over him? If he did everything he is supposed to do, why leave it hanging?"[45] Doubts about Powers did remain in the public mind because he received no public recognition for his efforts to withhold information from the Soviets. He was also snubbed by President Kennedy, who one year earlier had warmly welcomed two Air Force RB-47 fliers released by the Soviet Union. McCone remained hostile to Powers, and in April 1963 he awarded the Intelligence Star to all of the U-2 pilots except Powers. Finally on 25 April 1965, just two days before McCone's resignation became effective, Powers received the Star (which was dated 1963 on the back) from DDCI Marshall S. Carter.[46]

Powers' return from captivity raised the question of what his future employment should be. This issue had already been discussed one year earlier by John N. McMahon, executive of officer of the DPID, who noted that he and Col. Leo P. Geary (the Air Force project officer) were concerned about a major dilemma for the CLI and the US Government [approximately one-third page deleted].

Despite this negative recommendation, the Air Force agreed on 4 April 1962 to reinstate Powers effective 1 July, a decision that was approved by the Agency, State Department, and White House. Then Powers' divorce proceedings began, and the Air Force, concerned about adverse publicity, postponed reinstatement until the end of the proceedings. In the meantime Powers began working for Lockheed as a U-2 pilot. In March 1963, he met with Colonel Geary to discuss his future plans and decided to stay with Lockheed.[48] Powers remained at Lockheed until U-2 testing ceased in September 1969. Earlier in the year, he had published an account of his experiences on the U-2 project under the title *Operation Overflight.* Later he flew a light plane as a traffic reporter for a Los Angeles radio station and then a helicopter for a television station. On 1 August 1977, he and a cameraman from the station died when his helicopter crashed on the way to an assignment.[49]

CHANGES IN OVERFLIGHT PROCEDURES AFTER MAY 1960

One of the most important changes in the overflight program after the loss of Francis Gary Powers' U-2 was the institution of more formal procedures for the approval of U-2 missions. During the first four years of U-2 activity, very few members of the Eisenhower administration had been involved in making decisions concerning the overflight program. The President personally authorized all flights over the Soviet Union and was consulted by Richard Bissell and either the DCI or the DDCI about each such proposed mission. In addition to CIA officials, the President's discussions of individual U-2 missions or of the program as a whole generally included the Secretary of State or his Under Secretary, the Chairman of the Joint Chiefs of Staff, the Secretary of Defense or his deputy, and the President's secretary, Colonel (later General) Goodpaster.

The approval process under President Eisenhower was thus very unstructured. There was no formal approval body charged with reviewing overflight proposals; the President kept this authority in his hands and simply consulted with selected cabinet officials and advisers before reaching a decision [deleted].

The loss of Powers' U-2 in May 1960 led to major changes in the approval process [deleted] the approval process became more formal as the National Security Council became involved. Henceforth, proposed missions had to be submitted to the National Security Council (NSC) Special Group for approval. In the early 1960s, the Special Group consisted of the DCI, the Deputy Secretary of Defense, the Under Secretary of State, and the Military Adviser to the President. After the Military Adviser, Gen. Maxwell Taylor, became Chairman of the Joint Chiefs of Staff in 1962, his place on the Special Group was taken by McGeorge Bundy, the President's Special Assistant for National Security Affairs.50

Before requesting permission from the Special Group for a U-2 mission over denied territory, the CIA prepared a detailed submission giving justification for the proposed mission and maps showing the targets to be photographed, flight times, and emergency landing sites. Such submissions came to be known as "black books" because they were placed in black, looseleaf binders. The decision of the Special Group was generally final, although on occasion controversial issues were presented to the President for his decision.

This approval process did not come into play immediately after May 1960 because there was a long pause in U-2 operations as the detachments returned from overseas. It was not until late October 1960 that the next U-2 operation occurred, this time over Cuba. By this time the full approval procedure had been established, and the Special Group approved the mission (see chapter 5).

The approval process was not the only part of the U-2 program that changed after May 1960. The process for establishing requirements for overhead reconnaissance missions also became more formal. In August 1960 the US Intelligence Board took over the Ad Hoc Requirements Committee and merged it with the Satellite Intelligence Requirements Committee to form the Committee on Overhead Reconnaissance DCI Directive 2/7 tasked COMOR with the "coordinated development of foreign intelligence requirements for overhead-reconnaissance projects over denied areas." The DCID defined "overhead reconnaissance" to include "all reconnaissance for foreign-intelligence purposes by satellite, or by any vehicle over denied areas, whether by photographic, ELINT, COMINT, infrared RADINT, or other means." The only exception to COMOR's area of responsibility was "reconnaissance and aerial surveillance in direct support of actively combatant forces."[51]

By this time the Air Force had developed a large overhead reconnaissance program of its own, including a fleet of U-2s, and. occasionally, there were conflicts between the areas of responsibility of COMOR and the military services for collection requirements. The Air Force had already won a major victory in 1958, when it claimed that the White House had given responsibility for peripheral reconnaissance of the Soviet Union to the military. DCI Dulles, who was always reluctant to become involved in matters that seemed to lie in the military's area of responsibility, did not resist this claim, and the Ad Hoc Requirements Committee stopped preparing requirements for peripheral flights. This ended a major requirements committee study, which sought to estimate what could be gained from U-2 oblique photography along the entire border of the Soviet Union.[32] The last CIA U-2 mission along the Soviet Union's coasts occurred on 22 June 1958; thereafter, the only peripheral missions conducted by the CIA were those along the Soviet Union's [end of paragraph deleted].

Until the spring of 1961, there was virtually no coordination of military reconnaissance activities, even within the individual services. Each commander of a Theater or a Unified and Specified Command conducted his own independent reconnaissance activities. To meet the growing need for overall coordination of these activities at the national level, the Joint Chiefs of Staff (JCS) established the Joint Reconnaissance Center (JRC) under the J-3 (Operations) of the Joint

Staff The JRC immediately began to coordinate and obtain approval for approximately 500 missions per month, assigning each a risk factor of Critical, Sensitive, Unique, or Routine. The JRC then prepared a monthly Activities Book giving details of the proposed missions and briefed the Joint Chiefs of Staff on the more risky missions. The CIA received a copy of the Activities Book.

Most military reconnaissance missions were approved or disapproved at the JCS level, but the most sensitive missions were submitted through the Secretary of Defense to the Special Group for approval. In addition to this Department of Defense approval path, the military services could also submit requirements through the DCI using their representatives on COMOR. As a result, the military services had two channels for submitting reconnaissance missions to the Special Group. The Agency had only one—COMOR.[53]

The main conflicts between the requirements committee and the military services arose over missions in the Far East. In the early 1960s, North Vietnam had not been designated a denied area by the US Intelligence Board (USIB), so the military services could plan missions there without consulting COMOR. Such missions, however, came very close to China, which was a denied area and, therefore, came under COMOR's area of responsibility. Once the war in Southeast Asia escalated in 1964, the military services received responsibility for the entire area (see chapter 5).

To reduce the number of disputes between the competing CIA and Air Force reconnaissance programs and to manage the growing satellite program, the two agencies worked out an agreement to provide overall coordination for reconnaissance activities at the national level. The first such interagency agreement came in the fall of 1961, and it was followed by three additional agreements during the next four years.[54]

Interest in coordinating the reconnaissance efforts of the military services and the CIA also affected the field of photographic interpretation. In the wake of the loss of Francis Gary Powers' U-2 on 1 May 1960, the President's Board of Consultants on Foreign Intelligence Activities (PFIAB) had urged the establishment of an interagency group to study ways to improve the entire US intelligence community. Formed on 6 May 1960, the Joint Study Group on Foreign Intelligence Activities met for the next seven months under the leadership of Lyman Kirkpatrick, CIA Inspector General One of the study group's key recommendations in the report it issued in December 1960 was the creation of a national photointerpretation center that would bring together photointerpreters from the Agency and the military services. The report further recommended that the CIA be placed in charge of the new center. Ignoring Air Force claims that it should head such a center, President Eisenhower approved the report's recommendation, and, on 18 January 1961, National Security Council Intelligence Directive (NSCID) No. 8 established the National Photographic Interpretation Center (NPIC). Henceforth, the director of NPIC would be designated by the DCI and approved by the Secretary of Defense, and the deputy director would come from one of the military services. The first director of NPIC was Arthur S. Lundahl, head of the CIA's Photo-Intelligence Division.[55]

One additional major change in the U-2 program in

the years immediately following the May Day incident—although not directly related to the loss of Powers' U-2—was the departure of Richard Bissell from the CIA and the subsequent reorganization of the Agency's reconnaissance and scientific activities. The roots of Bissell's downfall went back to 1 January 1959, when he became Deputy Director for Plans and decided to place all Agency air assets in the DDP in order to maintain control of his overhead reconnaissance projects (the U-2 and its two proposed successors, the OXCART aircraft and the reconnaissance satellite). The previously independent Development Projects Staff became the Development Projects Division (DPD) of the DDP and now controlled all Agency air operations, including air support for covert operations. As a result, U-2's were occasionally employed for gathering intelligence to support DDP operations in addition to their primary mission of gathering strategic and tactical intelligence.

Although the reorganization made sense in terms of increasing the efficiency of Agency air operations, the use of the U-2 to support covert action disturbed Bissell's backers among the scientists advising Presidents Eisenhower and Kennedy, especially James Killian and Edwin Land. They were concerned that Bissell was becoming too involved in covert action and was not able to devote sufficient time to the overhead reconnaissance program. Then came the disastrous Bay of Pigs invasion in April 1961, which discredited Bissell with the Kennedy administration in general and the two scientists in particular. Later that year, Bissell lost another important source of support when Allen Dulles resigned as DCI in November 1961. During his final months as the Deputy Director for Plans, Bissell found himself involved in a major struggle with Killian and Land, who were serving on President Kennedy's Foreign Intelligence Advisory Board (successor to the Eisenhower administration's President's Board of Consultants on Foreign Intelligence Activities). These two influential Presidential advisers strongly advocated removing the Agency's overhead reconnaissance programs from the DDP and placing them in a new, science-oriented directorate, but Bissell resisted this proposal. With his position in the Agency becoming increasingly untenable, Bissell resigned on 17 February 1962, after turning down an offer from the new DCI, John A. McCone, to become the CIA's first Deputy Director for Research.[56]

Two days after Bissell's departure, the new Directorate came into existence, and it absorbed all of the Development Projects Division's special reconnaissance projects. Only conventional air support for the Clandestine Services remained with the DDP in the new Special Operations Division. The U-2 program was no longer connected with covert operations.

The first half of 1962 was a confusing period for the Development Projects Division. After losing the individual who had created and supervised it for seven years, the DPD also lost its feeling of autonomy when it was transferred from its own building to the new CIA Headquarters at Langley. Soon afterward, Col. Stanley W Beerli, who had headed the DPD since 1960, returned to the Air Force. Then on 30 July 1962, the overhead reconnaissance projects underwent a major reorganization with the formation of the new Office of Special Activities (OSA) to replace the DPD. The original organization of OSA with 10 division or staff heads reporting directly to the director of the office (at that time known as the Assistant

Director for Special Activities) proved too cumbersome, and, on 30 September 1962, a reorganization divided most of these offices between two major subordinates, the Deputy for Technology and the Deputy for Field Activities (see chart, page 193) .The Office of Special Activities (OSA) continued to control reconnaissance activities and related research and development after the Directorate of Research was enlarged and renamed the Deputy Directorate for Science and Technology (DDS&T) on 5 August 1963 (along with the other Directorates, DDS&T dropped the "Deputy" from its title in 1965 and became known as the Directorate of Science and Technology). In 1965 the head of OSA received a new title, Director of Special Activities. The Office of Special Activities remained in control of the CIA's overhead reconnaissance activities until 1974, when the Agency ended its involvement with manned reconnaissance aircraft.[57]

[1]For an overview of the controversy, see Roy E. Licklider, "The Missile Gap Controversy," *Political Science Quarterly* 85 (1970):600–615.
[2]Lawrence Freedman, *US Intelligence and the Soviet Strategic Threat*, 2nd ed. (Princeton: Princeton University Press, 1986), pp. 69–70.
[3]Ford Eastman, "Defense Officials Concede Missile Lag," *Aviation Week*, 9 February 1969, pp. 26–27.
[4]Freedman, *US Intelligence*, p. 70.
[5]"What About the Missile Gap?" *Time*, 9 February 1959, pp. 11–13.
[6]Andrew J. Goodpaster, Memorandum for the Record, 12 February 1959, WHOSS Alpha. DDEL (TS); Ambrose. *Eisenhower: The President*, pp. 513–514: Beschloss. *Mayday*, p. 173.
[7]Quoted in Ambrose, *Eisenhower: The President*, pp. 514–515; Beschloss, *Mayday*, p. 176.
[8]Mission folders 4120 (9 June 1959) and 4121 (18 June 1959), OSA records, [footnote material deleted] (TS Codeword).
[9]Andrew J. Goodpaster, Memorandum for the Record, 7 July 1959 (TS) idem, Memorandum of Conference with the President, 8 July 1959, WHOSS, Alpha DDEL (TS).
[10]Mission folder 4125 (9 July 1959), OSA records (TS Codeword).
[11]*OSA History,* chap. 19, annex 120, pp. 12–14 (TS Codeword).
[12]William E. Burrows, *Deep Black Space Espionage and National*

Security (New York: Random House, 1987), p. 101.
[13][footnote deleted]
[14]Licklider, "Missile Gap Controversy," pp. 608–609.
[15]Ambrose *Eisenhower: The President,* p. 568; Beschloss, *Mayday*, p. 233.
[16]Mission folder 8009 (5 February 1960), OSA records, [footnote material deleted] (TS Codeword: *OSA Chronology*, p. 25 (TS Codeword).
[17]*OSA Chronology*, p. 25 (TS Codeword); [footnote material deleted] 'The President's Board: 1956–60,' *Studies in Intelligence* 13 (Summer 1969): 118 (S).
[18]Mission folder 4155, 9 April 1960, OSA records, [footnote material deleted] (TS Codeword).
[19]Nikita S. Khrushchev, *Khrushchev Remembers: The Last Testament* (Boston: Little, Brown, & Co., 1974), pp. 443–444.
[20]Memorandum for Richard M. Bissell, Deputy Director (Plans), from Col. William Burke, Acting Chief, DPD, "Evaluation of Proposed CHALICE Operations," 4 March 1960, IC Staff, COMIREX records, [footnote material deleted] "CHALICE (General)" (TS Codeword).
[21]Memorandum for Richard M. Bissell, Deputy Director (Plans), from Colonel Burke, Acting Chief DPD, "Operational Priority of Proposed CHALICE Missions" 26 April 1960 IC Staff. COMIREX records [partial footnote deleted] CHALICE (General)" (TS Codeword).
[22]George B. Kistiakowsky, *A Scientist at the White House* (Cambridge: Harvard University Press, 1976), p. 328.
[23]*OSA History*, chap. 12, pp. 35–36 (TS Codeword).
[24]Ambrose, *Eisenhower: The President*, p. 569; Beschloss, *Mayday*, p. 10.
[25]Memorandum for Richard M. Bissell, Deputy Director (Plans), from [deleted] Acting Chief, DPD, "Evaluation of Proposed CHALICE Operations," 14 March 1960, TC Staff, COMIREX records [deleted] "CHALICE (General)" (TS Codeword).
[26]Mission folder 4154 (1 May 1960), OSA records (TS Codeword).
[27]Powers, *Operaiton Overflight*, p. 76.
[28][deleted] Message Received—Unfortunately, *Studies in Intelligence* 27 (Winter 1983): 29 (S).
[29]Powers *Operation Overflight* pp. 82–84; Beschloss, *Mayday*, pp. 26–28; Transcript of Debriefing Tapes of Francis Gary Powers, 13 February 1962, Board of Inquiry on the Conduct of Francis Gary Powers, Operations [deleted] files OSA records, [deleted] (S).
[30]Cunningham interview, 4 October 1983 (TS Codeword); *OSA History*, chap. 14 p. 55 (TS Codeword).
[31]Geary interview (S).
[32]Beschloss, *Mayday*, p. 39.
[33]Geary interview.
[34]Khrushchev, *Khrushchev Remembers: The Last Testament*, p. 507.
[35]*OSA History*, chap. 14, pp. 14–16 (TS Codeword); Beschloss, *Mayday*, pp. 43–66, 243–258.
[36]*OSA* History, chap. 12, pp. 46–47 (TS Codeword).

[37]*OSA Chronology*, p. 28 (TS Codeword).
[38]Mystery of the RB-47, '*Newsweek*, 25 July 1960 pp. 36–37; "Nikita and the RB-47," *Time*, 25 July 1960, pp. 30–31.
[39]At a meeting of high-level CIA NASA, and State Department officials on 31 May 1960 NASA was willing to continue its association with U-2 flights for the time being but the Administrator of NASA, Dr. Keith Glennan, believed that his agency "would be well advised to disengage from the U-2 program as rapidly as possible." James A. Cunningham, Memorandum for the Record "Telephone Conversation with Dr. Hugh Dryden, Deputy Director, NASA," 1 June 1960, DPD chrono [deleted] 60 OSA records (S).
[40]*OSA History*, chap. 12, pp. 47–49; chap. 16, p. 10 (TS Codeword).
[41]Powers, *Operation Overflight*, pp. 160–192; Beschloss, *Mayday*, pp. 331–335.
[42][deleted] Francis Gary Powers—The Unmaking of a Hero, 1960–1965," (draft), CIA History Staff, 1974, p. 19 (S).
[43]Powers, *Operation Overflight*, p. 307.
[44]Beschloss, *Mayday*, p. 352–354; Thomas Powers, *Man Who Kept the Secrets*, p. 328; Prettyman Board, DCI records (S).
[45]United States Congress, Senate, Foreign Relations Committee, *Executive Sessions of the Senate Foreign Relations Committee (Historical Series)*, vol. 12, 86th Congress, Second Session, "report on the U-2 Incident," 6 March 1962, p. 265 (declassified 1982).
[46]*OSA History*, chap. 14, p. 54 (TS Codeword); Beschloss, *Mayday*, p. 397.
[47]John N. McMahon to Chief, Cover Staff, DPD, 21 Mach 1961, Operation [footnote partially deleted] files, OSA records, [deleted] (S).
[48]*OSA History*, chap. 14, p. 52 (TS Codeword).
[49]Beschloss, *Mayday*, pp. 396–401. Beschloss claims that Powers was fired by Lockheed for criticizing the Agency in his memoirs (which he had shown to the Agency in draft form), but Kelly Johnson's "U-2R Log" records on 25 September 1969: "We have no flight test activity at all. I must let Gary Powers go. Have protected him for about seven years, but he doesn't have an ATR (Air Transport Rating), so we have no other job for him—not even flying the Beechcraft."
[50]The Special Group, which had been created by NSC Intelligence Document 5412/2 in 1955 to oversee covert activities, was originally known as the 5412 Committee. Later the Special Group became known as the 303 Committee and then the 40 Committee United States Congress, Senate, Select Committee to Study Governmental Operations with Respect to Intelligence Activities, *Foreign and Military Intelligence*, book I, (Washington, DC: US Government Printing Office, 1976), pp. 48–53.
[51]DCID 2/7, effective 9 August 1960 (S).
[52]Memorandum for DCI McCone from James Q. Reber, Chairman, COMOR, Proposed Procedures for Approval of Critical Reconnaissance," 1 March 1962. COMIREX records (TS Codeword).
[53]Ibid (TS Codeword).

[54]Problems of declassification prevent a more detailed discussion of this aspect of the reconnaissance program, which will be covered in a future history of satellite reconnaissance at a higher level of classification.
[55]Lundahl and Brugioni interview (TS Codeword).
[56]Killian interview (S); Land interview (TS Codeword), Richard M. Bissell to John A. McCone, 7 February 1962, DCI records [footnote partially deleted].
[57]*OSA Chronology*, pp. 34–35 (TS Codeword).

5

U-2 Operations After May 1960

The loss of Francis Gary Powers' U-2 over the Soviet Union on 1 May 1960 marked the end of the aircraft's use over the Soviet Bloc. Soon after the May Day incident, President Eisenhower ordered an end to overflights. Similarly, his successor, John F. Kennedy, told a 25 January 1961 press conference, "I have ordered that the flights not be resumed, which is a continuation of the order given by President Eisenhower in May of last year." This was not a binding pledge, as John A. McCone (who became DCI in November 1961) pointed out to President Kennedy's successor, Lyndon B. Johnson, on 15 January 1964 in response to the new President's request for information on U-2 overflight policies.

> *Contrary to popular assumption, President Kennedy did not make any pledge or give an assurance, at least publicly, that there would be no further overflights. He limited his response to a statement that he had ordered that the flights not be resumed. An order, obviously, is valid only until countermanded.*[1]

Technically, McCone was correct, but no President was likely to order a resumption of overflights of the Soviet Union without very good reason, and such a situation never developed, in part because satellite photography gradually began to fill the gap left by the end of U-2 coverage.

Although there were several proposals to resume overflights of the Soviet Union in the years that followed, none reached the mission planning stage. The Kennedy administration came closest to resuming overflights of the Soviet Union during the Berlin Crisis in the summer and fall of 1961. On 14 September 1961, Kelly Johnson noted in his project log:

> *Have had request from Mr. Bissell to propose ways and means for increasing safety of the U-2 on probable overflights. It seems that President Kennedy, who publicly stated that no U-2's would ever be over Russia while he was president, has requested additional flights. Some poetic justice in this.*[2]

One week later Colonel Geary called to order Lockheed to upgrade six older U-2s into U-2Cs with the more powerful engines on a priority basis, even if it meant taking people off the work on the successor aircraft in order to speed up the conversions.

Shortly thereafter, the resumption of overflights became a major topic of discussion within the intelligence community. On 25 September 1961, the Committee on Overhead Reconnaissance prepared a detailed "Justification for U-2 Photography over the USSR," which argued in favor of U-2 missions over selected, high-priority targets such as ICBM complexes. The COMOR paper stated that satellite photography did not provide sufficient detail to answer many critical questions about the Soviet ICBM program. To back up this contention, the report placed U-2 and satellite photography of the same Soviet targets side by side, clearly demonstrating the far superior resolution of the U-2's cameras. Not all members of COMOR supported the resumption of overflights, however. When COMOR formally recommended this course of action to the USIB on 1 October 1961, the State Department and CIA members dissented, having found "insufficient justification for resuming U-2 overflights of the USSR at this time."[3]

Nothing came of the proposal to resume overflights in the fall of 1961, as both the USIB and the Special Group came out against it, but, as long as U-2 photography remained clearly superior to satellite photography, the thought of obtaining U-2 coverage of the Soviet Union remained tempting. In February 1962, the USIB seriously considered a COMOR proposal to send a U-2 over Kamchatka to photograph Soviet antiballistic-missile facilities but finally decided to wait for the results of an Air Force peripheral mission. The board later accepted DCI McCone's recommendation to seek satellite rather than U-2 coverage of the area.[4]

With both the CIA and the State Department strongly opposed to sending the highly vulnerable U-2 over the Soviet Union, prospects for resuming flights remained slight unless the international situation worsened to such a degree that overflights would be worth the risks involved. Since this never happened, Francis Gary Powers' flight on 1 May 1960 proved to be the last CIA overflight of the Soviet Bloc. Yet, the U-2 remained useful, for it could operate successfully in other areas with less developed radar and air defense systems. After May 1960, the main focus of U-2 activity shifted to two new areas Latin America, where U-2s would play an extremely important role during the early 1960s, and the Far East, where CIA U-2s were active from 1958 until 1974, when the Agency's involvement in manned reconnaissance finally ended.

U-2 OPERATIONS IN LATIN AMERICA

U-2 Support to the Bay of Pigs Invasion

During late summer 1960, the Directorate of Plans was planning a counterrevolutionary invasion of Cuba for the following year. To support this effort, the Agency asked the National Security Council's Special Group to approve U-2 overflights of Cuba. Known as Operation KICK OFF, these flights were designed to obtain intelligence on Cuban air and ground order of battle and to provide geographic data far choosing an invasion site.

To allay fears that mechanical problems could lead to the loss of a U-2 over Cuba, the submission to the Special Group for overflights emphasized that, if a U-2 had a flameout anywhere over Cuba, it could still glide back and make a safe landing in Florida. The Special Group approved Operation KICK OFF but stipulated that only two overflights could be made. Detachment G staged the Cuban missions from Laughlin AFB near Del Rio, Texas, a base used by SAC U-2 aircraft. Agency photointerpreters went to Del Rio to read out the photography after these missions. The two flights, on 26 and 27 October 1960, were very long missions, covering 3,500 miles and lasting over nine hours. Because of cloud cover over Cuba, the results of both missions were poor. The Agency, therefore, asked the Special Group to approve additional missions. After receiving authorization, Detachment G conducted three missions (Operation GREEN EYES) on 27 November and 5 and 11 December 1960 with good results.

Overflights of Cuba continued under the new administration of President Kennedy. Under the codename Operation LONG GREEN, two overflights on 19 and 21 March 1961 photographed Cuba extensively to aid the final preparations for the invasion. Two weeks later Detachment G again deployed from Edwards ABB, California, to Laughlin AFB, Texas. Beginning on 6 April, Detachment G U-2s made 15 flights over Cuba to provide photographic coverage of the ill-fated Bay of Pigs invasion and its aftermath. These flights were known as Operation FLIP TOP[5].

Aerial Refueling Capability for the U-2

Long missions conducted over Cuba in late 1960 and over Southeast Asia in early 1961 pointed out the need to increase the range of the U-2. In May 1961, Lockheed began modifying Agency U-2s so that they could be refueled in flight to extend their operating range. The six Agency aircraft that were modified to achieve this capability received the designation U-2F. All Agency U-2 pilots then underwent training in the techniques of in-flight refueling.

Refueling a U-2 in flight was a very delicate task. When fully loaded with fuel, KC-135 tankers found it difficult to reduce airspeed to 200 knots, the safest speed for refueling a U-2. As for the U-2s, they were in a very vulnerable position when approaching a tanker at 200 knots because their frail wings could not stand much stress. As a result, U-2 pilots had to approach the KC-135 tankers very carefully in order to avoid the vortexes from the wingtips of the tanker and the turbulence caused by the four large jet engines. During the first few years of refueling operations, two U2s crashed after their wings broke off as they crossed into the turbulent area behind the tankers; one of the pilots was killed.[6]

The in-flight refueling capability was a useful modification to the U-2, but it could not dramatically extend mission length. The main limiting factor remained pilot fatigue, which prevented missions from lasting longer than approximately 10 hours.

U-2 Coverage During the Cuban Mission Crisis

Cuba remained a high-priority target even after the Bay of Pigs invasion failed in April 1961. Soon afterward, Detachment G U-2s began flying monthly missions over Cuba in a program known as Project NIMBUS. Most of the flights were staged from Laughlin AFB, Texas, but three were flown from Edwards AFB, Californa, using in-flight refueling to extend the range of the aircraft. By the spring of 1962, having received reports of increased Soviet activity in Cuba, the CIA requested permission for additional photographic coverage of the island. The Special Group authorized increasing the number of Cuban overflights to at least two per month, beginning in May 1962. At the same time, the National Photographic Interpretation Center began publishing a *Photographic Evaluation of Information on Cuba* series.[7]

By early August 1962, CIA analysts had noted a substantial increase in Soviet arms deliveries to Cuba during the preceding weeks. The first U-2 overflight in August, mission 3086 on the 5th, flew too soon to

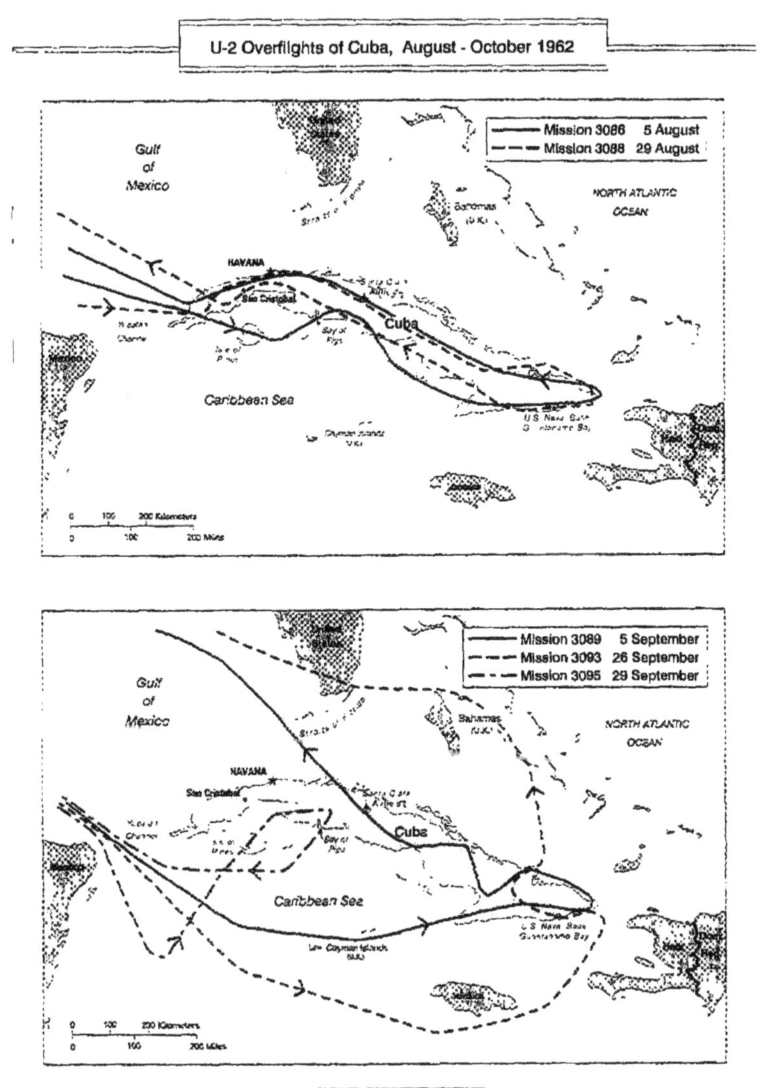
U-2 Overflights of Cuba, August - October 1962
Mission 3086 5 August
Mission 3088 29 August
Gulf of Mexico
NORTH ATLANTIC OCEAN
HAVANA
San Cristobal
Cuba
Caribbean Sea
Mission 3089 5 September
Mission 3093 26 September
Mission 3095 29 September
Secret NOFORN
724752 (R00426) 4 92

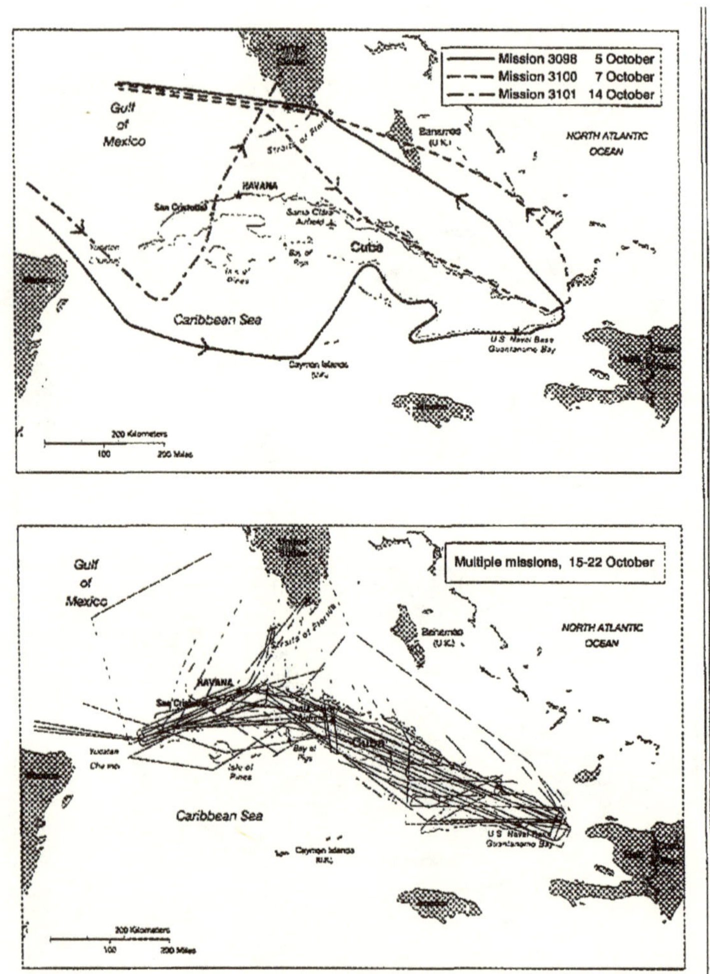

~~Secret NOFORN~~

724753 (R00426) 4 92

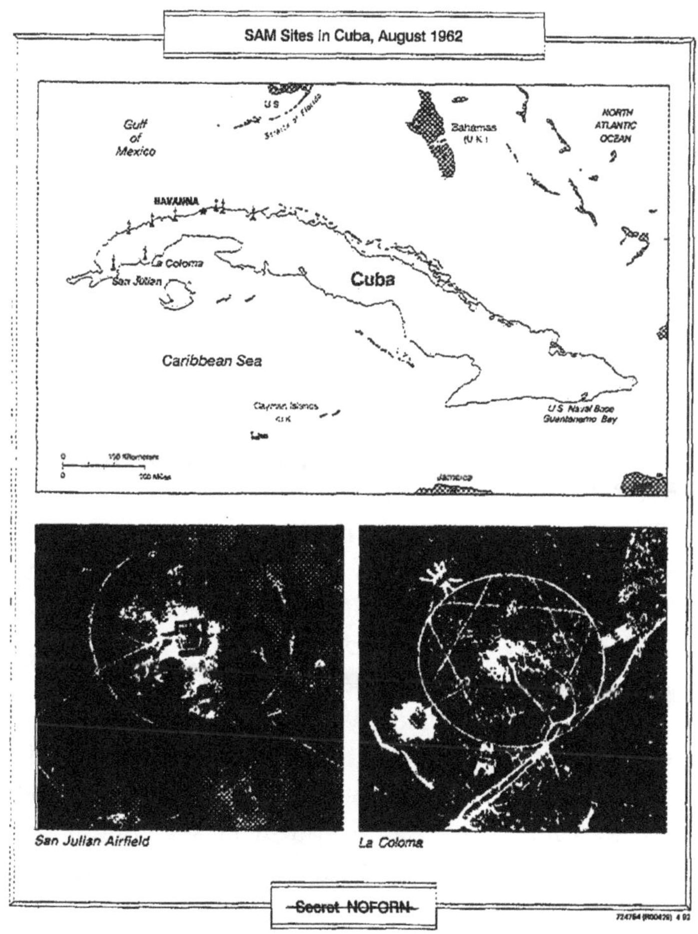

San Julian Airfield

La Coloma

detect the Soviet construction program just getting under way at various sites in Cuba. A second mission (3088) was originally set for 8 August, but bad weather forced repeated postponements until 29 August. This mission's photography provided the first hard evidence of the nature of the Soviet buildup in Cuba. Two days after the mission, the CIA reported in the *President's Intelligence Checklist* that there were at least eight surface-to-air missile (SA-2) sites in the western half of Cuba[8]. (The map on the following pages shows the routes taken by the two August overflights.)

On 5 September the next U-2 overflight (mission 3089) provided more evidence of the Soviet buildup. The mission's photography showed three more SAM sites and also revealed a MiG-21, one of the newest Soviet fighter aircraft, at the Santa Clara airfield.

The discovery of SAMs in Cuba had a twofold effect on the US reconnaissance effort over Cuba. First, it added substance to DCI McCone's fears that Cuba might become a base for Soviet medium-range ballistic missiles (he argued that SAM sites would only be set up to protect high-priority facilities such as missile bases). At this time, however, McCone's suspicions were not shared by other officials in the Agency or the administration. The second and most significant effect of the discovery of SAMs in Cuba was to make the administration far more cautious in its use of U-2s for reconnaissance of the island. As the loss of Francis Gary Powers' U-2 in May 1960 had demonstrated, the U-2 was very vulnerable to the SA-2 missile.

Within the administration, concern mounted about the U-2's vulnerability to SAMs in Cuba and the possibility that a loss could cause a major diplomatic crisis. Such fears increased as the result of two incidents in other parts of the world. On 30 August 1962, a SAC U-2 on a peripheral reconnaissance mission overflew Sakhalin Island in the Far East, prompting a Soviet protest on 4 September. The United States apologized for the intrusion. Then on 8 September, a U-2 [partial sentence deletion] (this CIA reconnaissance program is discussed later in this chapter in the section on Asian operations). Increasing concern about U-2 vulnerability led to an impromptu meeting on 10 September 1962 of Secretary of State Dean Rusk, National Security Adviser McGeorge Bundy, and DDCI Marshall S. Carter (in place of the DCI, who was on his honeymoon in France). The Secretary of State objected to the CIA's plans for two extended overflights covering the remaining areas of Cuba not covered by the last two missions. Rusk wanted peripheral flights over international waters kept separate from overflights of Cuban territory. He argued that the loss of an aircraft on a mission that combined both types of flights would make it difficult for the United States to stand on its rights to fly over international waters. Bundy and Carter therefore agreed to split the proposed reconnaissance program into four missions; two overflights and two peripheral flights, all planned for maximum safety. The overflights were thus designed to be quick "in-and-out" operations across the narrow width of the island instead of flights along the entire length of Cuba, as had been the case previously. (As the map on page 202 illustrates, the 5 September mission was the last one to fly along the length of the island.) As an additional precaution, flightpaths would be laid out to avoid known SAM sites. Although these changes greatly reduced the danger to the U-2, they slowed the gathering of information on the Soviet buildup by reducing each mission's coverage.[9]

To ensure that the photographs taken by these missions were of the highest quality, the CIA decided to conduct flights only when the weather along the flight routes was less than 25 percent overcast. Weather proved to be a major problem during the month of September. Unfavorable forecasts (along with a brief standdown of U-2 overflights after the loss [deleted] prevented the launching of any missions from 6 through 16 September. Moreover, when mission 3091 finally flew on 17 September, the favorable weather forecast proved inaccurate and heavy clouds prevented the mission from obtaining usable photography. Bad weather continued to rule out missions until 26 September, when mission 3093 covered eastern Cuba and found three additional SAM sites. Three days later mission 3095 flew over the Isle of Pines and Bay of Pigs area, finding one more SAM site and a coastal-defense cruise missile site[10].

The cautious series of U-2 flights in September had turned up many more SAM sites but no concrete evidence of the presence of surface-to-surface missiles. Growing impatient with the restrictions that had been placed on U-2 overflights of Cuba, DCI McClone told the Special Group on 4 October 1962 that their policy of avoiding SAM sites had restricted the Agency to using the U-2 only in Cuba's southeastern quadrant. He questioned "whether this was a reasonable restriction at this time, particularly since the SAM's were almost certainly not operational."[11] The Special Group then requested the preparation of an overall program for reconnaissance of Cuba in time for its next meeting on 9 October.

In the meantime, CIA U-2s continued the reconnaissance program that the Special Group had approved in

September. In early October two peripheral missions—3098 along the southeastern coast on 5 October and 3100 along the northern coast on 7 October (see maps)—discovered an additional five SAM sites. This brought the total to 19, but there was still no evidence of surface-to-surface missiles.

Evidence was mounting that the portion of Cuba that the September and early October missions had avoided was the most likely location for Soviet medium-range ballistic missiles (MRBMs). On 6 October 1962, the Committee on Overhead Reconnaissance recommended frequent and regular coverage of Cuba, pointing in particular to the need for renewed coverage of western Cuba:

> *The absence of coverage of the western end since August 29, coupled with the rate of construction we have observed, means that there may well be many more sites now being built of which we are unaware. Ground observers have in several recent instances reported sightings of what they believe to be the SS-4 (SHYSTER) MRBM in Cuba. These reports must be confirmed or denied by photo coverage[12]. Attached to this memorandum was a list of targets, with the area around San Cristobal at she top.*

On 9 October the Special Group met to discuss COMOR's recommendations, the most important of which was a U-2 flight over the "suspect MRBM site as soon as weather permits." This mission was also designed to pass over one of the SA-2 sites that was thought to be most nearly operational in order to determine the status of SA-2 defenses of Cuba. If this overflight did not provoke an SA-2 reaction, the study recommended "maximum coverage of the western end of the island by multiple U-2s simultaneously."[13] Because the danger posed by the SA-2 sites was one of the major topics at the Special Group meeting, DCI McCone brought along Col. Jack C. Ledford (USAF), head of the Office of Special Activities, who presented a vulnerability analysis that estimated the odds of losing a U-2 over Cuba at 1 in 6. The Special Group approved the recommended flight over San Cristobal.

As the Special Group meeting was breaking up, Deputy Secretary of Defense Roswell Gilpatric and the Air Force representative questioned the adequacy of the Agency's cover story, which was that its pilots were Lockheed employees on a ferry flight to Puerto Rico. The Air Force and DOD representatives argued that it would be better to use Air Force pilots and state in the event of a mishap that the overflight was a routine Air Force peripheral surveillance mission that had gone off course. McCone then asked Colonel Ledford's opinion of the proposed change Ledford agreed that the DOD cover story was better but pointed out that the SAC U-2s were much more vulnerable than those of the Agency, which had superior electronic countermeasures and a higher maximum altitude. Ledford then suggested that Air Force pilots use Agency aircraft after receiving familiarization training. After leaving the Special Group meeting, McCone and Gilpatric met with President Kennedy, who approved the San Cristobal mission and the use of Air Force pilots[14].

Two days later (11 October), Air Force and CIA representatives met to discuss the change in cover stories. Herbert Scoville, CIA Deputy Director for Research, agreed that in the long run the Air Force cover story was best but emphasized that an Air Force pilot should not be used until he had received adequate training. The conversation then turned to the issue of who would run the next mission, the CIA or the Air Force Strongly favoring Air Force control of the U-2 missions over Cuba, the DOD representatives called DCI McCone and obtained his consent. Shortly thereafter, McCone left Washington for California and did not return until 14 October. Air Force control of the Cuban overflights became official on 12 October, when President Kennedy transferred "responsibility, to include command and control and operational decisions, with regard to U-2 reconnaissance overflights of Cuba" from the CIA to the Department of Defense[15]. The Air Force then asked to borrow two of CIA's U-2Cs.

The Acting DCI, Lt. Gen. Marshall S. Carter, US Army, reacted strongly to the Air Force takeover of a major CIA operation. At one point he remarked, "I think it's a hell of a way to run a railroad. It's perfectly obviously a geared operation to get SAC in the act.[16]" In a series of conversations with high-ranking Air Force and administration officials, Carter argued against changing command and control of the flights at such a crucial time. The Agency operation, Carter pointed out, was already in place and working well, whereas the Air Force lacked experience in controlling U-2 overflights, particularly with the U-2C, which was not in the Air Force inventory. Carter also emphasized that Air Force pilots lacked experience with the more powerful J75 engines in the U-2C. He told Roswell Gilpatric, "To put in a brand new green pilot just because he happens to have on a blue suit and to completely disrupt the command and control and communication and ground support system on 72 hours' notice to me doesn't make a God damn bit of sense, Mr. Secretary."[17] DDCI Carter admitted that the Air

Force's cover story was probably better than the CIA's but suggested at one point, "Let's take one of my boys and put him in a blue suit."[18] Realizing, however, that the pilot would probably have to come from the Air Force, Carter concentrated his efforts on trying to convince DOD and administration officials to conduct art orderly transition by allowing the CIA to continue its operation for a few weeks using an Air Force pilot, and the Air Force gradually taking over command and control Carter's efforts were in vain. The Air Force insisted on immediate control of the operation, and administration officials were unwilling to become involved in what they perceived as a jurisdictional dispute. Presidential Assistant for National Security Affairs McGeorge Bundy told DDCI Carter that "the whole thing looks to me like two quarreling children."[19] Furthermore, no one wanted to speak out against a decision that the President had already made.

Once the decision was clearly irrevocable, the Agency gave its complete support to the Air Force in preparing for the upcoming overflight. A SAC U-2 pilot had already arrived unannounced at the CIA's U-2 Detachment at Edwards Air Force Base on 11 October, and the CIA U-2 detachment put him through a hasty training program to familiarize him with the U-2C. By Sunday, 14 October 1962, the weather over Cuba had cleared, and the first SAC overflight of the island took place.

When the U-2 returned, its film was rushed to the National Photographic Interpretation Center. By the evening of 15 October, photointerpreters had found evidence of the presence of MRBMs in the San Cristobal area. NPIC Director Arthur Lundahl immediately notified DDI Ray Cline, who in turn notified DDCI

Carter (DCI McCone had again left town). As the read-out progressed and the evidence became firmer, the DDI notified National Security Adviser Bundy and Roger Hilsman of the Department of State's Bureau of Intelligence and Research, who informed Secretary of State Dean Rusk. On the following morning, 16 October, DDCI Carter briefed the President on the results of the 14 October mission.[20]

Now that the presence of Soviet medium-range surface-to-surface missiles in Cuba had been confirmed, the rules for U-2 mission approval changed. The Strategic Air Command received blanket approval to fly as many missions as needed to cover Cuba completely, without again consulting the Special Group. During the week that followed the discovery of the missiles, SAC U-2s conducted multiple missions each day (see map). U-2 photography was supplemented by low-level photography taken by high-performance Navy and Air Force aircraft. Throughout the remainder of the Cuban Missile Crisis, the Agency's U-2 pilots remained idle, but the photointerpreters at NPIC did yeoman service in studying the thousands of feet of film returned by Air Force and Navy reconnaissance aircraft. President Kennedy used NPIC photographs to illustrate his address to the nation on 22 October 1962, when he revealed the Soviet missile buildup in Cuba and declared his "naval quarantine" to prevent the shipment of offensive weapons to Cuba.

On 27 October, at the height of the crisis, one of the U-2Cs lent by the Agency to the Air Force was shot down over Cuba, killing the pilot, Maj. Rudolph Anderson. This loss again illustrated the U-2's vulnerability to the SA-2 missile. Nevertheless, SAC U-2 overflights continued, both during and after the crisis. Responsibility for photographic coverage of Cuba remained with the Air Force; Agency pilots never flew another mission over the island.

Although SAC carried out most of the U-2 activity during the Cuban Missile Crisis, the Agency's U-2 missions had made vital contributions during the initial stages of the crisis. In all, Project IDEALIST pilots had spent 459 hours overflying Cuba during 1961 and 1962. They bad provided concrete evidence of the Soviet buildup on the island, evidence that was simply not available through any other means. Although by late 1962 photographic satellites had become an integral part of the overhead collection program, only U-2s could provide the highly detailed photography that photointerpreters needed to spot the early stages of work on missile sites. Attempts had been made to photograph Cuba with satellites, but to no avail because the satellites' normal orbits placed them over Cuba at the wrong time of day, after clouds had formed.

U-2s [title partially deleted]

Agency U-2s again conducted operations in the Western Hemisphere in December 1963. The Directorate of Plans had requested photographic coverage of [deleted] and neighboring [deleted] because of guerilla activities conducted by a pro-Castro movement [deleted]. Supplies for this movement appeared to be coming across the border from [deleted]. On 30 November 1963, the NSC Special Group approved overflights of the [deleted] Venezuela border to determine the scope and rate of buildup of guerilla forces. The Special Group stipulated that the entire effort was to be conducted without the knowledge of either the [deleted].

Within three days, several Detachment G aircraft and pilots deployed to Ramey AFB, Puerto Rico, from which they made six flights over the border areas between 3 and 19 December 1963 in an operation known as SEAFOAM. The results of the effort were inconclusive, and the task force returned to Edwards AFB on 22 December[21].

U-2 OPERATIONS IN ASIA

[paragraph deleted]

[Two full pages deleted]

[approximately one-third page deleted]

China Offshore Islands Dispute of 1958

During the summer of 1958, tension between the People's Republic of China and Nationalist China (Taiwan) increased to such an extent that on 18 June Detachment C mounted a U-2 mission to film the Chinese mainland coast and adjacent island areas. On 11 August, People's Liberation Army (PLA) artillery began bombarding the offshore islands of Quemoy and Little Quemoy, where the Nationalists had stationed large numbers of troops to ward off any invasion. On 23 August the Communists increased the shelling. After five days of intense bombardment, which made resupply of the islands from Taiwan impossible, the PLA commander ordered the Nationalist garrisons to surrender, intimating that an invasion was imminent. The Nationalists refused to surrender and received support from the United States in the form of warships from the 7th Fleet, which began escorting Nationalist ships carrying supplies to the beleaguered garrisons.

During this period, Detachment C U-2s flew four

missions over the mainland, searching for troop movements that would indicate that the PRC was planning to invade the islands. Photos from these missions showed no evidence of a PRC buildup, but the atmosphere in the region remained tense. Detachment C U-2s flew two more missions (9 September and 22 October) to monitor PRC troop movements and again found no indications of preparations for an invasion. The Offshore Islands Crisis receded in late October 1958 after the PRC learned that it would not receive support from the Soviet Union if the crisis escalated into a confrontation with the United States.[26]

While the Offshore Islands Crisis was still in progress, Detachment C began conducting flights in support of its weather reconnaissance cover story. On 14, 15, and 16 July 1958, U-2s flew high above Typhoon Winnie, which was causing great damage on Taiwan. These missions provided the first photography ever obtained of such a massive storm system. Photographs of the storm were the subject of articles in the magazine *Weatherwise* and the 21 July edition of *Aviation Week*. In September, Detachment C aircraft photographed two more typhoons.

[Two-thirds of a page deleted]

[approximately six lines deleted]

U-2Cs for Detachment C

Late in 1958, Lockheed began refitting the Agency's 13 remaining U-2s with the more powerful Pratt & Whitney J75/P-13 jet engine. The first of these U-2Cs arrived at Detachment C in the summer of 1959. During a test flight of this aircraft (article 360) on 24 September 1959, the pilot decided to set a new altitude record. Although the plane was equipped with a camera, it carried no film and did not have a full load of fuel, which made it considerably lighter than an operational U-2C. [deleted] In the process, however, the aircraft consumed more fuel than was called for in the test flight plan, causing the engine to flame out during the return to base. The pilot then made an emergency wheels-up landing at a glider-club strip near [location deleted].

The crash did not cause any injuries or serious damage to the aircraft, but it did bring unwanted publicity to the U-2 program. Much of the publicity resulted from the actions of Detachment C's security unit, whose conspicuous Hawaiian shirts and large pistols drew the attention of Japanese reporters. One reporter even flew over the area in a helicopter, taking pictures of the U-2. These photographs appeared in many Japanese newspapers and magazines.[28]

U-2 Crash [deleted]

Flights by Detachment C U-2s over [location deleted] continued during the first half of 1960 under Operation TOPPER. The first mission on 30 March was very successful. The second mission on 5 April took good photographs but encountered mechanical problems. At the start of the mission, the landing-gear doors failed to close completely, resulting in increased drag and higher fuel consumption. With no fuel gauge to warn the pilot of the critical fuel situation, the aircraft ran out of fuel far short [location deleted] forcing the pilot to make a crash landing in a rice paddy. The area was inaccessible to large vehicles, and the plane, article 349, had to be cut into pieces in order to remove it. With the help of local villagers, the retrieval team dissassembled the aircraft for transport to the base, where the pieces were loaded onto a C-124 under cover of darkness. The crash and subsequent recovery of the U-2 did not attract the attention of the press, there was only one report in a [deleted] newspaper, which simply referred to the crash of a jet plane. In appreciation for the assistance provided by the villagers, the [deleted] gave the headman funds to build a new school.[29]

End of Detachment C Operations

The loss of two aircraft in slightly more than six months left Detachment C with just two aircraft. Fortunately, the level of mission activity remained low because Detachment C was no longer conducting overflights of the Soviet Union.

One important remaining mission was high-altitude air sampling (HASP), in which specially equipped U-2s gathered upper-altitude air samples to look for evidence of Soviet nuclear testing. The direction of the prevailing winds made Detachment C ideally situated for this activity, which began in the fall of 1958 and continued in 1959. In late April 1960 Detachment C was preparing to stage [deleted] to conduct additional air-sampling missions, when the loss of Powers' U-2 temporarily halted all U-2 activities.

The publicity generated by the U-2 incident stirred considerable controversy in Japan, and there were soon demonstrations against the continuing presence of U-2s in Japan. On 6 June 1960, project headquarters decided on a phased-out withdrawal of Detachment C between 15 July and 1 September, but this timetable had to be accelerated when the Japanese Government formally requested the removal of the U-2s on 8 July[30].

Detachment G Missions Over Laos and North Vietnam

In the aftermath of the Powers loss, both of the

overseas U-2 detachments returned to the United States and their aircraft and personnel were incorporated into Detachment G at Edwards Air Force Base in California. This detachment was now responsible for providing coverage in Asia, and its first mission came in Laos. After the neutralist Laotian Government of Souvanna Phouma collapsed in early December 1960, reports began circulating that leftist antigovernment forces were using Soviet arms. Then on 30 December, a new Laotian Government appealed for UN aid against what it said was an invasion from North Vietnam and possibly Communist China. Alarmed over the possibility of the civil war expanding because of the introduction of foreign troops, the Eisenhower administration ordered Detachment G to gather more information on the events in Southeast Asia.

Five Detachment G pilots and planes were ferried to [location deleted] in the Philippines to conduct an operation known as [deleted]. During the period 3 to 18 January 1961, these U-2s made seven flights over Laos and North Vietnam. To search for the reported foreign troops, these missions concentrated on the lines of communications leading into Laos from North Vietnam and China. In addition, the U-2s scanned North Vietnamese airfields for Soviet aircraft to determine the magnitude of the airdrop operation allegedly supporting the Pathet Lao troops. NPIC sent photointerpreters to [location deleted] to obtain an immediate readout of each mission. The photography did not substantiate the Laotian claims, and on 26 January the Laotian Government retracted its charges of a foreign invasion. Detachment G's U-2s returned to California in early February 1961.[31]

During the final stages of Operation [deleted] there was a major threat to the security of the mission. The film from the flights made on 16 and 18 January had been sent to the United States for duplicate processing. Afterward the film was put aboard an Agency C-47 on 14 March to ferry it to Washington. During the flight one of the aircraft's engines failed, forcing the crew to jettison 43 boxes of highly classified film over mountainous terrain around Williamsport, Pennsylvania, to keep the craft airborne. After making an emergency landing at the Scranton-Wilkes-Barre Airport, the pilot reported the incident to Headquarters. The Office of Security immediately contacted the Pennsylvania State Police, who sealed off the wooded area. Agency security officers soon arrived to search for the boxes. They recovered all 43 containers; not one had broken.[32]

Detachment G's only other activity during the summer of 1961 was a solitary overflight of North Vietnam, known as Operation EBONY. In preparation for this mission, a U-2 deployed [deleted] 13 August 1961. Two days later it successfully conducted the overflight and subsequently returned to the United States.[33]

New Detachment [deleted]

[Entire section deleted]

[Two full pages deleted]

[deleted] the detachment also provided aircraft for use by American pilots flying missions in other parts of Asia. Indochina was an area of particular interest as American involvement there began growing during the early 1960s. [deleted] overflights of North Vietnam. During the first half of 1962, [deleted] pilots made seven overflights of North Vietnam from [delet-

ed]. Thereafter [deleted] pilots could use their own aircraft because the unit began staging teams and aircraft from Edwards AFB to [deleted].

Between 1962 and 1964, Agency U-2s staged a total of 36 photographic missions over North and South Vietnam. By April 1964, however, photographic requirements were changing from strategic reconnaissance to tactical support as the Viet Cong became more active, taking advantage of the weakness of the South Vietnamese central government following the coup that overthrew President Ngo Dinh Diem in 1963 and subsequent coups by disgruntled army officers. During this period the South Vietnamese "strategic hamlet" concept began breaking down, and the Viet Cong forces stepped up the pace of their attacks. As a result of the increasing level of combat in Indochina, the USIB gave responsibility for aerial reconnaissance of the areas where fighting was taking place to the SAC. Henceforth, SAC U-2s would be used over South Vietnam, parts of Cambodia within 30 miles of South Vietnam, all of Laos south of Paksane, and all of North Vietnam within 30 miles of South Vietnam or the coast. The remaining portions of Indochina remained the responsibility of the Agency's U-2s. Then in August 1964, following the Gulf of Tonkin Resolution, the Air Force assumed responsibility for all of Indochina.[45]

[3/4th of one page deleted]

[1/3rd page deleted]

Increasing Responsibilities, Inadequate Resources in Asia

The main focus of Agency U-2 activity in Asia remained the U-2s of [deleted]. In March and April

1963, the USIB met to consider COMOR proposals for aerial reconnaissance of Laos, North Vietnam, North Korea, [deleted]. All of COMOR's intelligence requirements could best be met by the U-2 because heavy cloud cover made it difficult to obtain satellite photography of the region. At the 28 May 1963 meeting of the Special Group, DCI McCone requested and authorization for a series of overflights to meet these requirements and stressed the need for additional [deleted]. The Special Group then established a "bank" of four authorizations for overflights [deleted] subject to monthly review by the Group.[51]

As a result of the increasing intelligence community interest in the Far East, both Agency U-2 detachments became very active in the region [deleted] conducted a number of missions over the border areas of China, North Vietnam, and Laos during April and May of 1963. At the same time, [deleted] became more adventurous, [deleted]

The increased level of U-2 activity in the Far East during the spring of 1963 exposed a serious weakness in Projects IDEALIST and [deleted] a shortage of aircraft. The Agency only had seven flyable U-2s when the [deleted] began in January 1962, and one of these aircraft had already been lost during an overflight in September 1962. To deal with this shortage, DCI McCone asked Defense Secretary McNamara and the Joint Chiefs of Staff on 10 June 1963 to transfer two U-2s from the Air Force to the CIA. The Defense Department quickly approved this request. Before the two Air Force aircraft were placed in service, however, the Agency had them upgraded with J75/P-13A engines and various electronic devices, a process that took more than four months.[52]

[Two-thirds of one page deleted]

President Johnson ordered a standdown of overflights [deleted]. This standdown was welcomed by [name deleted] which told [name deleted] that it wanted "to let some time go by" before more overflights were scheduled [location deleted] out that the only remaining qualified U-2 pilot had "disqualified" himself because of nervous tension. No new pilots could be qualified for U-2 flights before mid-August.

[location deleted] then demanded faster and higher flying aircraft as well as better antimissile equipment for the planes. This request led some CIA personnel to suspect that [deleted] had learned about Project OXCART, the successor to the U-2 that was still undergoing testing. [one third page deleted]

To counter the shortage of pilots in [deleted] DCI McCone suggested to the Special Group on 6 August 1964 that [deleted] be used to fly missions over [deleted]. The group agreed that the matter should be taken up with President Johnson. On the following day, however, Presidential National Security Assistant McGeorge Bundy informed McCone that, because Secretary of State Rusk and Secretary of Defense McNamara opposed the idea, he would not take it up with the President.[56]

Advanced ECM Equipment [deleted]

Demand for overhead photography [deleted] continued to grow, spurred in part by the results of earlier U-2 missions that revealed the presence of Soviet-made MiG-21s [deleted]. In addition, there were indications that [deleted] be producing its own SAMs. Furthermore, satellite photography revealed that preparations for the first [deleted] were almost complete at [deleted].

The need for photographs of [deleted] was considered so urgent that the Defense Department finally relented [one half page deleted].

The first overflight of [deleted] By mid-November, three more overflights had taken place, one over North Korea and [deleted] ground force installations would require about two man-years work, backed up by a larger expansion of photointerpretation effort."[58]

[almost a complete page deleted]

[two pages deleted]

[deleted] the Viet Cong and North Vietnamese launched their Tet offensive in South Vietnam. The 303 Committee (the new name for the Special Group after 1964) decided on I February 1968 to suspend a group of overflights scheduled for February and called for mission-by-mission approval "during this period of tension." The committee approved one additional overflight of [deleted] which was flown [deleted] on 16 March 1968, and two overflights of Cambodia, carried out on 27 March and 3 April 1968 by [name deleted] in its first operations since early 1966. These three missions turned out to be the last overflights by U-2s in the Far East. By this time U-2 flights over [deleted] had become so dangerous that the State Department opposed further overflights, and on 10 April 1968 the 303 Committee decided not to approve any mission that would fly closer than [deleted].

One reason why [deleted] overflights were stopped was the steady increase in [deleted] ability to track and engage U-2s, as evidenced by its success in downing five U-2s. By 1968 [deleted] along [deleted] were keeping a close watch on U-2 activity [deleted] and actively tracked U-2s as soon as they became airborne. The U-2s then had to face a growing PRC air defense system that not only consisted of SA-2 missiles but also the fast and high-flying MiG-21 [deleted] MiG-21 pilots had become adept at the power-zoom technique and were threatening almost every U-2 mission. The risks to U-2s now seemed too great.[65]

The decision to end Asian overnights was also rooted in the Johnson administration's change in its whole approach to the war in Indochina in the spring of 1968. On 31 March 1968, the President limited the bombing of North Vietnam in order to improve the chances for peace talks. The end of flights over [location deleted] was viewed as another way to improve the peace process.

[one major paragraph deleted]

[two full pages deleted]

Operation SCOPE SHIELD Over North Vietnam

In addition to the [deleted] peripheral missions against [deleted] flew a series of missions known as Operation SCOPE SHIELD to gather intelligence on activities in North Vietnam. The Indochina area had become the responsibility of the Air Force in 1964, but, under the terms of the cease-fire agreement negotiated with North Vietnam in January 1973, US military flights in the area were forbidden. The Nixon administration, therefore, tasked the CIA with monitoring North Vietnam's compliance with the cease-fire accords.

[deleted] Their highly sensitive missions had to remain at least 15 nautical miles away from the

North Vietnamese coast, and they initially flew at low altitude in a deceptive direction in order to avoid PRC radars. These constraints made the missions difficult because at low altitude the U-2 consumed more fuel and encountered more turbulence and the pilots' pressure suits tended to overheat.

The first mission on 30 March 1973 was only marginally successful because of cloud cover and haze, which prevented it from photographing most of its targets. A second mission on the following day had somewhat better luck with the weather, but problems with the film processing reduced the mission's coverage. Afterward, the monsoon season prevented any further missions until 21 July 1973. This mission obtained usable photography of SAM sites and North Vietnamese supply operations, although the resolution was not as high as it should have been because the H camera lens had not been properly focused. The last SCOPE SHIELD mission, on 6 January 1974, finally succeeded in obtaining high-quality photography. The mission provided complete coverage of shipping in Haiphong Harbor, SAM defenses, and North Vietnamese naval order of battle.[68]

IMPROVEMENTS IN U-2 TECHNOLOGY

Modification of U-2s for Aircraft Carrier Deployment

In mid-1963, the Office of Special Activities set in motion Project WHALE TALE to examine the possibility of adapting the U-2 aircraft for operations from an aircraft carrier [deleted] CIA planners believed that, if U-2s could be modified to operate from aircraft carriers, the United States could avoid the political problems involved in seeking permission to base U-2s in other nations. Kelly Johnson began working on changes to the aircraft, and Office of Special Activities Deputy Director James A Cunningham, Jr., a former Marine Corps aviator, asked the Navy for assistance.

The first test of the U-2's capability for carrier operations took place in August 1963 from the USS Kitty Hawk operating in the Pacific Ocean off San Diego, California. A U-2C, which had been loaded aboard the carrier at North Island Naval Base, took off from the flight deck with a full load of fuel and was airborne within 321 feet. No assistance from catapults was necessary. Although the takeoff was very successful, the attempted landing was not. The aircraft bounced, hit hard on one wing tip, and then just barely managed to become airborne again before reaching the end of the deck. Kelly Johnson realized that the airframe would have to be altered in order to make carrier landings possible. These alterations involved strengthening the landing gear, installing an arresting hook at the rear of the fuselage, and fitting "spoilers" on the wings to cancel the aerodynamic lift once the aircraft was over the flight deck. Aircraft thus modified were designated U-2G. While several aircraft underwent these modifications, [deleted] pilots began undergoing training in landing on aircraft carriers. The first successful carrier landing took place on 2 March 1964.[69]

[One major paragraph deleted]

There was never another Agency U-2 mission from an aircraft carrier. Although the idea of using a floating airbase to avoid political sensitivity proved feasible, the cost did not. Aircraft carriers are enormously expensive to operate and require an entire flotilla of vessels to protect and service them. The movement of large numbers of big ships is difficult to conceal and cannot be hastily accomplished, while the deployment of a solitary U-2 to a remote airfield can take place overnight.

A New Version of the U-2

By the summer of 1966, the number of flyable Agency U-2s had dwindled to six—two at [location deleted] in California—with three more at Lockheed undergoing repair. The Agency had originally ordered 20 U-2s in 1954–55 (the Air Force had purchased another 31 of these planes), and Kelly Johnson's crew at the Skunk Works had managed to assemble four additional craft for the Agency from leftover spare parts and usable sections of crashed aircraft. This brought the total number of U-2s acquired by the Agency to 24, for an average cost of [cost deleted] each.

At this point, the DCI and the Secretary of Defense on 1 August 1966 decided to place an order with Lockheed for eight more aircraft to be used in the Agency and Air Force U-2 programs—a completely new version of the aircraft. Kelly Johnson had been working on ways to improve the performance of the U-2 since early 1965 because he was concerned that all the modifications and additions to the aircraft over the years had made it so heavy that it had lost almost half of its range and several thousand feet in cruising altitude.[71] The new model, known as the U-2R, had a longer fuselage and a wider wingspan than the original U-2. The U-2R's wings were 103 feet long with 1,000 square feet of lifting surface, in contrast to the U-2C's 80-foot wings with only 600 square feet. The longer fuselage of the U-2R made it possible to provide two pressurized bays with an additional 2.2 cubic meters of equipment space and also achieve a better weight distribution. The net result of all these improvements was a much better performing aircraft. No longer did the U-2 pilot have to worry about keeping the aircraft's speed at altitude within a 6-knot window in the stall/buffet corner of the flight envelope. The envelope was now extended to 20 knots, which greatly improved flyability.

The U-2R used the upgraded Pratt & Whitney J75/P-13B engine and was able to fly higher—in excess of 74,000 feet—and faster—Mach 0 72 (410 knots), which is 12 knots faster than the U-2C. When flying at the higher altitude, however, the U-2R's range was less than the U-2C's. The restart capability of the P-13B engine was significantly better than the P-13A power plant. As a result, the U-2R could be restarted at 54,000 feet, which was 10,000 feet higher than the U-2C. Francis Gary Powers was one of the Lockheed test pilots who checked out this new aircraft when it first took to the air on 28 December 1967. The last of the U-2Rs was delivered on 11 December 1968.

The increased performance of the U-2R did not come cheaply. At [cost deleted] per aircraft, the new models cost almost [cost deleted] as much as the original U-2s. Much of the increased cost was due to inflation, but some was the result of technological advances. The initial order for eight of the new version of the U-2 was followed on 23 November 1966 by an order from the DCI and the Secretary of Defense for four more. This brought the total number of U-2Rs purchased by the CIA and the Air Force to 12.[72]

In addition to a new aircraft, the U-2 program received a new camera. Agency managers felt that, because the B camera was now 10 years old, the U-2R needed a camera that incorporated the many important advances that had occurred in recent years. The 112B—the modified version of the satellite program's stereo camera that had been used in the U-2G—had not proved totally successful. Despite its stereo capability, this camera's shorter focal length could not provide the scale of imagery needed to obtain the highly technical data desired by analysts. As a result, the Office of Special Activities asked the Hycon Manufacturing Company of Pasadena, California, to adapt its successful high-resolution 48-inch 9- by 9-inch format camera developed for the OXCART aircraft for use in the U-2R. This camera was actually a very advanced version of the original B camera with a new lens designed by James Baker. The new camera was designed to resolve objects smaller than 4 inches.

Hycon began work on the HR-333 camera in 1966. Unlike the OXCART camera, the new unit was to use the split 18- by 18-inch format of the B camera, so the lens had to be redesigned. James Baker's contribution to this effort was a 48-inch f/5.6 system that provided remarkably sharp imagery. Hycon completed the camera in time for it to be installed in the first U-2Rs delivered to the Agency in 1968, it is known as the H camera.[73]

Replacement of the Original U-2s With U-2Rs

As the new U-2Rs began coming off the production line at Lockheed in the autumn of 1968, CIA and the Department of Defense had to decide who would get the new aircraft. At a meeting on 13 November, DCI Richard Helms and Secretary of Defense Robert McNamara agreed that the Air Force and the Agency would each get six U-2Rs. The six older U-2s remaining from the original 1954–55 production were to be kept in flyable condition and be used as replacements if newer models were lost.

Despite the greatly increased capabilities of the new model of the U-2, the era of overflights of hostile territory was over. The U-2R would have six years of useful service with the Agency, but its missions did not include penetration flights over hostile territory

THE FINAL YEARS OF THE U-2

When the OXCART's brief operational career with the Agency ended in 1968, the U-2 was once again the center of the Agency's manned reconnaissance program. But by this time, reconnaissance aircraft had declined in importance as collection systems. Overflights were a thing of the past. Although [deleted] pilots were still flying missions targeted against [deleted] these missions did not overly [deleted] Increasingly, Agency U-2s flew missions that did not involve intelligence collection requirements.

Support to Other Agencies

Beginning in 1964, the Agency conducted a program known as RED DOT for the Department of Defense. RED DOT involved the development and testing of various color, black and white, and infrared films, emulsions, and processing techniques for use in manned and unmanned high-altitude reconnaissance systems. From 1968 until 1974, Detachment G U-2s photographed areas within the United States that were analagous to portions of the Soviet Union in order to test films and techniques for spotting certain targets. This analogous filming was particularly valuable in connection with agricultural areas and nuclear test sites.

Some U-2 missions supported agencies outside the intelligence community. In 1968 and 1969,

Detachment G U-2s flew high-altitude photographic missions in conjunction with the Apollo VII and IX spaceflights in response to a NASA request. These flights provided photography of the western United States for comparison with the photography taken by the Apollo crews. The Department of the Interior also requested U-2 support in early 1969 to help determine the extent of damage caused by a leak in an offshore oil well in California's Santa Barbara Channel. After preliminary assessment of the film at NPIC, the mission photography was given to the US Geological Survey for further study.

Also in early 1969, Detachment G began providing coverage of the western United States at the request of the Department of Commerce. U-2s filmed the Sierra snowfield to aid hydrologists in forecasting snowmelt and flooding potentials. Later that year, Detachment G supported the Office of Emergency Preparedness by photographing 61,000 square miles of the southern United States as part of a Hurricane Baseline Survey. These photographs could be used for future damage assessment following a major hurricane. A subsequent mission in fiscal year 1971 continued the Hurricane Baseline Survey by photographing the Gulf Coast. When a major earthquake struck the Los Angeles area on 9 February 1971, Detachment G U-2s flew four sorties to obtain damage-assessment photos.[74]

[paragraph deleted]

Overseas Deployment Exercises and Missions

With the exception of the [deleted] U-2s of [deleted] all of the Agency's U-2 assets were concentrated in Detachment G in California. To test the ability of Detachment G to respond to a crisis in Europe or the

Middle East, the Agency staged an overseas deployment exercise known as SCOPE SAINT each year (unless there was an actual operational deployment, as was the case in 1970, 1973, and 1974). The first of these exercises, SCOPE SAINT-I, took place on 9 October 1968, when Detachment G deployed a U-2G to [deleted]. The U-2 conducted several 6t5raining flights and then returned to California. SCOPE SAINT-II followed in April 1969 and demonstrated the feasibility of employing a C-141 aircraft to accompany a U-2 in flight to its destination. The C-141 carried support equipment to [deleted].

No overseas deployment exercise was necessary in 1970, for elements of Detachment G actually deployed overseas to provide photography of the Middle East. At the time, President Nixon's National Security Adviser, Henry A. Kissinger, was mediating between the Arabs and Israelis in order to obtain a cease-fire along the Suez Canal, where a virtual undeclared war was taking place. Once agreement was reached in August, Kissinger promised both sides that the United States would monitor the agreed upon 32-mile pullback from the waterway. Originally, Kissinger intended for photosatellites to do the monitoring. One satellite was tasked to photograph the Suez Canal area on 10 August, but the quality of its imagery lacked the detail needed to discover such small targets as gun emplacements and jeeps.

In early August, Kissinger asked the Air Force to provide U-2s to overfly the Canal, but the Air Force demurred, saying it would take several weeks to move a U-2 detachment from Del Rio, Texas, to the Middle East. At this point, DCI Helms told an NSC meeting that the Agency's Detachment G at Edwards Air Force Base could deploy aircraft [deleted] and begin filming the Suez area within the week, and it did. In fact, the first U-2 arrived in [deleted] only 71 hours after receiving notification to deploy. Between 9 August and 10 November 1970, Agency U-2s flew 29 missions over the cease-fire zone as part of Project EVEN STEVEN. Most flights used the B camera, but 12 were equipped with the new, high-resolution H camera The EVEN STEVEN U-2s also employed a dozen electronic-intelligence-collection packages, from System-X to System-XXIV. After 10 November 1970, Air Force SR-71s took over the task of photographing the cease-fire zone.[76]

The Middle East was again the cause of a Detachment G deployment in October 1973 when another Arab-Israeli war broke out. Two U-2s deployed [deleted] on 7 and 8 October 1973, to be ready for possible coverage of the conflict. Detachment G received no such tasking, however, and the last of the aircraft returned to California on 13 November. The 1973 war did lead to the overseas deployment of Detachment G U-2s in 1974, when the CIA was tasked to monitor the Israeli-Egyptian and later the Israeli-Syrian disengagement areas. On 21 April 1974, a Detachment G U-2 with appropriate support elements arrived at [location deleted] to conduct Operation [deleted]. Between 12 May and 28 July, the detachment conducted six overflights of the disengagement areas. During these missions the electronic warning systems of the U-2 registered numerous radar lockons, but no surface-to-air missiles were fired. On 1 August 1974, responsibility for the [deleted] missions as well as the aircraft itself came into the hands of the Air Force as part of the transfer of the entire Agency U-2 program at that time.[77]

The Phaseout of the Office of Special Activities

The Agency's U-2 program had been under review since the autumn of 1969 to determine if it should be continued along with the larger Air Force U-2 program. In December 1969, President Nixon decided to keep the Agency's program in existence through 1971 and asked for a formal review by the 40 Committee (the new name for the 303 Committee/Special Group). In August 1970, the committee recommended continuing the program through fiscal year 1972. On 12 August 1972, the 40 Committee again favored continuation of the CIA U-2 program. This recommendation was motivated primarily by a desire [deleted]. In June 1973, however, DCI James R. Schlesinger informed the 40 Committee that this project could be terminated without causing major difficulties [deleted]. On 30 August 1973, the 40 Committee approved the CIA's plans to terminate the U-2 program effective 1 August 1974. The Air Force would assume funding responsibility for the four U-2R aircraft assigned to the Agency and would take physical possession of them then or shortly thereafter. On 1 April 1974, Ambassador [name deleted] of the US intention to end the U-2 project, and the two countries then worked out a schedule for phasing out [deleted].

The transfer of all Agency U-2s to the Air Force eliminated Detachments [deleted]. Their parent organization, the Office of Special Activities, began its phaseout immediately thereafter. The 20-year career of the U-2 with the CIA had come to an end.

[56 full pages deleted here]

[1]Memorandum for President Johnson from DCI McCone, "Response to Query Concerning U-2 Overflight Policy," 15 January 1964, DCI records, [footnote partially deleted] (TS Codeword).

[2]Johnson, "Log for Project X," 14 September 1961. In preparation for the possible resumption of overflights, Kelly Johnson began thinking about what to do in a worst case scenario like that of 1 May 1960. He noted in the project log on 21 September 1961:

One of the greatest technical problems and, of course, a great moral one, is how we insure destroying the aircraft and the pilot should the mission fail. I have proposed a time-altitude fusing setup for multitude bombs, that looks like it should do the trick. Beerli [Col. Stanley Beerli, USAF, Director of the Office of Special Activities] doesn't want anything to do with this, but we will go ahead and develop it in case someone decides it is necessary.

[3]Memorandum for USIB from COMOR, "Justification for U-2 Photography over the USSR," 25 September 1961, IC Staff, COMIREX records, [deleted] "COMOR (General)" (TS Codeword); Memorandum for USIB from COMOR, "Requirements for Resumption of U-2 Overflights of the USSR," 1 October 1961, IC Staff, COMIREX records, [deleted] (TS Codeword).

[4]Memorandum for the Special Group from COMOR, "Illustrations of Policy Restraints on the Collection of Information through Overflight of Denied Areas during 1962," 14 December 1962, IC Staff, COMIREX records [deleted] (TS Codeword); James S. Lay, "The United States Intelligence Board, 1958–1965," (draft) CIA History Staff MS-2, 1974, p. 385 (TS Codeword). One year later Saryshagan was the topic of US Intelligence Board deliberations. In October 1963 the board asked COMOR to prepare recommendations on the need for an electronic intelligence-gathering mission against the Soviet ABM installations at Saryshagan. The proposed mission would not, however, violate Soviet airspace, instead, the U-2 would fly over the portion of the People's Republic of China closest to Saryshagan . Lay, "USIB History," pp. 393–94 (TS Codeword).

[5]*OSA History*, chap. 16, pp. 13–15 (TS Codeword).

[6]Ibid., p. 11–12 (TS Codeword).

[7]Ibid., pp. 19–20 (TS Codeword).

[8]Richard Lehman, "CIA Handling of the Soviet Buildup in Cuba, 1 July–16 October 1962." 14 November 1962 (Hereafter cited as Lehman Report), DCI records, [partial footnote deletion] (TS Codeword).

[9]Lehman Report, pp. 12–13 (TS Codeword).

[10]DCI John A McCone, Memorandum for the Record, "U-2 Overflights of Cuba, 29 August through 14 October 1962," 27 February 1963, DCI records, [deleted] (S). Although this DCI memo states that "the delay in completing the photographic coverage was due solely to the unfavorable weather predicted during this period," a more contemporary COMOR memo reported a standdown of U-2 overflights until 16 September as a result of the loss of mission No. GRC-127 over China on 8 September. Memorandum for DDCI Carter from James Q. Reber, Chairman, COMOR, "Historical Analysis of U-2 Overflights of Cuba," 24 October

1962, IC Staff, COMIREX records, [deleted] "Cuba Requirements, 1961–63" (TS Codeword).

[11]Minutes of the Special Group meeting, 4 October 1962, in Memorandum for DCI McCone from J.S. Earman, Inspector General. "Handling of Raw Intelligence Information During the Cuban Arms Buildup," 20 November 1962, DCI records, [deleted] (TS Codeword).

[12]Lehman Report, p. 30 (TS Codeword).

[13]Ibid, p. 31 (TS Codeword).

[14]Brig. Gen. Jack C. Ledford, USAF Ret, interview by Gregory W. Pedlow, Washington, DC, 20 February 1987 (S); Memorandum for DCI McCone from Herbert Scoville, Jr., Deputy Director (Research), "The Chronology of Events Leading to the Transfer of Cuban Overflight Responsibility," 28 February 1963, DCI records, [deleted] (S).

[15]Memorandum for DCI McCone from McGeorge Bundy, "Reconnaissance Overflights of Cuba," 12 October 1962, DCI records [deleted] TS).

[16]Telephone conversation between DDCI Carter and McGeorge Bundy, 13 October 1962, DCI records, [deleted] (TS Codeword).

[17]Telephone conversation between DDCI Carter and Roswell Gilpatric, 12 October 1962, DCI records [deleted] (TS Codeword).

[18]Telephone conversation between DDCI Carter and Gen. William McKee, 12 October 1962, DCI records [deleted] (TS Codeword).

[19]Telephone conversation between DDCI Carter and McGeorge Bundy, 12 October 1962, DCI records, [deleted] (TS Codeword)

[20]For a more detailed account of NPIC's discovery of the Soviet missiles in Cuba, see Dino Brugioni, *The Cuban Missile Crisis—Phase I, 29 August16 October 1962*, DDS&T Historical Series, NPIC-1 (CIA: NPIC, 1971) (S).

[21]*OSA History*, chap. 16, pp. 35–36 (TS Codeword).

[22-24][footnotes deleted]

[25]Mission folder 1773, (10 June 1958), OSA records [footnote partially deleted] (TS Codeword); *OSA History*, chap. 15, pp. 25–26 (TS Codeword).

[26]*OSA History*, chap. 15, p. 27 (TS Codeword).

[27]Ibid., chap. 18, p. 6–7, 12; chap. 15, p. 29 (TS Codeword).

[28]Ibid., chap. 15, p. 30 (TS Codeword).

[29]Ibid., chap. 15, pp. 32–33 (TS Codeword).

[30]Ibid., chap. 15, pp. 33–36 (TS Codeword).

[31]Ibid., chap. 16, p. 17 (TS Codeword).

[32-50][footnotes deleted]

[51]Lay, "USIB History," vol. 3, pp. 391–392 (TS Codeword).

[52-54][footnotes deleted]

[55]*OSA History*, chap. 17, pp. 53–55 (TS Codeword); Mission folder C174C (7 July 1964), OSA records, [deleted] (TS Codeword) [footnote partially deleted]

[56]OSA History, chap. 17, pp. 58–59 (TS Codeword).

[57]Lay, "USIB History," vol. 6, pp. 751, 753–755.

[58-66][footnotes deleted]

[67]Ibid., pp. 44–45 (TS Codeword).

[68]Ibid., pp. 48–51 (TS Codeword).
[69-70][footnotes deleted]
[71]Johnson "Log for Project X" 2 February 1965, June to October 1965, 20 October 1965; Johnson. U-2R Log January to August 1966.
[72]*OSA History,* chap. 5, pp. 34–36 (TS Codeword); OSA History 2, chap. 6, pp. 1–2, (TS Codeword).
[73]"OSA History-2," chap. 5, pp. 10–12.
[74]Ibid., chap. 3, pp. 3–29 (TS Codeword).
[75]Ibid., pp. 5–6, 10–11 (TS Codeword).
[76]Ibid., pp. 15–20 (TS Codeword).
[77]Ibid., pp. 31–34 (TS Codeword).
[78]Ibid., chap. 10, pp. 1–4 (TS Codeword).

7

Conclusion

U-2 OVERFLIGHTS OF THE SOVIET UNION

Before the first U-2 overflights in the summer of 1956, project managers believed that their aircraft could fly virtually undetected over the Soviet Union. They did not expect this advantage to last very long, however, because they also expected the Soviets to develop effective countermeasures against the U-2 within 12 to 18 months. Recognizing that time was against them, the U-2 project managers planned a large number of missions to obtain complete coverage of the Soviet Union as quickly as possible. At this time, the U-2 program focused solely on the collection of strategic intelligence.

Once operations began, however, project managers found themselves operating under severe constraints. Contrary to the CIA's expectations, the U-2 could not fly undetected. Its overflights led to Soviet diplomatic protests and numerous attempts at interception. Not wishing to aggravate the Soviet Union during periods of tension or to harm relations during more favorable intervals, President Eisenhower placed strict limits on overflights, personally authorizing each one and greatly limiting their number. Yet, the President never went so far as to eliminate the overflight program. As Commander in Chief, he valued the intelligence that the U-2 overflights collected, especially at times when the press and Congress alleged that the United States was falling behind the Soviet Union militarily, first in bombers and then in missiles. As a result of the President's ambivalence toward overflights, the years 1956–60 were marked by long periods during which no overflights occurred, followed by brief bursts of activity.

The low level of overflight activity did not prevent the U-2 from accomplishing a lot in the four years it flew over the Soviet Union and Eastern Europe. Twenty-four U-2 missions made deep penetration overflights of the Soviet Union six by Detachment A from Germany, three by Detachment C from the Far East and Alaska, and 15 by Detachment B [deleted] including the unsuccessful Powers mission.

The amount of information these missions gathered was impressive. By the summer of 1960, the U-2 project had developed more than 1,285,000 feet of film—a strip almost 250 miles long. The U-2s covered more than 1,300,000 square miles of the Soviet Union, approximately 15 percent of its total area. Information from U-2 photographs was used to prepare [deleted] separate photoanalytical reports.[1]

Numbers alone cannot describe the importance of the U-2 overflight project. In a 28 May 1960 memorandum, after Powers was shot down, DCI Allen W. Dulles described the program's accomplishments. "Five years ago, before the beginning of the U-2 program, half knowledge of the Soviet Union and uncertainty of its true power position posed tremendous problems for the United States. We were faced with the constant risk of exposing ourselves to enemy attack or of needlessly expending a great deal of money and effort on misdirected military preparations of our own." Dulles went on to describe the U-2's contribution in gathering information on four critical aspects of the Soviet Union's power position its bomber force, its missile force, its atomic energy program, and its air defense system.[2]

The first major contribution of intelligence collected from U-2 overflights was the exposure of the "bomber gap" as a myth. Contrary to the US Air Force's claims, the Soviet Union was not building a large force of long-range bombers. Armed with information from U-2 overflights, President Eisenhower was able to resist pressure to build a large US bomber fleet to meet a nonexistent Soviet threat.

The "bomber-gap" controversy was soon followed by a "missile-gap" controversy, provoked by an extensive Soviet propaganda campaign that claimed a substantial Soviet lead in developing and deploying ICBMs. U-2 missions searched huge stretches of the Soviet Union along the rail network, looking for ICBMs deployed outside the known missile testing facilities. These missions enabled the CIA to conclude, as Dulles explained to Congress in May 1960, that "the Soviet ICBM program has not been and is not now a *crash* program; instead, it is an orderly, well-planned, high-priority program aimed at achieving an early ICBM operational capability."[3] As with the controversy over Soviet bomber strength, information from U-2 photography enabled President Eisenhower to resist pressure to accelerate the US missile deployment program by building obsolescent liquid-fueled missiles rather than waiting to complete the development of more reliable solid-fueled missiles.

U-2 missions also gathered considerable data on

the Soviet Union's atomic energy program, including the production of fissionable materials, weapons development and testing activities, and the location and size of nuclear weapons stockpile sites. Such U-2 photography also revealed no evidence that the Soviet Union had violated the nuclear testing moratorium.

One of the greatest contributions of the U-2 program was to increase the capabilities of the US deterrent force. Before the U-2 overflights, most target information was based on obsolete materials dating back to World War II or shortly thereafter. With the assistance of U-2 photography, the Defense Department could allocate weapons and crews more efficiently and identify many new targets U-2 photos also proved invaluable in determining the precise location of targets. One further contribution to the capabilities of the US deterrent force was the information that U-2s collected on the Soviet air defense system. U-2 photography located Soviet fighter airfields and gained intelligence on new fighter models. Special electronic intercept and recording equipment carried on many U-2 missions enabled the CIA to analyze the technical characteristics, operational techniques, and radar order of battle of the Soviet Union's electronic defenses. This information was vital both for planning the routes for US deterrent forces and for developing electronic countermeasures.

The U-2 program not only provided information on individual Soviet weapons systems, but also helped analysts assess basic Soviet intentions, particularly during crisis situations, as Dulles wrote in May 1960

> *Whenever the international situation becomes tense because of a problem in some particular area, we are concerned whether the situation*

> *might get beyond control—that someone on the other side might suddenly and irrationally unleash big war. Our knowledge of Soviet military preparations, however, resulting from the overflight program, has given us an ability to discount or call the bluffs of the Soviets with confidence. We have been able to conclude that Soviet statements were more rhetorical than threatening and that our courses of action could be carried through without serious risk of war and without Soviet interference.*[4]

Dulles closed his report on the U-2's accomplishments by putting the program in perspective as part of the entire national intelligence effort, noting that "in terms of reliability, of precision, of access to otherwise inaccessible installations, its contribution has been unique. And in the opinion of the military, of the scientists and of the senior officials responsible for our national security it has been, to put it simply, invaluable."

The impact of the U-2 overflights on international relations is harder to measure. On the one hand, the intelligence they gathered was a major factor in keeping the United States from beginning a costly and destabilizing arms race in the late 1950s and early 1960s by showing that the Soviet Union was not engaged in major buildups of strategic bombers and intercontinental ballistic missiles. On the other hand, violations of Soviet airspace by U-2s strained relations with Moscow at times and led to the collapse of the 1960 summit meeting. On balance, however, the impact of the U-2 on superpower relations was positive. Without the intelligence gathered by the U-2, the Soviet Union's strategic military capabilities would have remained a mystery, making it very difficult for the President to resist pressure from the military, the Congress, and the public to carry out major increases in strategic weapons, which would have poisoned relations with the Soviet Union far more than the small number of overflights did.

[Three-fourths of a full page deleted]

U-2s AS COLLECTORS OF TACTICAL INTELLIGENCE

The low level of mission activity over the project's original target—the Soviet Union—was initially very frustrating for CIA project managers, but the U-2 soon found new missions not originally envisioned for the program. With its strategic-intelligence-collection role often on hold, the U-2 became highly useful as a collector of tactical intelligence during crisis situations.

Beginning with the Suez Crisis of 1956 and continuing with subsequent Middle Eastern wars, [deleted] and culminating in support to the growing US involvement in Indochina, U-2 photography provided accurate and up-to-date intelligence to US policymakers and field commanders, assisting them in crisis management and the planning of military operations. Agency U-2s also assisted in monitoring cease-fire agreements in the Middle East, with operations occurring after an undeclared war in 1970 and the 1973 Middle East war.

By the time the OXCART became fully operational, manned strategic reconnaissance of the Soviet Union was no longer seriously considered. The political risks were too high, especially since the quality of intelligence from reconnaissance satellites was increasing steadily. Thus, the OXCART's only operational use was for collecting tactical intelligence in the Far East. Like the U-2, the OXCART gathered valuable intelligence during crisis situations. Thus, in January 1968, OXCART photography revealed the location of the USS Pueblo and showed that the North Koreans were not preparing any large-scale military activity in conjunction with the ship's seizure.

ADVANCES IN TECHNOLOGY

One very important byproduct of the CIA's manned reconnaissance program was the many advances in technology that it generated. Thanks to simplified covert procurement arrangements and the lack of detailed and restricting specifications, creative designers such as Kelly Johnson produced state-of-the-art aircraft in record time. The U-2, designed to carry out reconnaissance missions for two years at best, proved so successful that, even after its original area of activity became too dangerous for overflights at the end of four years, the aircraft served the CIA well for another 14 years and still is in service with other government agencies.

The OXCART is an even better example of the technological advances generated by the CIA's reconnaissance program. Although the OXCART was designed almost 30 years ago and first flown in 1962, its speed and altitude have never been equaled. The development of this aircraft also led to the use of new materials in aircraft construction. Unfortunately, the technological breakthroughs that made the OXCART possible took longer than expected. By the time the aircraft was ready for operations, the missions originally planned for it were not practicable. The tremendous technological achievement represented by the OXCART ultimately led to the aircraft's demise by inspiring the Air Force to purchase its own version of the aircraft. The government could not afford to maintain two such similar reconnaissance programs. The elimination of the Agency's OXCART program did not, however, spell the end of the usefulness of the world's most advanced aircraft, its offspring, the SR-71, is still in service.

In addition to the aircraft themselves, many other items associated with the reconnaissance program have represented important advances in technology. The flight suits and life-support systems of the U-2 and OXCART pilots were the forerunners of the equipment used in the space program. Camera resolution improved dramatically as the result of cameras and lenses produced for the CIA's reconnaissance program.

COOPERATION WITH THE AIR FORCE

In this history, which concentrates on the CIA's involvement in overhead reconnaissance, it is easy to overlook the important role that the US Air Force played in the U-2 and OXCART programs. From the very beginnings of the U-2 program in 1954, the Agency and the Air Force were partners in advancing the state of the art in overhead reconnaissance. Air Force personnel served at ail levels of the reconnaissance program, from project headquarters to the testing site and field detachments. The Air Force supplied the U-2's engines, at times diverting them from other high-priority production lines. Perhaps most important of all, the Air Force provided pilots for the U-2s after the Agency's original attempt to recruit a sufficient number of skilled foreign pilots proved unsuccessful. Finally, the day-to-day operations of the U-2s could not have been conducted without the help of Air Force mission planners, weather forecasters, and support personnel in the field detachments. The cooperation between the Agency and the Air Force that began with the U-2 and continued with Project OXCART remains a major feature in US reconnaissance programs today.

IMPACT OF THE OVERHEAD RECONNAISSANCE PROGRAM ON THE CIA

CIA's entry into the world of overhead reconnaissance at the end of 1954 ultimately produced major changes in the Agency. Classical forms of intelligence—the use of covert agents and clandestine operations—gradually lost their primacy to the new scientific and technical means of collection. As soon as the U-2 began flying over the Soviet Union, its photographs became the most important source of intelligence available. The flood of information that the U-2 missions gathered led to a major expansion of the Agency's photointerpretation capabilities, which finally resulted in the creation of the National Photographic Interpretation Center to serve the entire intelligence community.

The U-2's tremendous success as an intelligence-gathering system led the Agency to search for follow-on systems that could continue to obtain highly reliable information in large quantities. Thus, the CIA sponsored the development of the world's most advanced aircraft—the OXCART—and also pioneered research into photosatellites. Less than a decade after the U-2 program began, the Agency's new emphasis on technical means of collection had brought about the creation of a new science-oriented directorate, which would ultimately rival in manpower and budget the Agency's other three directorates combined.

The negative aspect of this new emphasis on technology is exploding costs. The Agency's first strategic reconnaissance aircraft, the U-2, cost less than [cost deleted]. With the U-2's successor, the OXCART, each aircraft cost more than [deleted] and the cost explosion has continued with each new generation of reconnaissance satellites.

Perhaps the greatest significance of the CIA's entry into the world of overhead reconnaissance in December 1954 was the new national policy that it signaled. Although US military aircraft had frequently violated Soviet airspace in the decade after World War II, such shallow-penetration overflights, concentrating primarily on order-of-battle data, had been authorized and controlled by US field commanders, not by the President. In the autumn of 1954, however, President Dwight D. Eisenhower—determined to avoid another Pearl Harbor—authorized the construction of a new aircraft designed solely to fly over the Soviet Union and gather strategic intelligence. Peacetime reconnaissance flights over the territory of a potential enemy power thus became national policy. Moreover, to reduce the danger of conflict, the President entrusted this mission not to the armed forces, but to a civilian agency—the CIA. From that time forward, overhead reconnaissance has been one of the CIA's most important missions.

[1]DCI Allen W. Dulles, Memorandum for Brig. Gen. Andrew J. Goodpaster, "Statistics Relating to the U-2 Program," 19 August 1960, Operation [deleted] files, OSA records, [deleted] (TS Codeword).
[2]The original draft of this document was probably written by James Q. Reber. It was then revised by DCI Dulles. "Accomplishments of the U-2 Program." 27 May 1960, Operation [deleted] files, OSA records, [deleted] (TS Codeword).
[3]Ibid, p. 3 (TS Codeword).
[4]Ibid, pp. 9–10 (TS Codeword).

Appendix A

Acronyms

AEC	Atomic Energy Commission
AFR	Air Force Base
AFDAP	Air Force office symbol for the Assistant for Development Planning under the Deputy Chief of Staff for Development
[deleted]	
ARC	Ad Hoc Requirements Committee
ARDC	Air Research and Development Command (USAF)
[deleted]	
ATIC	Air Technical Intelligence Center (USAF)
BSAP	Boston Scientific Advisory Panel
BUORL	Boston University Optical Research Laboratory
COMINT	Communications Intelligence
COMIREX	Committee on Imagery Requirements and Exploitation
COMOR	Committee on Overhead Reconnaissance
DB	"Dirty Bird"
DCI	Director of Central Intelligence
DCID	Director of Central Intelligence Directive
DDCI	Deputy Director of Central Intelligence
DDI	Deputy Director for Intelligence
DDP	Deputy Director (or Directorate) for Plans

DDS&T	Deputy Director for Science and Technology
DPD	Development Projects Division
DPS	Development Projects Staff
ECM	Electronic Countermeasures
EG&G	Edgerton, Germeshausen & Grier, Incorporated
ELINT	Electronic Intelligence
FCRC	Federally Controlled Research Center
HASP	High-Altitude Air Sampling Program
IAC	Intelligence Advisory Committee
IAS	Indicated air speed
IC	Intelligence community
ICBM	Intercontinental ballistic missile
IR	Infrared
ISP	Intelligence Systems Panel (USAF)
JRC	Joint Reconnaissance Center
MATS	Military Air Transport Service (USAF)
MRBM	Medium-range ballistic missile
NACA	National Advisory Committee for Aeronautics
NAS	Naval air station
NASA	National Aeronautics and Space Administration
NIE	National Intelligence Estimate
NPIC	National Photographic Interpretation Center
NSA	National Security Agency
NSC	National Security Council
NSCID	National Security Council Intelligence Directive
ODM	Office of Defense Mobilization
ORR	Office of Research and Reports
OSA	Office of Special Activities
OSI	Office of Scientific Intelligence

PBCFIA	President's Board of Consultants on Foreign Intelligence Activities
P-E	Perkin-Elmer Company
PFIAB	President's Foreign Intelligence Advisory Board
PI	Photointerpreter
PIC	Photographic Intelligence Center
PID	Photo-Intelligence Division
PSAC	President's Science Advisory Committee
RAF	Royal Air Force
RFP	Request for Proposal
SAB	Scientific Advisory Board (USAF)
SAC	Science Advisory Committee
SAC	Strategic Air Command
SA/PC/DCI	Special Assistant to the DCI for Planning and Coordination
SAM	Surface-to-air missile
SEI	Scientific Engineering Institute
SENSINT	Sensitive Intelligence (USAF)
SLAR	Side-looking aerial radar
TAS	True air speed
TCP	Technological Capabilities Panel
USIB	United States Intelligence Board
WADC	Wright Air Development Command (USAF)
WRSP	Weather Reconnaissance Squadron, Provisional

Appendix B

Key Personnel

AYER, Frederick, Jr.
Special assistant to Trevor Gardner in the Office of the Secretary of the Air Force, Ayer was a strong advocate of overhead reconnaissance by balloons and an early supporter of Lockheed's CL-282 design.

BAKER, James G.
Harvard astronomer and lens designer, Baker was a leading designer of high-acuity aerial lenses during World War II and continued this work after the war. He also headed the Air Force Intelligence Systems Panel and served on the Technological Capabilities Panel's Project Three committee that urged the development of the U-2 aircraft Baker designed the lenses for the U-2's cameras.

BISSELL, Richard M., Jr.
Head of all CIA overhead reconnaissance programs from 1954 until 1962, a former economics professor at MIT and high official of the Marshall Plan, Bissell became Allen W. Dulles's Special Assistant for Planning and Coordination in January 1954 and received responsibility for the new U-2 project at the end of that year. Later he also headed the first pho-

tosatellite project and oversaw the development of the OXCART. In 1959 Bissell became Deputy Director for Plans but kept the reconnaissance projects under his control. He resigned from the CIA in February 1962.

CABELL, George Pearre

Air Force general and DDCI from 1953 until 1962. Because of Cabell's many years of experience in aerial reconnaissance, DCI Dulles delegated most of the responsibility for the reconnaissance projects to him.

CARTER, Marshall S.

Army general who served as DDCI from 1962 until 1965. During the period leading up to the Cuban Missile Crisis, Carter served as Acting DCI on a number of occasions while DCI McCone was out of town. In October 1962 he fought unsuccessfully to keep the CIA involved in flying reconnaissance missions over Cuba. Carter became the Director of the National Security Agency in 1965.

CHARYK, Joseph R.

An aeronautical engineer who had followed careers first in academia and then the aerospace industry, Charyk became the Chief Scientist of the Air Force in January 1959. Five months later he moved up to Assistant Secretary of the Air Force for Research and Development, and the following year he became Under Secretary of the Air Force. In these positions he was involved in coordination with the CIA on both the U-2 and OXCART projects. In 1963 Charyk left government to become the first chairman of the Communications Satellite Corporation.

CUNNINGHAM, James A., Jr.

An ex-Marine Corps pilot, he became the administrative officer for the U-2 project in April 1955. Cunningham handled the day-to-day management of the U-2 program and brought only the more complex problems to Richard Bissell's attention. Later he served as the Deputy Director of the Office of Special Activities and then Special Assistant to the Deputy Director for Science and Technology.

DONOVAN, Allen F.

An aeronautical engineer who had helped to design the P-40 fighter while working at the Curtiss-Wright Corporation, Donovan was one of the founders of the Cornell Aeronautical Laboratory after World War II. He served on several Air Force advisory panels and was a strong advocate of the proposed Lockheed CL-282 aircraft. Later he became vice president of the Aerospace Corporation.

DOOLITTLE, James H.

A vice president of Shell Oil Company and an Army Air Force reserve general, Doolittle headed General Eisenhower's Air Staff during World War II. After the war Doolittle served on many Air Force advisory panels, and in 1954 he chaired a special panel investigating the CIA's covert activities. Doolittle also served on the Technological Capabilities Panel and the President's Board of Consultants on Foreign Intelligence Activities.

DUCKETT, Carl E.

Headed the Directorate of Science and Technology from September 1966 until May 1976, first as Acting Deputy Director and then as Deputy Director beginning in April 1967. During his tenure, the emphasis in the CIA's overhead reconnaissance program shifted from aircraft to satellites.

DULLES, Allen W.

DCI from 1953 until 1961. Although initially reluctant to see the CIA involved in aerial reconnaissance, which he viewed as the military's area of responsibility, Dulles became a strong supporter of the U-2 program when he saw how much intelligence it could gather on the Soviet Union. Because his own interests lay more in the area of human intelligence, he left the management of the reconnaissance program in the hands of DDCI Cabell and project director Richard Bissell.

GARDNER, Trevor

During World War II, Gardner worked on the Manhattan Project, and later he headed the General Tire and Rubber Company before starting his own research and development firm, the Hycon Company, which built aerial cameras. Gardner served as the Secretary of the Air Force's Special Assistant for Research and Development and then as the Assistant Secretary for Research and Development during Eisenhower's first term of office. Gardner's concern about the danger of a surprise attack helped lead to the establishment of the Technological Capabilities Panel. Gardner also urged the building of Lockheed's CL-282 aircraft.

GEARY, Leo P.

Air Force colonel (later brigadier general) who was James Cunningham's Air Force counterpart in the U-2 program. He was instrumental in diverting engines from other Air Force projects for use in the U-2, and his 10 years with the U-2 project provided a high degree of continuity.

GOODPASTER, Andrew J.

An Army colonel who served as President Eisenhower's Staff Secretary from 1954 to 1961. During this period, he was the CIA's point of contact in the White House for arranging meetings with the President on the subject of overhead reconnaissance. Goodpaster's later career included service as the supreme commander of NATO and then commandant of the US Military Academy at West Point.

HELMS, Richard M.

DCI from 1966 to 1973. During his tenure as DCI, the CIA's manned reconnaissance program came under heavy pressure because of competition from the Air Force's reconnaissance program.

JOHNSON, Clarence L. (Kelly)

One of the nation's foremost aeronautical designers, Kelly Johnson graduated from the University of Michigan's School of Aeronautics in 1933 and began working for the Lockheed Aircraft Corporation. During World War II he designed the P-38 fighter, and after the war his design successes continued with the F-104 jet fighter, the Constellation airliner, and the CIA's two strategic reconnaissance aircraft, the U-2 and the OXCART A-12.

KIEFER, Eugene P.

An Air Force officer with a degree in aeronautical engineering who in 1953 informed a friend at Lockheed of the Air Force's search for a high-altitude reconnaissance aircraft, thus, leading to the initial design of the CL-282. After leaving the Air Force, Kiefer became Richard Bissell's technical adviser for the OXCART and photosatellite programs.

KILLIAN, James R., Jr.

President of the Massachusetts Institute of Technology, Killian headed a high-level and very secret study of the nation's ability to withstand a surprise attack. While this project was still under way, he and Edwin Land persuaded President Eisenhower to support the development of a high-altitude reconnaissance aircraft, the U-2. Later, Killian headed Eisenhower's Board of Consultants for Foreign Intelligence Activities, served as his Cabinet-level science adviser, and chaired the President's Science Advisory Board. Killian was also chairman of the President's Foreign Intelligence Advisory Board under John F. Kennedy.

LAND, Edwin H.

An extremely talented inventor famous for the development of polarizing filters and the instant-film camera. Land also devoted considerable time and energy to voluntary government service. During World War II, Land worked for the Radiation Laboratories, and after the war he served on numerous Air Force advisory panels. As the head of the Technological Capabilities Panel's study group investigating US intelligence-gathering capabilities, Land became a strong advocate of the development of a high-altitude reconnaissance aircraft (thc CL-282) under civilian rather than Air Force control. Land and James Killian persuaded President Eisenhower to approve the U-2 project and later the first photosatellite project. Land also served on the President's Board of Consultants for Foreign Intelligence Activities.

LEGHORN, Richard S.

An MIT graduate in physics, Leghorn joined the Army Air Force in 1942 and went to work for reconnaissance expert Col. George Goddard. By the time of the invasion of Europe, Leghorn was chief of reconnaissance for the 9th Tactical Air Force. After the war, Leghorn began preaching the need for "pre-D-day" reconnaissance in order to gather intelligence on the Soviet Bloc. He returned to the Air Force during the Korean war and later worked for Harold Stassen's Disarmament Office. In 1956 he became the head of the Scientific Engineering Institute, [deleted] working on ways to reduce the U-2's vulnerability to radar detection. In 1957 he founded Itek Corporation.

LUNDAHL, Arthur E.

A Navy photointerpreter during World War II and afterward Lundahl became the chief of the Photo-Intelligence Division in 1953. To support the U-2 project, be established a separate photointerpretation center under Project HTAUTOMAT. Under his leadership the Photo-Intelligence Division grew rapidly and achieved office status as the Photographic Intelligence Center in 1958. In 1961 Lundahl became the first head of the National Photographic Interpretation Center, which combined the photointerpretation efforts of the CIA and the military services.

McCONE, John A.

DCI from 1961 to 1965. A strong supporter of the CIA's manned reconnaissance program, McCone presided over the OXCART's main period of development and pushed for a greater role for the CIA in its joint reconnaissance programs with the Department of Defense.

MILLER, Herbert L.

Miller worked in the Office of Scientific Intelligence's nuclear branch and became Richard Bissell's first deputy for the U-2 project. He later left the Agency to work for the Scientific Engineering Institute.

NORTON, Garrison

An assistant to Trevor Gardner, Norton became an early supporter of the Lockheed CL-282 and started the CIA's interest in overhead reconnaissance by informing Philip Strong about the aircraft. Norton later became Navy Assistant Secretary for Research and Development and was involved with the OXCART program.

OVERHAGE, Carl F. J.

After working on the development of Technicolor, Overhage went to work for Kodak. He headed the Beacon Hill Panel in 1952 and later became director of Lincoln Laboratories.

PARANGOSKY, John N.

Parangosky worked for Richard Bissell's Development Projects Staff in the mid-1950s. He served as deputy chief of the Adana U-2 unit in 1959 and became project manager of the OXCART program from its inception through the test flight stage.

PERKIN, Richard S.

President of the Perkin-Elmer Corporation, Perkin was a close friend of James Baker and was also a member of several advisory panels, including the BEACON HILL project. He helped Baker decide what cameras to use in the first U-2 aircraft.

POWERS, Francis Gary
An Air Force Reserve Officer who became a CIA U-2 pilot in 1956, Powers flew 27 successful missions before being shot down over the Soviet Union on 1 May 1960. After his return to the United States in exchange for Soviet spymaster Rudolf Abel in 1962, Powers was cleared of all allegations of misconduct in his mission, capture, trial, and captivity. He became a test pilot for Lockheed and later piloted light aircraft and helicopters for radio and television stations. He died in a helicopter crash on 1 August 1977.

PURCELL, Edward M.
A physicist who won a Nobel prize in 1954 for his work in nuclear resonance, Purcell served on a number of advisory bodies, including the USAF Scientific Advisory Committee and Edwin Land's Technological Capabilities Panel study group. It was Purcell's ideas for reducing the radar cross section of the U-2 that led to the OXCART program. Purcell also contributed to the satellite programs.

RABORN, William F., Jr.
DCI from 1965 to 1966, Raborn pushed for the deployment of OXCART to the Far East but failed to sway the top officials of the Johnson administration.

REBER, James Q.
After serving as the Assistant Director for Intelligence Coordination in the early 1950s, Reber became the chairman of the Ad Hoc Requirements Committee in

1955 and continued to chair this committee after it was taken over by the US Intelligence Board in 1960 and renamed the Committee on Overhead Requirements. In 1969 he became the chairman of the USIB's SIGINT Committee.

RODGERS, Franklin A.
Formerly of MIT, Rodgers was the chief engineer at the Scientific Engineering Institute who converted the theories of Edward Purcell into practical systems to reduce the radar image of the U-2 and especially the OXCART.

SCHLESINGER, James R.
DCI from February to July 1973, Schlesinger supported the Nixon administration's proposal to terminate the Agency's U-2 program.

SCOTT, Roderic M.
An engineer with Perkin-Elmer who worked with James Baker in designing the first cameras for use in the U-2. Scott helped design the 30001 camera for the OXCART.

SCOVILLE, Herbert, Jr.
In February 1962 Scoville became the first Deputy Director for Research, which took over control of the Agency's reconnaissance programs from the Deputy Director for Plans. Frustrated by the lack of support from the DCI and the other directorates, he resigned in June 1963.

SEABERG, John
An aeronautical engineer who was recalled to active duty with the Air Force during the Korean war,

Seaberg drafted the first specifications for a high-flying jet reconnaissance aircraft in 1953.

STEVER, H. Guyford
A professor of aeronautical engineering at MIT, Stever served on numerous Air Force advisory panels and later became the Air Force's chief scientist.

STRONG, Philip G.
Chief of collection in the Office of Scientific Intelligence, Strong kept himself well informed on developments in overhead reconnaissance and attended many Air Force advisory panel meetings as an observer. In 1954 he learned about the Lockheed CL-282 design and passed the information on to Edwin Land's study group investigating US intelligence-gathering capabilities.

WHEELON, Albert ("Bud") D.
Wheelon became the Deputy Director for Science and Technology in August 1963 following the reorganization and renaming of the Deputy Director for Research. He held this position until September 1966.

Annotated Bibliography

———. *The Trial of the U-2: The Exclusive Authorized Account.* Chicago: Translation World Publishers, 1960. The transcription of the trial of Francis Gary Powers, held before the Military Division of the Supreme Court of the U.S.S.R., in Moscow, August 17–19, 1960. Contains 24 pages of photos of the trial, debris of the downed U-2 and other exhibits from the trial.

Beschloss, Michael R. *May-Day: Eisenhower, Khrushchev and the U-2 Affair.* New York: Harper & Row, 1986.

Burrows, William E. *Deep Black: Space Espionage and National Security.* New York: Random House, 1986.

Miller, Jay. *Lockheed U-2.* Austin: Aerofax, 1983. Technological analysis of the U-2.

Pace, Steve. *Lockheed Skunk Works.* Osceola, Wisc.: Motorbooks International, 1992.

Pocock, Chris. *Dragon Lady: The History of the U-2 Spyplane.* Osceola, Wisc.: Motorbooks International, 1989.

Powers, Francis Gary. *Operation Overflight: The U-2 Spy Pilot Tells His Story for the First Time.* New York: Holt, Rinehart & Winston, 1970. The autobiography of Francis Gary Powers, who was shot down over Russia.

Rich, Ben and Janos, Leo. *Skunk Works: A Personal Memoir of My Years At Lockheed.* Boston; Little, Brown & Co., 1994. The inside story of the secret development of the warplanes of the Cold War, from the U-2 to the Stealth fighter.

Wise, David and Ross, Thomas B. *The U-2 Affair.* New York: Random House, 1962.

ABOUT THE EDITOR

Thomas Fensch is the editor of the Top Secret series and is the publisher of New Century Books.

He has written or edited over twenty books of non-fiction, published since 1970.

His previous books include:

Steinbeck and Covici: The Story of a Friendship
Conversations With John Steinbeck
Conversations With James Thurber
The Man Who Was Walter Mitty:
The Life and Work of James Thurber
Of Sneetches and Whos and the Good Dr. Seuss:
Essays on the Writings and Life
of Theodor Geisel
Writing Solutions:
Beginnings, Middles & Endings

Thomas Fensch holds a Ph.D. degree from Syracuse University and lives near Houston.